高等学校商务英语系列教材

外贸函电与单证

Business English Correspondence and Documents

（修订本）

主　编　李　蓉　赵凤玉
副主编　阳有明　覃　璇　赵莉莉

清华大学出版社
北京交通大学出版社
·北京·

内 容 简 介

本书共分 4 部分 18 章,从理论上系统地介绍了外贸活动中外贸函电与电子邮件的特点、格式、组成部分、写作原则及注意事项等,并通过信函和邮件样信,逐一展现了建立业务关系、询价、报盘、还盘、订货、支付、包装、装运、保险、索赔等各个磋商环节,系统地介绍了外贸英语函电的专业用语、写作特点、写作技巧,并通过理论联系实际的方法,训练学生正确使用信函常用的句型和词汇,达到熟练地翻译和撰写业务信函的目的。

本书适合高等院校经贸方向的学生使用,也适合有志于从事国际贸易的人士参考使用。

本书封面贴有清华大学出版社防伪标签,无标签者不得销售。
版权所有,侵权必究。侵权举报电话:010-62782989 13501256678 13801310933

图书在版编目(CIP)数据

外贸函电与单证/李蓉,赵凤玉主编. ——修订本. ——北京:北京交通大学出版社:清华大学出版社,2014.9(2021.8 重印)
ISBN 978-7-5121-2077-8

Ⅰ. ①外… Ⅱ. ①李… ②赵… Ⅲ. ①对外贸易-英语-电报信函-写作-高等学校-教材 ②进出口贸易-原始凭证-高等学校-教材 Ⅳ. ①H315 ②F740.44

中国版本图书馆 CIP 数据核字(2014)第 201271 号

外贸函电与单证
WAIMAO HANDIAN YU DANZHENG

责任编辑:张利军	特邀编辑:李秀云
出版发行:清华大学出版社 邮编:100084 电话:010-62776969
北京交通大学出版社 邮编:100044 电话:010-51686414
印 刷 者:北京时代华都印刷有限公司
经　　销:全国新华书店
开　　本:185 mm×260 mm　印张:18.5　字数:480 千字
版 印 次:2020 年 1 月第 1 版第 1 次修订　2021 年 8 月第 5 次印刷
印　　数:8 001~10 000 册　　定价:48.00 元

本书如有质量问题,请向北京交通大学出版社质监组反映。对您的意见和批评,我们表示欢迎和感谢。
投诉电话:010-51686043,51686008;传真:010-62225406;E-mail:press@bjtu.edu.cn。

前言 Preface

外贸函电在涉外经济活动中起着联络业务、沟通交流的作用，对市场的开拓和贸易的发展起着积极的作用。《外贸函电与单证》从进出口业务实际出发，以国际贸易流程为主线，将国际贸易业务知识与英语融于一体，旨在帮助学生在了解并熟悉外贸各个环节的同时，能与客户进行有效的沟通。此外，由于信息技术的发展，电子邮件已广泛应用于信息交流，大大加快了信息传播的速度，因此本书以邮件为主进行信函的展示。本书首先从理论上系统地介绍外贸活动中外贸函电与电子邮件的特点、格式、组成部分、写作原则及注意事项等，然后通过信函和邮件样信，逐一展现了建立业务关系、询价、报盘、还盘、订货、支付、包装、装运、保险、索赔等各个磋商环节，系统地介绍了外贸英语函电的专业用语、写作特点、写作技巧，并通过理论联系实际的方法，训练学生正确使用信函常用的句型和词汇，达到熟练地翻译和撰写业务信函的目的。

本书分为4部分：第1部分系统介绍与外贸函电相关的理论知识及其他常用的商务写作文体；第2部分由易渐难地从寻找客户、磋商订单、签订合同、处理纠纷和其他贸易信函等方面逐一展现外贸业务的各个环节，介绍了建立业务关系、询价、报盘、还盘、订货、支付、包装、装运、保险、索赔、代理等内容；第3部分则结合对外贸易的各个环节，提炼常见的单据，通过展现贸易过程中常见的各类单据，帮助学生熟悉和掌握相关的外贸单证；第4部分为外贸函电实训部分，以实训的方式让学生切实掌握各类信函和邮件的写作。

本书把外贸函电与相关的国际贸易实务课程的内容有机地衔接起来，在内容的编排上充分体现以学生为中心的原则，向学生展现真实的外贸业务环节，诱发学生的学习兴趣，激发学生的学习主动性。特别是实训部分的贸易单证，为实践教学提供了相应的素材，便于学生将学习与实习、就业联系起来，充分调动学生学习的积极性和参与性。本书适合高等院校经贸方向的学生使用，也适合有志于从事国际贸易的人士参考使用。

本书是2014年广西高等教育教学改革工程项目（一般A类）课题"地方高校商务英语核心类课程资源整合与教学方法优化"（2014JGA149）和2014年广西高等教育教改工程项目（一般B类）《基于数字化平台的广西独立学院立体化英语写作评改模式的研究与实践》（2014JGB400）的阶段性成果，由桂林理工大学外国语学院的李蓉、赵凤玉担任主编，桂林理工大学外国语学院的阳有明、广西师范大学漓江学院外语系的赵莉莉、Oklahoma City University的覃璇担任副主编。全书具体的编写分工为：赵莉莉负责编写第1~4章；李蓉负责编写第5~9章及第11~15章；赵凤玉负责编写第10章及第4部分；阳有明和覃璇负责后期电子文稿的创作与编辑。在本书的编写过程中，傅广生教授、莫运夏教授、胡金副教授提供了宝贵的意见；桂林理工大学外语学院英语系的部分老师也参与了资料收集与整理，在此表示衷心的感谢。此外，本书的顺利出版也离不开桂林理工大学教材科有关领导和同仁的关心和支持，在此一并致谢。

  为答谢广大教师对本书的厚爱，方便教学，编者特向选用此书做教材的教师免费提供每章练习的参考答案，有需要的教师可发邮件至编者的邮箱 huangxinyilr@163.com 及 757427905@qq.com 索取。

  由于编者水平有限，书中疏漏之处在所难免，敬请广大读者、学界同仁赐教指正。

编 者

2020 年 1 月

目录 Contents

Part 1 An Introduction to Business Correspondence

Chapter 1 Introduction to the Business Correspondence ················ 2
Chapter 2 The Forms of Business Correspondence ················ 7
Chapter 3 The Components in Business Correspondence ················ 19
Chapter 4 The Writing Principles in Business Correspondence ················ 31
Chapter 5 Other Business Writing ················ 41

Part 2 Business Correspondence in International Visible Trade

Chapter 6 Looking for Potential Customers ················ 62
Chapter 7 Discussing Price ················ 76
Chapter 8 Signing a Contract ················ 92
Chapter 9 Dealing with Complaints ················ 157
Chapter 10 Other Business Partnership ················ 175

Part 3 Simulation Training in Major Documents

Chapter 11 Official and Organizational Documents ················ 200
Chapter 12 Financial Documents ················ 209
Chapter 13 Commercial Documents ················ 218
Chapter 14 Shipping Documents ················ 226
Chapter 15 Insurance Documents ················ 237

Part 4 Simulation Training in Business Correspondence

Chapter 16 Simulation Training in Business Correspondence (1) ················ 244
Chapter 17 Simulation Training in Business Correspondence (2) ················ 260
Chapter 18 Simulation Training in Business Correspondence (3) ················ 272

参考文献 ················ 290

Part 1

An Introduction to Business Correspondence

Chapter 1

Introduction to the Business Correspondence

Questions for Discussion

1. Why is business correspondence so important in our daily life?
2. How many kinds of business letters do you know?
3. What are the features of business correspondence?

Section 1 Definition of Business Correspondence

Generally speaking, correspondence, including letters, e-mails, newsgroups, Internet forums, blogs, etc., refers to non-concurrent, remote communication through exchange of letters between people. A businessperson writes and receives letters in his or her day-to-day transactions, which may be called business correspondence. Business correspondence or business letter is a written communication between two parties for the purpose of achieving specific business objectives. For example, a businessman may write letters to supplier of goods and also receive letters from the suppliers; on the other hand, a customer may write letters to the businessperson for seeking information about availability of goods, price, quality, sample etc. or placing an order for purchase of goods. Therefore, business letters can be defined as a medium or means through which views are expressed and ideas or information is communicated in writing in a process of business activities. According to a Chinese chief executive of an import and export company, the prior job for one who aims to become a foreign trade salesperson is to improve his or her capability to write business letters effectively.

Business correspondence is also written by people in connection with their work, for example, a businessperson, an executive or a manager might find it necessary to write to the members of his or her staff, complimenting them on their good performance, or rebuking them for negligence of some kind or other. Meanwhile, he or she might have to discuss internal administrative matters with managerial colleagues, or make reports to seniors and/or directors.

Section 2 Functions of Business Correspondence

Nowadays business operations are not restricted to any locality, state or nation because production takes place in one area while consumption takes place everywhere. Thus, business letters should be promotional, motivational, informational, and persuasive. The purpose is to:

1. Maintain Proper Relationship

Business activities are not confined to any one area or locality in the modern society, as the businessmen and customers are scattered throughout the country. Thus, there is a need to maintain proper relationship among them by using appropriate, economical and convenient means of communication. In this case, business letters play an important role, in which the customers can write to the businessperson seeking information about products and the businessperson in turn can supply various information to customers. This helps them to carry on business on national and international basis economically and conveniently.

2. Create and Maintain Goodwill

The messages containing in business letters will exert certain impact on the readers. The professional and appropriate expressions and writing skills in business letters might give readers good impression and thus arouse their trust in the products and service of a company. This might be really valuable for the success of a deal.

3. Serve as Evidence

It is impossible for a trader to memorize all facts and figures in a conversation that normally takes place among businesspersons. Through letters, he can keep a record of all facts for organizing the transactions of the international trade. Thus, letters can also serve as evidence in case of dispute between two parties.

4. Expand Business

Business letters are used to convey the vast amount of information regarding competing products, prevailing prices, promotion, market activities, etc., so as to complete day-to-day business operations. If the trader has to run from place to place to get information, it will simply result in loss of time. But through business letters, he can make all inquiries about the products and the markets. He can also receive orders from different countries and, thus enhance sales.

Section 3 Types of Business Correspondence

Business correspondence is the most formal method of communication. It is addressed to a particular person or organization. Therefore, we cannot discuss business correspondence writing without considering the trade process of import and export. The following table shows correspondence between the exporter and the importer in international transactions.

	The Exporter's Letters	The Importer's Letters
1	A letter for establishing business relationship	A letter for establishing business relationship
2	Replies from the potential customers	Replies from the potential customers
3		Letters of enquiry
4	Offer	
5		Counter-offer
6		Placing an order
7	Acknowledgment	
8		Payment terms
9	Packing	Packing
10	Shipment	Shipment
11	Insurance	Insurance
12		Complaints
13	Settlement with the complaints	

In addition, there are also other kinds of business letters which are not for trade but for other business or communication, such as memos, proposal letters, a covering letter, curriculum vitae (CV), resignation letter, recommendation letter, notice of meeting, minutes of meeting, and so on.

Section 4 Essential Qualities of a Good Business Letter

No one can succeed in business without being able to write GOOD business letters. A "good" business letter is the one that is written in GOOD English (or whatever other language is used) in clearly understandable words, and the one that is brief and to the point and, above all, is persuasive. What's more, the quality of paper used in the letter, its size, color etc. also need special attention, because it creates a positive impression in the mind of the receiver. We may classify the qualities of a good business letter into writing qualities and format qualities.

1. Writing Qualities

The writing qualities of a good business letter refer to the quality of language, its presentation, etc. These facilitate quick processing of the request and that leads to prompt action. The various writing qualities of a good business letter are discussed as follows:

(1) Simplicity. Simple and easy language should be used for writing business letters. Difficult words should be strictly avoided, as one cannot expect the reader to refer to the dictionary while reading letter.

(2) Clarity. The language should be clear, so that the receiver will understand the message immediately, easily and correctly. Ambiguous language creates confusion. The letter will serve the purpose if the receiver understands it in the same manner in which it is intended by the sender.

(3) Accuracy. The statements written in the letter should be accurate to the best of the sender's knowledge. Accuracy demands that there are no errors in the usage of language — in grammar, spellings, punctuations, etc. An accurate letter is always appreciated.

(4) Completeness. A complete letter is one that provides all necessary information to the readers. For example, in sending an order we should mention the desirable features of the goods, i.e., their quality, shape, color, design, quantity, date of delivery, mode of transportation, etc.

(5) Relevance. The letter should contain only essential information. Irrelevant information should not be mentioned while sending any business correspondence.

(6) Courtesy. Courtesy wins the heart of the reader. In business letters, courtesy can be shown/expressed by using words like please, thank you, etc.

(7) Neatness. A neat letter is always impressive. A letter, either handwritten or typed, should be neat and attractive in appearance. Overwriting and cuttings should be avoided.

2. Format Qualities

The format qualities of a good business letter refer to the appearance of the letter. It includes the quality, color and size of the paper used. Good quality paper gives a favorable impression in the mind of the reader, and helps in documenting the letters properly. The various format qualities of a good business letter are mentioned as follows:

(1) Quality of paper. The paper used should be in accordance with the economic status of the firm. From an economical point of view, quality paper should be used for original copy and ordinary paper may be used for duplicate copy.

(2) Color of the paper. It is better to use different colors for different types of letters, so that the receiver will identify the letters quickly and act promptly.

(3) Size of the paper. Standard size paper (A4) should be used while writing business letters. The size of the paper should be in accordance with the envelopes available in the market.

(4) Folding of letter. The letter should be folded properly and uniformly. Care should be taken to give minimum folds to the letter so that it will fit the size of the envelope. If window envelope is used then folding should be done in such a way that the address of the receiver is clearly visible

through the transparent part of the envelope.

(5) Envelope. The size and quality of the envelope also need special attention. The size of the letter should fit the size of the envelope. The business firms use different types of envelopes, such as ordinary envelope, window envelope, laminated envelope, etc. In window envelope there is no need to write the address of the receiver separately on the envelope. It is clearly visible through the transparent part on the face of the envelope known as window. In laminated envelope, a thin plastic sheet or cloth is pasted on the inner side that gives extra protection to letters from being damaged during transit.

Exercise

I Fill in the blanks with proper words.

1. Business letters serve as a/an _____ in case of dispute in business transactions.
2. It is _____ for the businessmen to remember all facts without correspondence.
3. Business letters build _____ for a businessman.
4. Business letters are written to _____ information.
5. A business letter is the most _____ mode of communication.
6. Apart from ordinary envelopes, we may also use _____ or _____ envelopes for sending business letters.
7. To make a letter courteous, words like _____ and _____ should be used.
8. A business letter should contain only _____ information.
9. Accuracy demands no error in the usage of _____.
10. Business letters should be always neat and _____ in appearance.

II Write "T" for true statements and "F" for false statements.

1. A letter is a form of written communication. (   )
2. Through business letters, personal contact can be maintained between buyer and seller. (   )
3. Business letters lead to decline the goodwill of the firm. (   )
4. A letter is a convenient and economic mode of communication. (   )
5. Business letters do not help in removing misunderstanding between buyer and seller. (   )

Chapter 2

The Forms of Business Correspondence

Questions for Discussion

1. What are the differences between the block form and the indented form?
2. How many line spaces are usually set between parts in business correspondence?

Although daily business messages like e-mail or telephone are dominant nowaday, the printed business letter is still the preferred way to convey important information. A carefully crafted letter can be a powerful communication tool in the trade. To make sure that you are writing professional and effective business letters, it is necessary for you to use the acceptable business letter format and template. There are at least four kinds of format for business correspondence: block form, modified block form, simplified form and indented form.

Section 1 Block Form

In block form, the commonly used one, every part is aligned along the left margin. What's more, line spaces will be set up between parts.

The following is the layout of block form.

Letterhead *(6-10 line spaces, depending on whether a letterhead is used)*

(About 2 inches or 2 lines below letterhead)

Date

   (2-3 line spaces)

Inside address

   (1 line space)

Salutation

   (1 line space — new paragraph)

Subject line
    (1 line space — new paragraph)
Body
Paragraph 1
    (1 line space — new paragraph)
Paragraph 2
    (1 line space — new paragraph)
Paragraph 3
    (2 line spaces)

Complimentary close

    (3 line spaces)

Signature
    (2 line spaces)

Your name (typed)
Your tittle
    (1 line space)
Enclosure

Sample 1   The Block Form

BRIGADE QUARTERMASTERS CO., LTD.
1234 Kennesaw Drive
Atlanta, Georgia 30332

August 24, 2014

Captain James T. Kirk
Starship Enterprise
Crab Nebula, Sector 031-P29

Dear Captain Kirk,

It has come to my attention that your company, the Cooking Store, has been late with paying the invoices for the past three months.

In order to encourage our customers to pay for their invoices before the due date, we have implemented a discount model where we'll give you 2% off your invoice if you pay us within 10 days after receiving the invoice.

I hope that everything is going well with you and your company. You are one of our biggest customers, and we appreciate your business. If you have any questions, you can feel free to contact me at (555) 555-5555.

Sincerely,

George P. Burdell
Account Executive

Enclosure

Section 2   Modified Block Style

  The modified block style is a traditional and quite popular layout. This form is similar to the block form. However, complimentary closing and signature should appear to the right margin of the paper.
  The following is the layout of modified block style.

Letterhead *(6-10 line spaces, depending on whether a letterhead is used)*
(About 2 inches or 2 lines below letterhead)

Date
  (2-3 line spaces)

Inside address
    (1 line space)
Salutation
    (1 line space — new paragraph)
Subject line
    (1 line space — new paragraph)
Body
Paragraph 1
    (1 line space — new paragraph)
Paragraph 2
    (1 line space — new paragraph)
Paragraph 3
    (2 line spaces)

                              Complimentary close

                                (3 line spaces)

                                Signature
                                (2 line spaces)

                                Your name (typed)
                                Your tittle
                                (1 line space)

Enclosure

Sample 2   The Modified Block Form

                BRIGADE QUARTERMASTERS CO., LTD.
                       1234 Kennesaw Drive
                     Atlanta, Georgia 30332

August 24, 2014

Captain James T. Kirk

Starship Enterprise
Crab Nebula, Sector 031-P29

Dear Captain Kirk,

It has come to my attention that your company, the Cooking Store, has been late with paying the invoices for the past three months.

In order to encourage our customers to pay for their invoices before the due date, we have implemented a discount model where we'll give you 2% off your invoice if you pay us within 10 days after receiving the invoice.

I hope that everything is going well with you and your company. You are one of our biggest customers, and we appreciate your business. If you have any questions, you can feel free to contact me at (555) 555-5555.

                                                          Sincerely,

                                              George P. Burdell
                                              Account Executive

Enclosure

 ## Section 3   Simplified Form

    The simplified form is almost similar to block form, that's to say, all letter parts begin at the left margin. However, the difference lies in that this format includes a subject line but omits the salutation and signature.

    The following is the layout of simplified form.

                          Letterhead *(6-10 line spaces, depending on whether a letterhead is used)*
          (About 2 inches or 2 lines below letterhead)

Date
    (2-3 line spaces)

Inside address
    (1 line space)
Subject line
    (1 line space — new paragraph)
Body
Paragraph 1
    (1 line space — new paragraph)
Paragraph 2
    (1 line space — new paragraph)
Paragraph 3
    (2 line spaces)

Complimentary close

    (3 line spaces)

Your name (typed)
Your title
    (1 line space)
Enclosure

Sample 3　The Simplified Form

CLAIMS DIVISION, LAW DEPARTMENT
City of Austin
P.O. Box 96, Austin, Texas 78767-0096

February 14, 2014

Lindsay Office Products
P.O. Box 1879
Spokane, Washington 98989

Subject: Furniture and equipment order

Please ship the following items from your sales catalog dated January 31, 2014.

ITEM	CATALOG #	COLOR	QTY	PRICE
Conference Desk	HN-33080-WB	Sandalwood	2	$478.60 each
Shelf	HN-36887-WK	Sandalwood	2	$431.40 each
Executive Chair	HP-56563-SE	Toasted Tan	4	$422.00 each
File Cabinet	HN-5344C-K	Beige	2	$135.90 each
Letter Tray	K5-299907-A	Black	6	$16.95 each

The items ordered above should be shipped COD to this address:

CLAIMS DIVISION, LAW DEPARTMENT
City of Austin
P.O. Box 96 Austin, Texas 78767-0096

The costs above reflect a discount of 50/10, with net due in 30 days after the invoice date. The merchandise is to be shipped by your company's own truck line at a rate of 7 percent of the total net cost.

We are remodeling our offices and have a target completion date of March 30, 2014. If there is any reason you see that you can keep your part of this schedule, please let me know immediately.

Sincerely,

Berenice Chamala
Supervisor, Clerical Services

 ## Section 4   Indented Form

In this form, each line of the inside address is in the body part four or five letters indented from the left, and the first line of each paragraph is also indented.

The following is the layout of indented form.

> **Letterhead** *(6-10 line spaces, depending on whether a letterhead is used)*
> *(About 2 inches or 2 lines below letterhead)*
>
> **Date**
> *(2-3 line spaces)*
>
> **Inside address**
> *(1 line space)*
> **Salutation**
> *(1 line space —new paragraph)*
> **Subject line**
> *(1 line space —new paragraph)*
> **Body**
>   **Paragraph 1**
>   *(1 line space —new paragraph)*
>   **Paragraph 2**
>   *(1 line space —new paragraph)*
>   **Paragraph 3**
>   *(2 line spaces)*
>
>   **Complimentary close**
>
>   *(3 line spaces)*
>
>   **Signature**
>   *(2 line spaces)*
>
>   **Your name (typed)**
>   **Your tittle**
>   *(1 line space)*
>
> **Enclosure**

Sample 4   The Indented Form

BRIGADE QUARTERMASTERS CO., LTD.
1234 Kennesaw Drive
Atlanta, Georgia 30332

August 24, 2014

Captain James T. Kirk
    Starship Enterprise
        Crab Nebula, Sector 031-P29

Dear Captain Kirk,

    It has come to my attention that your company, the Cooking Store, has been late with paying the invoices for the past three months.

    In order to encourage our customers to pay for their invoices before the due date, we have implemented a discount model where we'll give you 2% off your invoice if you pay us within 10 days after receiving the invoice.

    I hope that everything is going well with you and your company. You are one of our biggest customers, and we appreciate your business. If you have any questions, you can feel free to contact me at (555) 555-5555.

                                                    Sincerely,

                                                George P. Burdell
                                                Account Executive

Enclosure

Section 5 Envelope Addressing

Addressing an envelope correctly helps get your letter to the correct destination on time. If you're writing an address on an envelope to a business contact, it's especially important to make it accurate, legible and good-looking so that you look professional. Similar to the inside address, there are also two forms: block form and indented form. Keep in mind that you should write the sender's address on the top left corner in separate lines, and the recipient's on the bottom right corner.

1. Block Form

```
China National Machinery Import & Export Corp.
No. 1 (W) Fuchengmenwai Avenue
Beijing, 100037
People's Republic of China                                     Stamp



                                              Apple
                                              1 Infinite Loop
                                              Cupertino, CA 95014
                                              USA
```

2. Indented Form

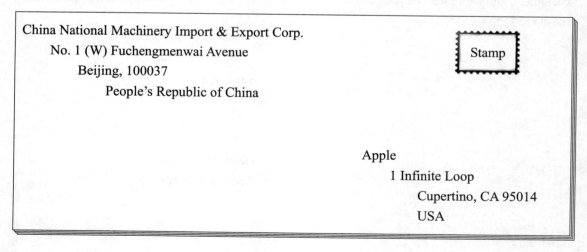

The Forms of Business Correspondence **Chapter 2** 17

Note:
Use all capital letters in the address and return address, for capital letters are easier to read. Use standard abbreviations for streets (ST, BLVD, RD, etc.) and for states, but don't use punctuation in the address.

I Fill in the blanks with suitable words.
1. The complementary close must be in accordance with the _____.
2. Below the signature and name of the writer, his _____, which informs the main idea, is also written.
3. In the body part of the body of the letter _____ is written.
4. Dear Sir is the form of _____.
5. The body of the letter is usually divided into _____ part(s).

II Choose the best answer to each of the following questions based on the information of the forms of business letters.
1. In the Indented Form Business Letter, YOUR ADDRESS should be at the top with the left edge of the address aligned with the _____.
   A. center of the page   B. right margin   C. left margin   D. bottom
2. At the top of the page, the date should line up and have the same alignment as _____.
   A. the greeting   B. your address
   C. the inside address   D. the subject line
3. The alignment of the inside address and salutation should be _____.
   A. centered   B. next to the right margin
   C. flush left   D. typed in capital letters
4. The salutation of a business letter always followed by _____.
   A. a semi-colon   B. a colon
   C. a period   D. a question mark
5. What should one always avoid in formal letters?
   A. Starting the first sentence of the letter with the word "How".
   B. Using a red-colored font.
   C. Paragraphs with more than one or two sentences.
   D. Abbreviations.
6. The closing and signature lines alignment should be placed _____ in the indented form.
   A. the left edge of text aligned with the center of the page
   B. the left edge of text aligned with the right margin of the page

C. the right edge of text should be aligned with the left margin of the page

D. the right edge of the text justified and bold

7. The salutation of a business letter is always "_____" unless you know the name of the person to whom you are writing.

 A. Dear sir,   B. Dear Sirs,   C. Dear Sirs,   D. Dear Sir;

8. In the Indented Form Business Letter, how far should the paragraphs be indented?

 A. One-quarter inch.   B. One-half inch.   C. One inch.   D. Two inches.

9. How many line spaces should there be between the closing and the name of the writer of the letter?

 A. One.   B. Two.   C. Three.   D. Four.

10. How many line spaces should there be between paragraphs?

 A. One.   B. Two.   C. Three.   D. Four.

Chapter 3

The Components in Business Correspondence

Questions for Discussion

1. What are the components of a formal business letter?
2. What requirements should we follow for each component?
3. Do you know any differences between British and American English in letter writing conventions?

A business letter creates an impression of professionalism on the part of the business and sender. A properly structured letter provides clarity for the reader to look for the date, reference number and other elements; meanwhile, the proper structure would earn the recipient's respect. The body itself, structured with an introduction, body and conclusion, creates a purpose and an action for the next step, which shows that you have taken time to write clearly. Therefore, you should know that a business letter, generally, contains the following 16 components.

(1) Letterhead.
(2) Date.
(3) Reference line.
(4) Special mailing notations.
(5) On-arrival notations.
(6) Inside address.
(7) Attention line.
(8) Salutation.
(9) Subject line.
(10) Body of the letter.
(11) Complimentary close.
(12) Signature.
(13) Identification initials.
(14) Enclosures.
(15) Copy circulation.
(16) Post script.

Among the 16 elements, letterhead, date, inside address, salutation, body, complementary close and signature are necessary while the rests are optional.

1. Letterhead

Letterhead, or return address, usually contains the following information.

(1) Company name (always in all capitals).

(2) Street address or post office box number.

(3) City, state, ZIP code.

(4) Area code and phone number.

(5) Cable address or fax.

(6) Trade mark or logo of the business (optional).

For example:

 MANOR HOUSE HOTEL

Farnham Green, Warnside, Upminster, UB23.

Tel: 091 8976.   Fax: 091 9008.

E-mail: manhot@man.itx

A business letter produced on a typewriter might be typed on a prepared sheet of paper, which has a printed "letterhead" with details of the organization on whose behalf the letter is being written. Letterhead can be setup and inserted into or typed into e-mails. However, it is far too common a mistake for the addressor's address to be omitted from e-mails. A sender might expect the addressee to reply by e-mail, but the addressee might not wish to do so. Or it might not be feasible for the addressee to do so; for example, if a printed catalogue or samples of products need to be sent with the "response" letter.

2. Date

The date is frequently placed in the top right-hand corner, just two to three lines below the letterhead. However, some writers prefer to have the date typed in the top left-hand corner. In business letters, the date can be written in many acceptable ways like 6 September 2014, 6th September 2014 or September 6, 2014. However, it is usually not abbreviated. That is to say, we write "September 6, 2014" instead of "Sept. 6, 2014". The format of the date differs from country to country. It is common to use American (Month/Day/Year) or British (Day/Month/Year) format for receivers from different areas. Therefore, in order to avoid misunderstanding, we should not write "06/09/2014" for it means "9 June 2014" to the American but "6 September 2014" to the British.

3. Reference Line

If the recipient specifically requests information, such as a job reference, invoice number, or letter number, type it on one or two lines, immediately below the Date. If you're replying to a letter, refer to it here. A business letter often — but not always — includes a typewritten "reference" or "code" to identify it. For example:

Ref.: Job # 625-01
Ref.: Your letter dated 1/1/2014

4. Special Mailing Notations

Special notations appear two lines below the date or reference line. When an inside address is included, the special notation appears between the date or reference line and the inside address. Capital letters are used to ensure visibility. For instance:

SPECIAL DELIVERY
CERTIFIED MAIL
AIRMAIL

5. On-arrival Notations

You might want to include a notation on private or business correspondence, such as a resignation letter and include the same on the envelope. Remember to type in all uppercase characters, if appropriate. Examples are as follows:

PERSONAL
CONFIDENTIAL
PRIVATE AND CONFIDENTIAL
REGISTERED MAIL

6. Inside Address

The inside address is the recipient's address. It usually includes the following information.
(1) The addressee's courtesy title — Mr., Mrs., Ms., Miss, or Dr. — followed by his/her full name.
(2) The addressee's business title.
(3) The name of the organization.
(4) The street address, post office box, suite number, mail drop, or other mailing information.
(5) The city, state, and full ZIP code.

When writing the addressee's name/title or organization name, you'd better pay attention to the following points.
(1) Write the name exactly as the person or business does in her/his/its correspondence to you. For example:

Maine St. Investments (not Main Street Investments)
Mr. William B. Sachs (not Wm. B Sachs or W.B. Sachs or Willie B. Sachs)

(2) Include addressee's job title and department if known. For instance:

Ms. Eleanor A. Hill
Director of Training
Creative Dining

When the name of the intended reader is unknown, the letter should be addressed to a position title. If the letter is written to an organization, it should be addressed to the name of the organization (or the department within it).

(3) Avoid double titles and use "Dr. Ann Smith" or "Ann Smith, M.D." (not Dr. Ann Smith, M.D.), and break a long company name into two lines for balance.

When writing street names and numbers, use figures (except for One) for street numbers and spell out street names that are numbers 1 through 10, e.g. 915 West Seventh Street; add the letters "d", "st", or "th" to numbers over 10 that represent street names, e.g. 707 West 16th Street. Preferably, spell out "street", "avenue", "building", and directional words such as "east" and "northwest".

As to the state and ZIP codes, please note to type the ZIP code on the same line with city and state, leaving two spaces between state and ZIP. And you can use the standard two-letter state abbreviations (both capitals, no period thereafter) preferred by the US Post Office(see Note). Spelling out the state name is also correct.

The example of inside address is as follows:

Ms. Betty Johnson

Accounts Payable

The Cooking Store

765 Berliner Plaza

Industrial Point, CA 68534

Because letter length dictates the number of blank lines that are inserted between the date or reference line and the inside address, it appears two to four lines below the date or reference line. It is written on the left hand side of the sheet below the reference number. If you type an Attention Line, skip the person's name.

7. Attention Line

An attention line is used when the inside address does not include either the name of an individual or the name of the department. It appears two lines below the inside address at left margin. The word attention may have an initial capital letter or appear in all capitals and followed by a colon. For example:

Attention: Mr. Todd W. Baldwin

ATTENTION: REAL ESTATE REPRESENTATIVE

Many companies now omit the attention line and type the name of the person or department above the company name in the inside addresses. Whenever possible, omit the attention line, but address the letter directly to an individual in the organization, by name and title.

8. Salutation

The salutation helps to establish the tone of the correspondence. The salutation appears two spaces beneath the inside address and usually begins with the conventional greeting "Dear" followed by the title and name of the addressee. When you are writing to a person whose name and sex you know, use "Dear+Mr./Mrs./Ms./Miss+Surname". No punctuation follows the salutation in open punctuation style; in standard punctuation style, a colon (formal letters) or comma (informal letters) follows the salutation. When none of the non-gender alternatives seems appropriate, a simplified letter format (omitting the salutation) may be used. Another solution is to omit the gender title, e.g., Dear Chris Smith. For different addressees, different salutations should be used. The following table shows common salutation.

Addressee	British English	American English
Company or institution	Dear Sirs,	Dear Gentlemen:
Man (name unknown)	Dear Sir,	the same as British English
Woman (name unknown)	Dear Madam,	
Name and sex unknown	Dear Sir or Madam,	
Man	Dear Mr. Blair,	
Married woman or widow	Dear Mrs. Blair,	
Unmarried woman	Dear Miss Blair,	
Woman (the modern way)	Dear Ms. Blair,	
Woman (marital status unknown)	Dear Ms. Blair,	
Married couple	Dear Mr. and Mrs. Blair,	
Friend/acquaintance	Dear Jackie,	
Punctuation	After the salutation there is a comma (,).	After the salutation there is a colon (:).

9. Subject Line

A subject line helps identify the subject of the letter. It appears 1 line space below salutation, flush left or indented according to format of body paragraphs. A subject line is often typed either in capital and small or in all-capital letters, beginning with the word "Subject", "Re", "Underlined" or "Capitalized". Each is followed by a colon. Examples can be seen as follows:

RE: MEADOW GLEN MALL TAB
Re: Late Delivery of Order 123
Subject: Your order No. C317/8 dated 12th March 2014
Subject: Order No. 1232 for Tea-sets
Underlined: <u>Sale Contract No. 234</u>
Capitalized: SALE CONTRACT NO. 234

10. Body

This is the main part of the letter. It begins on second line below salutation or subject line. Most business letters are single-placed with double-line space between paragraphs. It usually contains three parts.

(1) Opening part. It is the introductory part of the letter. In this part, attention of the reader should be drawn to the previous correspondence, if any.

(2) Main part. This part usually contains the subject matter of the letter. It should be precise and written in clear words and to the point.

(3) Concluding Part. It contains a statement of the sender's intentions, hopes or expectations concerning the next step to be taken. Further, the sender should always look forward to getting a positive response.

11. Complimentary Close

The complimentary close (omitted in the simplified letter format) appears two lines below the last line of text. Its alignment varies with the format of the letter. In block letters, the complimentary close appears flush with the left margin. In modified and indented letters, it appears in the center, flush with the right margin. "Yours sincerely", "Respectfully yours", or "Respectfully" are complimentary closes for very formal letters (those addressed to dignitaries and high officials); "Best wishes", "Kindest regards", "Regards", "Best regards", and "Cordially" for informal letters. "Sincerely yours" is the American style while "Yours sincerely" is the British style.

The complimentary close should convey the level of formality and degree of personal feeling that the writer has for the reader. For example:

    Respectfully yours (very formal)
    Sincerely (typical, less formal)
    Very truly yours (polite, neutral)
    Cordially yours (friendly, informal)

What is more, it must be in accordance with the salutation. For example:

Salutation	Complementary Close
Dear Sir/Dear Madam	Yours faithfully
Dear Mr. Raj	Yours sincerely
My Dear Akbar	Yours very sincerely (very informal relations)

12. Signature

The signature block contains the handwritten signature of the writer, the full typed name of the writer, and the title of the writer. It appears four or five lines beneath the complimentary close (or at a like distance below the last line of text of simplified format letters). The company name is optional; it is only needed when the letter represents a company policy, position, or decision; and the company name should be typed entirely in all capitals two lines below the complimentary close.

13. Identification Initials

Identification Initials or Reference initials (the writer's initials and the secretary's/typist's initials) appear two lines below the last line of the signature block and flush with the left margin. If only the secretary's/typist's initials are used, they are usually lowercase. If the writer's initials are included, they are in all capitals, followed by a slash mark or colon, and then followed by the secretary's/typist's initials in lowercase. Common styles are shown below.

TLM/rgn (the writer's initials and the secretary's/typist's initials)

TLM: rgn

Rgn (the secretary's/typist's initials)

14. Enclosure Notation

An enclosure notation reminds readers of enclosures and appears directly under reference initials. The following are examples of enclosure notation forms: "Enclosure", "Enc.", "Enclosures (3)", "3 Enclosures", and "Enclosures 3".

This is also required when some documents like cheque, draft, bills, receipts, lists, invoices etc. are attached with the letter. These enclosures are listed one by one in serial numbers. For example:

Encl: (i) The list of goods received

(ii) A cheque for Rs. One Thousand dtt. Feb. 27, 2014 (Cheque No. 56792)

15. Copy Circulation (C.C.)

Copy Circulation, denoted as C.C., is required when copies of the letter are also sent to persons apart of the addressee. It appears two lines below the enclosure notation, flush with the left margin. Persons receiving the letter in addition to the addressee are listed in alphabetical order. For example:

C.C. i. The Chairman, Electric Supply Corporation

ii. The Director, Electric Supply Corporation

iii. The Secretary, Electric Supply Corporation

C.C.: Edward Albers&G.C. Fischer&Merilee Tobias

16. Postscripts

Postscripts (additions to the letter after it has been typed or items for emphasis) appear two lines below the last line of courtesy copy notation. The use of the initials PS or PPS is optional.

Supplementary Information

The list of Standard Two-letter Abbreviations for Addressing Envelopes

AL	Alabama	LA	Louisiana	OK	Oklahoma
AK	Alaska	ME	Maine	OR	Oregon
AZ	Arizona	MD	Maryland	PA	Pennsylvania
AR	Arkansas	MA	Massachusetts	RI	Rhode Island
CA	California	MI	Michigan	SC	South Carolina
CO	Colorado	MN	Minnesota	SD	South Dakota
CT	Connecticut	MS	Mississippi	TN	Tennessee
DE	Delaware	MO	Missouri	TX	Texas
DC	District of Colombia	MT	Montana	UT	Utah
FL	Florida	NE	Nebraska	VT	Vermont
GA	Georgia	NV	Nevada	VI	Virgin Islands
GU	Guam	NH	New Hampshire	VA	Virginia
HI	Hawaii	NJ	New Jersey	WA	Washington
ID	Idaho	NM	New Mexico	WV	West Virginia
IL	Illinois	NY	New York	WI	Wisconsin
IA	Iowa	NC	North Carolina	WY	Wyoming
KS	Kansas	ND	North Dakota	OH	Ohio
KY	Kentucky				

Exercise

I Decide whether the following statements are true (T) or false (F) when writing a business letter.

1. It is normal to write "Mr. John Tan" in the first line of the receiver's address, and underneath to write "Dear Mr. Tan" without the initial. (   )
2. The subject heading usually comes after "Dear Mr. Tan". (   )

3. In a modern business letters Dear Mrs. Lee and Yours sincerely are followed by a comma. (   )
4. Even if you know the person's name, you don't have to use it; you can still use "Dear Sir/Madam". (   )
5. You should not use abbreviations in letters and e-mails. (   )
6. Short simple sentences are better than long complex ones. (   )
7. Memos have a different structure to letters. (   )
8. Bullets and numbers can't be used in letters, as they're too informal. (   )
9. "Enc." is used when you are sending something in addition to the letter, e.g. a cheque. (   )
10. In modern business documents punctuation is not used in the receiver's address. (   )

II **Please read the following badly-written formal business letter and try to finish the exercises 1-4.**

Lee's Furniture Mart
62/66 Downtown, Moreville DT23. Tel: 608 0097

The Manager,
Seaview Guest House,
Parade DT12.

Dear Sirs,
The furniture you ordered has arrived at hour showrooms. Please telephone the undersigned personally to say weather you will collect it or we should deliver it to you; we shall be unhappy with either. Remember we want your money when you get the furniture so have it ready. Your early reply will be appreciated.
Yours sincerely, Manger

---

1. Write down ten faults and errors in the letter.
   (1) _____
   (2) _____
   (3) _____
   (4) _____
   (5) _____
   (6) _____
   (7) _____
   (8) _____
   (9) _____
   (10) _____

2. Rewrite the letter with all ten faults and errors corrected.

3. Answer the following questions.
(1) Why is it so important for the appearance of a business letter to be attractive?
_____
_____
_____

(2) What is "indentation" and why do some letter-writers use it?
_____
_____
_____

4. Choose the best answer.
(1) The addressee of a business letter is _____.
    A. the person or organization from which it is received
    B. the person or organization on behalf of which it is written
    C. the person or organization to whom it is to be sent
    D. the person who writes and/or signs it

(2) The greeting "Dear Sir or Madam" needs to match with the close "_____".
    A. Yours faithfully,
    B. Yours sincerely,
    C. Faithfully to you both,
    D. Yours truly,

(3) The first paragraph of a business letter usually _____.

    A. contains only one sentence
    B. states what the writer wants the addressee to do
    C. starts with the addressee's name
    D. gives the reason why the letter has been written
(4) The term "justification" in relation to a business letter means _____.
    A. that the writer has good reason for the facts contained in it
    B. that it contains all the proof necessary to convince the reader
    C. that it only just fits on one sheet of paper
    D. that all lines containing sufficient words end at the right-hand margin
(5) A prefix _____.
    A. is a senior boy or girl at school
    B. is added to the front of a word to form a new word
    C. involves the use of glue or an adhesive
    D. is added at the end of a word to form a new word

III Please make improvement to the following letter in which some parts of the layout is impropriate.

INTEGRATED COMPUTER TECHNOLOGY CO., LTD.

Rm 808, Kyo-Won-Kong-Jea 35-2 Yeoido

Young Dung Po

Seoul

South Korea

Tel: 822-782-4641   Fax: 822-785-4245

16 June 2014   KJ: rh

Enclosures 2

CC: Kim Sang-Chul

Moon Young-Seung

Subject: Integrated Circuit Boards

Dear Dr. Brenda Yeoh

We have just received your order for 400 integrated circuit boards (item No. KR10779). Unfortunately, these circuit boards are no longer produced as they have been replaced by our Model KR2000, which is cheaper, more reliable and more efficient than the circuit boards you ordered. With this in mind, we imagine that you will be happy to change your order.

The prices of the KR2000 and peripheral equipment are as follows:

KR2000 integrated circuit board: @US$23,200

KT200X "Toolkit": @US$15,500

KC200X connectors: (2 per pack) @US$10,000

I should be grateful if you could contact me to tell me what you wish us to do about your order.

Yours faithfully

Kim Jungsup

For INTERGARATED COMPUTER TECHNOLOGY CO., LTD.

Attention Dr Brenda Yeoh, PhD

ATT Computers Corp. Pte Ltd.

88 Kitchener Road, #02-15

Jalan Besar Plaza

Singapore 208512

PS: Forgot to mention it, but there are lots of bargains in the brochure and price list that I'm sending you.

Chapter 4

The Writing Principles in Business Correspondence

Questions for Discussion

1. What are the principles we should be aware of when writing business correspondence?
2. How can we reveal these principles in language use of business letter?

Business communication means the use of effective language for conveying a commercial or industrial message to achieve a predetermined purpose. Of all forms of written communication, letters are the most common and considered as the most personal. "6C" principles, the basic principles of writing business correspondence, refer to the evaluation of foreign letters in the word choice, sentence structure, content, tone, attitude and other aspects of writing English letters. "6C" principles include Courtesy, Conciseness, Concreteness, Clarity, Correctness, and Completeness.

Section 1 Courtesy

Courtesy is an important feature of foreign correspondence, as it is the basic principle of social relationship. Courtesy is like a lubricant, which removes friction and makes life smooth and helps to win friends. Therefore, courtesy leads to stronger business relationships. Especially in business correspondence, discourtesy damages both friendship and business. Developing courtesy in a business letter, generally speaking, includes three aspects: being polite, being positive and being personal.

1. Being Polite

No matter how aggravating the circumstances are, you should always write courteously as this style of writing fosters a positive relationship with your reader and is more likely to bring about a favorable response. To be polite in your business writing, you need to write in a style that:

(1) reflects an appropriate reader-writer relationship,
(2) does not convey a sense of superiority/anger/condescension, or
(3) does not embarrass the reader.

Some examples are given in the table below.

Writing that	Examples	Tone
an appropriate reader-writer relationship	With effect from 14 July, your goods must be delivered at 7:00 am sharply. I seek your cooperation in this respect.	impolite
	My suggestion is that we deliver your goods promptly at 7:00 am instead of the usual 6:30 am. I hope this arrangement is convenient for you.	polite
not convey a sense of superiority, anger or condescension	If you had read Section IV of your policy, you would know that you are not covered for accidents which happen on water.	angry
	As a review of Section IV of your policy indicates, you are covered for accidents which happen on the grounds of your home only.	composed
not embarrass the reader	As you did not respond within 10 days, it should be clear to you that you did not qualify for the free gift.	rude
	You probably did not notice that your order was mailed after our special gift offer had expired.	polite

2. Being Positive

Being positive in your writing also helps to generate a more favorable response to your message. Positive words are helpful especially when persuasion and goodwill are needed. Positive words emphasize the pleasant aspect of the goal and tend to put the reader in the right frame of mind. However, negative words tend to produce the opposite effect. They may stir up your reader's resistance to your goals. So in business correspondence you'd better:

(1) use positive words and phrases, and
(2) stress what can be done.

Some examples are given in the table below.

Writing that	Examples	Tone
positive words/phrases	There are no more places for the May 15 seminar and there will be no similar seminar organized until October.	negative
	Due to its popularity, all places for the May 15 seminar have been filled. A similar seminar will be organized in October and we will be happy to reserve a place for you, if you like.	positive
what can be done	We regret to inform you that we must deny your request for credit.	negative
	For the time being, we can serve you only on a cash basis.	positive

3. Being Personal

The style and tone of your letter will also be improved if you could be more personal in your writing. The ways to achieve this include:

(1) adopting a "you" attitude,
(2) using personal pronouns, and
(3) avoiding pompous words/phrases.

The "you" attitude in business letter writing is a style of writing that looks at things from the reader's perspective and expresses genuine consideration for the reader. To project this attitude in your writing, you need to recognize and understand the reader's situation and you should be interested in helping in a sincere and courteous way. When writing with the "you" attitude, you need to emphasize what the reader wants to know, respect the reader's intelligence and protect the reader's ego.

Some examples are given in the table below to demonstrate ways in making your writing more personal.

Writing that	Examples	Tone
an "you" attitude	We are happy to announce that we have increased the size of our store building.	straightforward informative
	Now you will find a wider choice of merchandise in the greatly enlarged building.	personal, engaging
personal pronouns	If there should be any questions concerning this matter, please call the number listed on the letterhead above.	formal detached
	We look forward to working with you. Meantime, if there is anything further that we can do for you, please let us know.	personal friendly
pompous words/phrases	I want to cogitate further on the matter before giving a definitive answer.	pompous
	I want to think about the matter a little more before I give a final answer.	unpretentious

 ## Section 2 Conciseness

Conciseness refers to "conveying complete message with the help of minimum words possible". It is a pre-requisite of business correspondence as it is said in the field of business that "time saved is money saved". Hence, a concise letter saves time and expense of both parties. Being concise means using the fewest possible words to get a message across to the reader. Long-winded writing can be annoying because unnecessary words, irrelevant details and muddled expressions waste the reader's time. However, concise writing does not mean sacrificing clarity or essential information. Conciseness is still about using the fewest possible words to get the same message across in the clearest possible way. Transmission of maximum information by using minimum of words should be the aim in the letter writing. Attention of the reader can be caught with clarity and conciseness. Unnecessary details and redundant expressions are to be avoided. Being concise in business letter need you to avoid redundancy and wordy expressions, and use strong verbs and the active voice.

1. Avoid Redundancy

A repeated word can make the whole information boring. Sometimes repetition is necessary in case to lay stress on particular information but this should not be practiced without more than one reason. In order to avoid redundancy, do not use two words with the same meaning in the same sentence. In the following examples, the word in italics with underline is redundant and should be left out:

my *personal* opinion   prompt *and speedy*

after three hours *later*   attached *hereto*

2. Avoid Wordy Expressions

Note how the expressions below can be shortened without losing any meaning.

Cluttering Words	Concise Substitutions
at the present time	now
in the near future	soon
in very few cases	seldom
I am of the opinion that	I think

3. Use Strong Verbs and the Active Voice

Strong verbs are those which describe actions directly. By contrast, weak verb forms are those which have action words as well as nouns. Hence, weak verb forms use more words to describe the same action as its equivalent strong verb. Weak verb forms should be avoided also because they tend to be abstract and usually require the passive voice.

Weak Verb	Strong Verb
give assistance to	assist
make an acquisition	acquire
have a discussion	discuss
conduct an investigation	investigate
We must aim for a reconciliation of our differences.	We must reconcile our differences.
The establishment of a rehabilitation center has been accomplished.	The company has established a rehabilitation center.

Section 3 Clarity

The purpose of clarity is achieving accuracy. For the audience to understand the information easily, the information must be very clear. In effective business correspondence, familiar and easy words and short and effective sentences and paragraph construction help the audience understand. The use of jargons and complex sentences leads to misunderstandings. If there is a choice between jargons and familiar words or a simple sentence and a complex sentence, one must choose familiar words and simple words. A simple expression and clear thinking are the most important virtues of effective writing. As Mathew Arnold rightly advised, "Have something to say and say it as clearly as you can". Using indirect sentence structure, preferring short, simple words, and keeping sentences short will be helpful to make business clear.

1. Use Indirect Sentence Structure in Bad News and Persuasion

When you want to express the message of bed news or try to persuade your partner to accept your ideas, you should usually write in an indirect order. The indirect order is especially effective when you must say "no" to a request or when you convey disappointing news. The main reason for this approach is that negative messages are received more positively when an explanation precedes them.

Do's	Don'ts
Many thanks for your letter	You state
We are glad to note that	You are wrong in saying
We appreciate your writing	It is difficult to believe
We regret to inform that	We can't accept your request
We are sorry that	We are forced to refuse
We are grateful for the suggestions you have made	We demand

2. Prefer Short and Simple Words

Short, familiar words communicate more clearly than longer and less used words. Long words may look impressive, but they may not be understood and may distract the reader from the message.

Instead of	Use or Write
terminate	end
remunerate	pay
endeavour	try

cogitate	think
procure	buy
scrutinize, probe	study, inspect
stipulate	specify
necessitate	require
This machine has a tendency to develop excessive and unpleasant audile symptoms when operating at elevated temperatures.	This machine tends to get noisy when it runs hot.

However, the above examples, and all other possible examples, must be used with caution. While the objective is to use simple and shorter words, you do not do so at the expense of other considerations, such as the use of concrete and specific words. For example, the word "ask" may be shorter than "enquire" or "demand", but these last two words have shades of meaning which are concrete and specific. To ask for an explanation is different from to demand an explanation. The key point is that if your meaning can be expressed more clearly by a shorter or simpler word, and then you should use this word. Do not use longer words just because you want to impress your reader.

3. Keep Sentences Short

Shorter sentences and paragraphs are easier to understand and likely to contain fewer errors.

Unnecessary words that add nothing to the meaning and the impact of the sentence or paragraph should be omitted. Most business communication experts recommend writing with an average sentence length of 20 to 25 words. Sentences over 40 to 50 words long should be reconsidered to decide whether they should be rewritten.

Of course, sometimes longer sentences can, and should, be written. This is necessary in order to complete a thought or idea, to provide variety in sentence length, and to subordinate less important information. But in writing long sentences, care should be taken to ensure that they are clear and the important point is not lost.

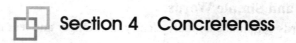 Section 4　Concreteness

Concreteness is the most important aid to clarity because general statements make little impression upon the average mind. Concrete communication means being specific, definite, and vivid rather than vague and general. Often it means using denotative rather than connotative words. Using concrete expressions is one of the most important features of modern business English. Concrete words create visual images which are easy to comprehend. On the other hand, abstract words refer to general ideas and things, qualities and conditions. The benefits to business professionals of using concrete facts and figures are obvious; your readers know exactly what is required or desired. Using concrete language has some extra advantages. When you supply specifics for the reader, you increase the likelihood that your message will be interpreted the way you intend to. In business writing, you should use concrete and specific words.

Abstract	Concrete
a significant loss	a 83 percent loss
good attendance record	93 percent attendance record
the majority	72%
at the soonest possible time	by 8 p.m., Friday
substantial amount	$ 2.7 million
a relatively new product	a new product introduced in 2014

Section 5   Correctness

Correct use of grammar, punctuation and spellings are a must for business correspondence. Errors in business letters might give a negative impression on the reputation of the company and the writer. Therefore, business writer should pay attention to three characteristics of correctness: use of correct level of language and paralanguage (such as grammar, spelling, terminology choices), use of correct facts, figures and words and use of correct mechanics of writing (like formats). Incorrect grammar, punctuation and spelling are likely to lead to highest level of misunderstandings and trade disputes.

Section 6   Completeness

When a message is transmitted in business letters, the audience (reader/listener) desires complete information to be presented. A muddled message or half message creates confusion in the mind of the audience. A chain of who-what-when-where-why questions must be addressed in the process of information presentation. When these questions are addressed, the scope of confusion in the mind of the audience becomes minimal. These questions also help the writer/speaker deal with other business activities of letter writing. For example, if a customer enquires about a particular product, it is the responsibility of the person-in-charge to give detailed information in a short span of time along with some additional information that the customer is not aware of. This process helps in building good business relation. Therefore, all the necessary information and data should be included in the business letters for achieving desired objective.

Exercise

I. Match the following statements with the principles.

1. The receiver understands the message in the same way as intended by the sender.
2. There should be no errors in the usage of language in business letter.
3. Relevant information should be provided in business letter.
4. Words of anger should not be used in any business letters.
5. You include all the facts and details of the order in the body of your letter.

A. Completeness
B. Courtesy
C. Correctness
D. Clarity
E. Conciseness

II. Each pair of the following statements expresses the same idea. Choose the more appropriate one and write down the principle.

1. a. Your prompt shipment of our order will be highly appreciated.
   b. You are requested to ship our good without any delay.
   Principle: _____
2. a. The credit will remain valid until the end of this month.
   b. The credit will remain valid until May 31, 2014.
   Principle: _____
3. a. This machine has a tendency to develop excessive and unpleasant audible symptoms when operating at elevated temperature.
   b. This machine tends to get noisy when it runs hot.
   Principle: _____
4. a. We have established through our bank an irrevocable L/C in your favor.
   b. We have established through our bank an irrevocable L/C in your favor which will reach you in June 15 and remain valid until the end of June.
   Principle: _____
5. a. Upon arrival at the head office, your auditor is to go to the boardroom.
   b. When your auditor arrives at the head office, he is to go to the boardroom.
   Principle: _____

III. Rewrite the following sentences according to the principle of courtesy.

1. I am in receipt of your order for 250 pairs of Nike "Conga" sports shoes.

2. We receive your enquiry of 20 August.

3. You must furnish us with details as to the credit that may be safely allowed to the firm whose name is given on the slip.

4. It's your duty to inform us whether your business relations with Messrs J. A. Hussain and Co. during the past would lead you to advise us to allow them 3 months' credit.

5. Tell us whether they are in the wholesale trade or not.

6. We suggest that whenever you have goods to place with us you send them to us as soon as possible.

IV Rewrite the following sentences according to the principle of consideration.

1. We cannot devote much time to your visit as the March Sales figures are being complied and we are very busy.

2. We do not have the time to send our Sales Representative to see you. He is busy dealing with larger accounts than yours.

3. It is not our fault if you do not check whether the goods are satisfactory on delivery.

4. Since you can't supply goods of the type and quality required we can't place our orders.

5. Your prices are too high; therefore we can't place the order.

6. I regret to inform you that we cannot refund your deposit unless you return the goods within a week.

7. You failed to send your order to us before the new prices were introduced.

8. We will decline your order.

V. Rewrite the following sentences according to the principle of conciseness.

1. Will you ship us any time during the month of December, or even November if you are rushed, for November would suit us just as well?

2. The end result of our mutual cooperation is that the project will be completed during the winter months.

3. The agency is not able to release the report at the present time.

4. As a matter of fact, the X-210 copier is not really the kind of machine the company needs, since the X-200 has the capability of meeting virtually all of our needs.

VI. Rewrite the following sentences according to the principle of clarity.

1. Your proposal for payment by time draft is acceptable to us under Order No. 115.

2. We have ordered a hundred cupcakes for the children dipped in chocolate.

3. Please bring the speaker a cold glass of water.

4. To be sure the report would be delivered on time; URGENT was written across the front of the envelope.

5. Having agreed to a solution, the meeting ended.

6. Upon receipt of your order, the contract will be sent.

7. We sent you 5 samples yesterday of the goods which you requested in your letter of May 25 by air.

Chapter 5

Other Business Writing

Questions for Discussion

1. How many types of commonly used business writing are there?
2. What are the features of letters of public relation and good will?
3. What are the differences among memo, minute and agenda?
4. How to produce an effective business report?

Section 1 Letters of Public Relation and Goodwill

The letters will be used to show the gratitude, concern, or congratulation on some special occasions, and thus should be timely, considerate, and sincere. The popular topics will cover:
- reply to the proposed visit;
- showing gratitude for the reception;
- congratulations and reply;
- boarding arrangement;
- invitation.

Sample 1 Proposed Visit

Subject: proposed visit during May

Dear Helen,

As I am planning a visit to Qingdao during May 17 to 22, I wonder if it is possible to include a visit to your company and factory then. I am very interested in introducing a new line to you as well as seeing your latest products. Please let me know if this time schedule is OK with you. There will be 3 of us in the party and it would be great if you could suggest a hotel.

Looking forward to seeing you.

Sample 2　Replies to the Proposed Visit

Subject: Proposed visit during May

Dear Tom,

I am glad to hear that you will visit Qingdao and the timing is fine. Please let me know your flight number and I will arrange to pick you up. There are several hotels you can choose from. I have attached a list for you.

I look forward to seeing any new designs you have for us.

We have recently launched some new products you may be interested in.

Looking forward to seeing you.

Sample 3　Showing Gratitude for the Reception

Dear Helen,

Thank you so much for meeting us at the airport and for looking after us so well during our visit.

I hope that you can manufacture our new designs according to our specifications and within the cost limits. Please let me know the progress you are making on this. We are really enjoying the tour of the factory and certain that some of your new products interest us. We will get in touch with you about that very soon.

Again, thank you very much for the warm hospitality we've received, not just from you, but from everyone we met.

Looking forward to hearing from you.

Sample 4　Congratulations

Dear all,

Our warmest congratulations to Eric Johnson, who has recently received the industry's award for the best TV commercial of the year. A recent graduate from Tsinghua University, Eric joined us in

2014 and immediately attracted the attention of writers and artists with his avant garde style. He says he enjoys working in our country setting, where he and his bride can enjoy the inspiration of the mountain.

The award is granted each year for the commercial that industry writers and artists vote as the most effective in the use of visual media. Eric will receive his award at the annual banquet of screen and TV writers in February.

Our best wishes to Eric and to all our writers who set today's standard of excellence. Your futures look very bright.

All the best,

Fred

Sample 5 Boarding Arrangement

Dear Sir or Madam,

I would like to book 3 single rooms from May 9 to 12. Could you please tell me what your rates are? If possible, I would like 2 smoking rooms and 1 non-smoking room. Could you please confirm whether you have any rooms available for those 3 nights? Also please let me know what the check-out time is on the 12th.

I look forward to hearing from you soon.

Sincerely yours,

Alice

Sample 6 Invitation

Subject: Shanghai visit

Dear Mr. Chan,

Following our pleasant discussion last week, I would like to invite you to visit our head office and manufacturing factory in Shanghai. As proposed, your visit would cover 2 days starting from the 17th Nov. to the 18th.

The Shanghai facility is designed to produce top-class components which can meet even the most rigorous international quality requirements. Through the extensive use of advanced hardware and software, the whole facility only needs 20 staff for system control and supervision.

The following agenda is for your review.

    November 17th
    9:00–9:30   arrival
    9:45–11:45   headquarters visit
    12:00–1:30   welcome lunch
    2:00–4:30   meeting with CEO
    5:30   dinner

    November 18th
    9:00–9:30   factory visit and manufacturing introduction
    11:45–1:30   lunch
    2:00–3:30   distribution center visit
    4:00–5:30   discussion
    6:00   dinner

We trust these arrangements will be satisfactory and look forward to the confirmation of your visit. We are confident this visit will demonstrate our strong capability and provide the proof of our reliability as a future supplier with your organization.

We look forward to hearing from you soon!

Section 2 Memo

Memo, or a memorandum, is a brief written message, proposal or reminder from one person or an organization to another. One major difference between memos and letters is that memos have "MEMO" as the title, as well as the title line. Because readers often decide whether to read the memo solely on the basis of this title line. Another difference between letters and memos is that you sometimes write memos that serve as short reports. In such case, the format of a memo changes accordingly. For instance, in a memo serving as a progress report for a project, you might include subheadings and sub-subheadings.

The typical parts of a memo are heading and body part and heading segment should also include the complete and exact date on which the memo was written, and the subject matter (what the memo is about).

The format of a memo is as follows:

MEMO

To:
From:
Date:
Subject:

Message

Sample 1 Memo

To: Co-workers
From: Mike
Date: June 25, 2014
Subject: Customer presentation

The P&G marketing presentation you prepared this Monday to demonstrate our product line was wonderful!

Your sincerity, enthusiasm, salesman skill and expert knowledge impressed Mr. Han and thus sealed the deal with him.

Thank you for your outstanding work and endeavor in the job, the bonus check will be distributed next week.

My sincere congratulation to all of you!

Sample 2   Memo

To: Mary McGee, Alistair Warwranka, George Lipton
CC: Dorothy Barrie
From: The Boss
Date: June 1, 2014
Re: Need for New Memo Format

I've noticed that we don't seem to be able to communicate important changes, requirements and progress reports throughout the company as effectively as we should do. I propose developing one consistent memo format, recognizable by all staff as the official means of communicating company directives.

While I know this seems like a simple solution, I believe it will cut down on needless e-mail, improve universal communication and allow the staff to save necessary information for later referral.

Please talk among yourselves to determine the proper points of memo writing and return the input to me by 12 noon. I will then send out a notice to the entire staff regarding the new memo format.

Thank you for your prompt attention to this.

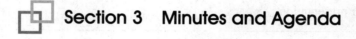

Section 3   Minutes and Agenda

Agendas and minutes are the basic records of an actual business meeting. Many organizations keep a copy of all their meeting agendas and minutes in a spiral notebook, available to anyone in the organization who wishes to read through or examine the events of past meetings. While an

Other Business Writing Chapter 5 47

electronic record is useful, having a permanent hard copy of your group's history will provide an easily accessible record.

Keep the correct minutes and make them available for future reference. Such referencing is essential when there is a question about who said what at a meeting or the details of a particular vote. The minutes become legal documents of the organization. The collected documents need to be well preserved because they will become an excellent history of the organization.

An agenda is the framework that helps meetings run effectively and efficiently. It is a step-by-step outline of the topics to be covered at the meeting. Effective agendas enhance group accomplishments, such as ensuring adequate consideration of all issues, events and projects, keeping the discussion focused and on track and making effective use of participants' time.

Minute Template

Name of the meeting — date
(1 line space)
Meeting details
Meeting called to order at ... am/pm by ...
(1 line space)
Members present:
(1 line space)
Members not present:
(1 line space)
Approval/Reading of minute:
(1 line space)
Business details
Motion from ...:
Vote:
Resolved:
Amendment: (optional)
(2 lines space)

Meeting adjourned at ... am/pm

Sample Minutes 1

Park Avenue Writers Meeting — 8 August, 2014

Meeting called to order at 4:30 pm by meeting chair Jessalyn Boyce

Members present: Chair Jessalyn Boyce/Grace Grayson/Natalie Wilcox/Jon Mitchell/Luna Stanford/Sierra Winchester/Adam Monroe/Dick Richards/Nick Nicholas

Members not present: Andrew Anderson (pre-arranged)/Andrea Anderson (pre-arranged)

Reading of Agenda
Motion: To approve the agenda for 8 August, 2014
Vote: Motion carried
Resolved: Agenda for the meeting on 8 August, 2014 approved without modification
Approval of Minutes
Motion: To approve the minutes for 1 August, 2014
Vote: Motion carried
Resolved: Minutes from the meeting on 1 August, 2014 approved without modification

Business
Motion from Jon Mitchell: To select Luna Stanford's manuscript for critique
Vote: 6 in favor, 2 against, 1 abstain
Resolved: Motion carried; Luna Stanford's manuscript accepted for critique
Motion from Luna Stanford: To replace the meeting table using committee funds
Vote: 3 in favor, 4 against
Resolved: Motion failed
Amendment: Nick Nicholas volunteered to repair the table at no cost
Motion from Sierra Winchester: To subscribe to Writer's Digest, using committee funds
Vote: Motion carried
Resolved: Subscription to Writer's Digest to be purchased with committee funds
Amendment: Subscription will be in the name of Chair Jessalyn Boyce at special two-year rate

Meeting adjourned at 5:15 pm.

Sample Minutes 2

Sally's Bakery Business Meeting — 9 February, 2014

Meeting called to order at 2:30 p.m. by bakery owner Sally Honer

Employees present:
Ashley Logan, Manager
Taylor Cooper, Assistant Manager

Abby Morgan, Associate
Mark Sellers, Baker
Sharon Bess, Baker

Members not present:
(none)

Approval of minutes:
Motion: To approve the minutes for 5 January, 2014
Vote: Motion carried
Resolved: Minutes from the meeting on 5 January 2014 approved without modification

Business:
Motion: Owner Sally Honer made a motion to hold baking training seminar on February 26th
Vote: 4 for, 1 opposed
Resolved: Motion carried
Motion: Baker Mark Sellers made a motion to host taste testing session during February 26th training seminar
Vote: 5 for, 0 opposed
Resolved: Motion carried
Motion: Associate Abby Morgan made a motion to get rid of worst seller, red velvet cupcakes
Vote: 2 for, 3 opposed
Resolved: Motion failed

Meeting adjourned by Sally Honer, bakery owner, at 3:50 p.m.

Sample   Minutes 3

Franze Co. Monthly Board Meeting — 13 February, 2014

Meeting called to order at 12:00 p.m. by CEO Taylor Cooper

Members present:
Taylor Cooper, CEO
Logan Shafter, CFO
Morgan Ely, Senior Vice President, Marketing
Elyse Chan, Senior Vice President, Engineering
Joyce Comer, Senior Vice President, Consulting

Lindsay Rogan, Communication Strategist
Mark Epstein, Senior Vice President, Human Resources
Shane Hale, Engineering Specialist
Nick Mitchell, International Consulting Representative
Ryan Marke, Senior Vice President, Recruiting

Members absent:
(none)

Approval of minutes:
Motion: Approve minutes from 14 January, 2014 board meeting
Vote: Motion carried
Resolved: Minutes from the meeting on 14 January, 2014 approved without modification

Business:
Motion from Morgan Ely to submit the latest issue of company newsletter, The Newswire, for national award
Vote: 10 in favor, 0 opposed, 0 abstained
Resolved: Motion carried
Motion from Shane Hale to attain 10% more engineering materials for company
Vote: 4 in favor, 6 opposed
Resolved: Motion failed
Motion from Mark Epstein to hire 5 interviewed candidates to fill vacant positions in the company
Vote: 6 in favor, 4 opposed
Resolved: Motion carried

Meeting adjourned at 1:14 p.m. by CEO Taylor Cooper

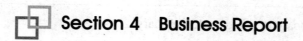

Section 4　Business Report

  Business reports are documents that present data and information to specific readers. When starting a business report you should first determine what it is about and who it is for. In general, to write the business report you should, first, write the introduction and executive summary, in which you define the problem you are hoping to solve, state your purpose and describe your objectives. Next, write a section that describes your key issues and supporting evidence. Reference the research and resources you identified in Step 3. Highlight any key insights that you found while analyzing the data for your report, and then write a section that includes your conclusions. Finally, provide a list of recommended next steps after your target audience reads the report. In particular, you should do the following jobs.

(1) Determine the scope for your business report. The scope of your report is also known as your purpose. According to Alan Thompson, author of several business books, many companies make the mistake of making their report either too general or too vague. To avoid this, ensure the scope of your business report aligns with your company's strategic objectives.

(2) Determine your target audience, or who the majority reading your business report will be. When you write your report, you will need to write in a voice that speaks to your target audience. Some considerations to keep in mind when determining your audience are the education level, company position, decision making capability, knowledge of the topic and demographic information of your readers.

(3) Gather your research. Once you have defined your scope and target audience, gather all research you have that will support your report. Depending on the topic of your business report, you may reference your company's financial statements and sales figures; market research studies; competitor research; internal processes; interviews; or competitive advantages.

(4) Structure your report. Analyze the research and information you have that supports the purpose of your report. Create an outline that has an introduction and executive summary, key issues and supporting evidence, insights and conclusions and recommendations.

Simple Format of a Business Report

Terms of Reference
This section gives background information on the reason for the report. It usually includes the person requesting the report.

Procedure
The procedure provides the exact steps taken and methods used for the report.

Findings
The findings point out discoveries made during the course of the report investigation.

Conclusions
The conclusions provide logical conclusions based on the findings.

Recommendations
The recommendations state actions that the writer of the report would like to take based on the findings and conclusions.

Sample Business Report 1

Terms of Reference
Margaret Anderson, Director of Personnel has requested this report on employee benefits satisfaction. The report was to be submitted to her by 28 June.

Procedure
A representative selection of 15% of all employees was interviewed in the period between April 1st and April 15th concerning:

Overall satisfaction with our current benefits package;
Problems encountered when dealing with the personnel department;
Suggestions for the improvement of communication policies;
Problems encountered when dealing with our HMO.

Findings
Employees were generally satisfied with the current benefits package.

Some problems were encountered when requesting vacation due to what is perceived as long approval waiting periods.

Older employees repeatedly had problems with HMO prescription drugs procedures.

Employees between the ages of 22 and 30 report few problems with HMO.

Most employees complain about the lack of dental insurance in our benefits package.

The most common suggestion for improvement was for the ability to process benefits requests online.

Conclusions
Older employees, those over 50, are having serious problems with our HMO's ability to provide prescription drugs.

Our benefits request system needs to be revised as most complaints concerning in-house processing.

Improvements need to take place in personnel department response time.

Information technology improvements should be considered as employees become more technologically savvy.

Recommendations

Meet with HMO representatives to discuss the serious nature of complaints concerning prescription drug benefits for older employees.

Give priority to vacation request response time as employees need faster approval in order to be able to plan their vacations.

Take no special actions for the benefits package of younger employees.

Discuss the possibility of adding an online benefits requests system to our company Intranet.

Formal Format for a Business Report

Title Page
The title page includes the name of report, the author's name and date. You can also write the reason of report on the title page to inform the reader about the problems or solutions offered.

Letter of Transmittal
This is used to announce the release of the business report and give the reader its necessary background.

Content Page
This page includes the table of contents of the major titles or heading mentioned in the report. You should include the letter or memo of transmittal in the table of contents. If there are sub headings in the report, try to include them too. You should mention the page number on which the main heading and sub heading lie. The page numbers should be written an inch from the bottom of the page.

List of Illustrations
This page is used to mention the illustrations included in your business report. When it includes only figures, title the page "List of Figures" or if it includes only tables then mention, "List of Tables".

Executive Summary
The executive summary is used to summarize the background of the report in one page for managers who do not have time to read your business report. The executive summary should include purpose and scope of the report and the major conclusions and recommendations suggested. Mention only the information that is worth writing in the executive summary.

Methodology

Explain the methods followed in your research to come to a valid conclusion. You need to mention if you did a group survey or searched for information through the internet or library or involved an outside agency to carry out the research for you.

Report Body

This is the major chuck of business information report when writing business information. The headings and page numbers should match according to the table of contents. The report body should contain the following contents.

- Introduction. The introduction will explain your audience why they are given this report to read and what is covered in the main body.
- Main Body. The heart of your report lies within the main body. All your important data and information that needs to be mentioned while writing a report need to be covered in the main body. You need to put forth your best writing skills when writing a report.
- Conclusion. The conclusion will analyze your result and bring your business report together. Keep the conclusion short and to the point.

Recommendation

This will provide your reader the possible suggestions that will help address the issues mentioned in the business report. You should mention the recommendations using bullets and numbered points. You should be thoroughly sure about the recommendations made as they may be followed by the reader.

Appendix

You need to mention all the sources of research in detail. These details will prove helpful in supporting your recommendations.

Sample   Business Report 2

Report on Eco-Homes Project

1. Title of Business Report
- Title: Eco-Homes Project Initiative
- Objective: Compile data and analysis for development for housing project Eco-Homes at location and address of the project.
- Report by: Dr. Larry Marshall, CEO EcoVision Projects, Empire Construction and Infrastructure Group.

- Key Contents: A Detailed plan, proposition, execution schedule and analysis of the project idea of an eco-friendly settlement put forth by Dr. Jason Smith, New Projects Department, Empire Construction and Infrastructure Group (Mother Company).
- Reporting and Analysis Time: 1 month.
- Project Implementation Time: 17 months.
- Assumptions: The time frame and execution is framed, taking into consideration the seasonal elements of climate and other turnover ratios, experienced in the previous financial year.

2. Letter of Transmittal

Attached, letter of transmittal, conveying the idea by Dr. Smith, consisting of the core features of report.

3. Table of Contents
- Summary and Synopsis of the Project
- Introduction
- Discussion and Details
- Conclusion
- Recommendations

4. Summary and Synopsis

The Eco-Homes Project Initiative is an underway project which has been conceived by the Empire Group. The basic ideology of the initiative is eco-friendly living. The Empire group intends to build a mega residential complex which is spread over 35 acres of land, and house around about 150 households, which are self-sufficient in several ways. The complex thrives on the basis of inbuilt agricultural center, animal husbandry center, building gardens, fuel cell and bio-gas-propane generators of electricity, massive solar panels which provide heat to the homes and also electricity. The complex will span over the 35 acre premise and will consist of 3 core residential centers 15 solar panel driven green houses, 2 orchards, 5 gardens, 3 pastures and 3 animal husbandry centers cum dairies and a staff of 33 people.

5. Discussion and Details

Some common points, details and conclusions that were drawn in the meeting of project engineers, company architects, cost accountants and the CFA's go as follows:

- The project will bring substantial revenue if all 150 houses are sold off at a price of _amount_ per house hold. The project will be a highly big commercial success as it is not just situated in the city, once the customer buys the housing facility his usual bills that include electricity and water bill will be cut down to half. The only con that is foreseen is that the sale value is huge.
- There are 5 phases of the project, namely, the basic foundation phase, housing complex 1

phase, followed by 2 and 3, with the last phase of the development of all the support and infrastructure facility. It is estimated that every phase would go on for 3 months plus a backup of 2 months has been provided.
- The sales for real estate would begin with the completion of housing complex 1, followed by complex 2 and 3. By the end of complex 3, the real estate market rates would have increased by 7.8%. This price escalation however is not included in any of the calculations.
- The cost sheets showing cost projections for the project have been attached.
- 5 year maintenance, free of cost has been provided for the complex. An operation cost of about $500 per 2 months is to be paid by every household to keep the operations going.

6. Conclusion

The project team recommends that this project should be taken up and executed as fast as possible as the real estate market is and the eco-friendly products have been consistently showing positive rises in the past 5 years.

7. Recommendation

In order to reduce operational cost of $500 for every two months, which is incurred by the residents, the project team recommends more research and development. It is a selling point that can be put forth to boost sales.

I Please fill in the following letters with the appropriate words.

Letter 1

June 20, 2014

To: Shun-Yuan INTL INC
Attn: Mr. Fred Lin

Dear Fred,

RE: Our visit in HK

Jack and I will _____ your factory on Monday July 7. I have _____ out a preliminary list of _____ to be discussed during our visit. Those are as follows:

Other Business Writing **Chapter 5** 57

1. Quality _____;
2. Survey;
3. Packing _____;
4. Cost and _____.

Please let me know _____ you can _____ us at the Lai Lai Sheraton or fax us directions to go to the factory.

Thanks

Lynn Lorsch

Letter 2

To: Mr. Jorge Rodrigues

Invitation Letter

We would _____ to invite your service engineer Mr. Eudelio to come _____ here to HK to _____ the problems of the Pumps we bought from your factory last month. We _____ he can arrive here before July 7 and it may need to _____ 7-10 days for the repairing.

We are awaiting his coming soon.

Thanks

John

II **Read the information below and then write a memo to all the staff in your company.**

You are William Wang, making requests to change the time of weekly meeting. Write a memo about the response form Jorge. Such a memo should include purpose statement, summary and discussion. You may make up any necessary details.

III **Simulated exercises.**

Please work in groups to produce a report "On Student's Satisfaction with Rear-service

Department", you are supposed to design a questionnaire and follow the format of the following report.

1. Title Page
- Title: Students' satisfaction with the canteen of GUT
- Objective: to have students' opinions and help to improve the environment and the food quality in our canteen
- Report by:
- Date of Reporting and Analyzing: April 13, 2014
- Date of Implementation: April 16, 2014

2. Terms of Reference
To Mr. Li, the director of the logistics department. We do the survey in order to improve the quality of the food and management. The report is to be submitted to him by 18April.

3. Procedure
(1) The subject of our survey is determined.
(2) More than one hundred students were asked to fill the questionnaire between April 9th and April 14th.
(3) Lots of feedbacks are gathered data are compiled.
(4) Suggestions for the improvement of the food and management are given.
(5) Summary is made.

4. Findings
After asking 100 students in our campus about our canteen, we can divide generally their opinions into the following three aspects.

First, some students think the food in our canteen is not in line with their taste, especially for those who have special demand on food such as dumpling. Besides, some say that they think the dishes in canteen are very expensive. Last but not the least, there are some complain that the canteen is not clean. Sometimes they find that the desks are with soup or rice that should be cleaned timely. What's the worst they find some dirty things in our dishes.

5. Conclusion
(1) Our 100 respondent have different opinions.
(2) 35% of respondents are not satisfied with the food.
(3) 55% of respondents consider the price of dishes is too expensive. Relevant departments need to take effective actions to deal with students' complaints.
(4) 10% of respondents complain that the environment in campus canteen is terrible. We need

to try our best to improve our service.

6. Recommendations
According to the questionnaire, we'd like to give you some advice as follows:
(1) Cut down the food price to a reasonable level;
(2) Offer the fresh food to students;
(3) Supply the nutritious food;
(4) Maintain the staff hygiene in working place;
(5) Speed up the food offering;
(6) Take measures to stop the food wasting.

7. Appendices
(1) Questionnaire on School Canteen
(2) The Analysis of Questionnaire

Part 2

Business Correspondence in International Visible Trade

Chapter 6

Looking for Potential Customers

Lead-in: Case Study

Case One
A shoes importer wants to extend his range and gets the information about the exporter from his business connection; please send the inquiry to the exporter to show the desire to establish the business relationship.

Case Two
Hangzhou Textile Import and Export Corporation learns from the Commercial Counselor's Office of the US Embassy that an American company Xinli Textile Inc. intends to have the import of cotton bed-sheets and pillowcases, and the Chinese corporation seizes the opportunity to write a letter to establish the business relationship.

Section 1 Establishing Business Relationship

Inquiry means asking, which falls into two catalogues — the first inquiry and the general letter of inquiry. Inquiries mean potential business, so both the buyer and the seller should take great care in writing or replying the letter.

The first inquiry referred as "to establish relationship" comes from both seller and buyer, and is the letter the businessmen approach each other for the first time. Companies are more likely to be agreeable to business proposals if they are given every possible detail from the very beginning. To serve the purpose, the first inquiry should include the following information.

(1) How you get the potential partner's name and address.

(2) A self introduction and/or some indication of the demand in your area for the goods which the supplier (or seller) deals in.

(3) Information as to what the buyer would like the prospective supplier to provide. Normally the buyer will be interested in a catalogue, a price list, discounts, methods of payments, delivery time, and where appropriate, samples. When the buyer has many points on which information is required,

it may be useful to enumerate the inquiry. To ensure smooth and successful transactions, it is also essential to ask for credit information about the prospective dealers such as capital, capacity and character.

(4) A closing sentence to inspire the further relation.

The general inquiry letter actually covers the topics of various types, which will be discussed in the following chapters.

Sample 1 First Inquiry from the Buyer

> **To:** "sales department" <Kee & Co., Ltd.1999@hotmail.com>
> **From:** "Tony Smith" <Smith2000@hotmail.com>
> **Subject:** Establishing business relationship

> Dear Sirs,
>
> We have obtained your name and address from Dee & Co., Ltd, and we are writing to enquire whether you would be willing to establish business relations with us.
>
> We have been importers of shoes for many years. At present, we are interested in extending our range and would appreciate your catalogues and quotations.
>
> If your prices are competitive we would expect to place volume orders with you.
>
> We look forward to your early reply.
>
> Yours faithfully,
>
> Tony Smith
> Chief Buyer

Sample 2 First Inquiry from the Seller

> **To:** "purchase department" <Hangzhou Textile Import and Export Corporation@hotmail.com>
> **From:** "Lily" <Xinli Textiles Inc.@gmail.com>
> **Subject:** Establishing relationship

Dear Sirs/Madams,

From the Commercial Counselor's Office of the US Embassy we have learned that you wish to import cotton bed-sheets and pillowcases from China.

We are the leading exporter of textile products in China and have entered into business relationship with more than 70 countries in the world. Because of the softness and durability, our cotton bed-sheets and pillowcases are rapidly becoming popular.

You will find the attached catalogue, which we hope will be of interest to you. Also attached for your reference is our latest price list.

Should you be interested in any of our product please contact us.

Look forward to your early reply.

Sincerely yours,

Lily Hu
Export Manager

Section 2 Replies from the Potential Customers

In reply to the first inquiry be sure to first state clearly which letter you refer to, then inform your client whether you are interested in the products or not. If the products are of interest to you ask for the other details about the goods you need, and lastly end your letter with a complimentary sentence.

Sample 1 Reply from the Seller

To: "Tony Smith" <Smith2000@hotmail.com>
From: "Ann" <Kee & Co., Ltd.1999@hotmail.com>
Subject: Establishing business relationship

Dear Mr. Smith,

Thank you for your letter of the 20th of this month. We shall be glad to enter into business relations with your company.

In compliance with request, we are sending you, under separate cover, our latest catalogue and price list covering our export range.

Payment should be made by irrevocable and confirmed letter of credit.

Should you wish to place an order, please e-mail or fax us.

Yours sincerely,

Ann
Chief Seller

Sample 2   Reply from the Buyer

To: "Lily" <Xinli Textiles Inc.@gmail.com>
From: "Michel" <Hangzhou Textile Import and Export Corporation@hotmail.com>
Subject: Establishing relationship

Dear Lily,

We are glad to receive your letter of August 5, 2014 and would like you to send us details of your various ranges, including sizes, colors and samples of the best quality of material used.

If they are of the standard we require, we will place a substantial order. We would also like to know if you are offering any trade discounts.

Thank you.

Yours sincerely,

Mickel LEE
General Manager

Supplementary Information

1. Channels Approaching to the Prospective Dealers
Channels through which the prospective dealers abroad may be approached are illustrated as follows:

(1) Banks.

(2) A chamber of commerce. A chamber of commerce is an organization of businessman. One of its tasks is to get business information and to find new business opportunities for its members.

(3) Commercial Counselor's office or other commercial institutions at home and abroad.

(4) Advertisements in newspapers, magazines, and the Internet.

(5) Attendance at the export commodities fairs or exhibitions.

(6) The introduction from business connections and mutual visits by trade delegations or groups.

(7) Internet.

2. Trade Discount
Trade discount is a deduction from the list price allowed by a manufacturer, wholesaler to a retailer, or distributor to a retailer, or one firm to another in the same trade, usually there are cash discount and quantity discount (the same as "price scale", e.g. US$10/pc for 100 pcs; US$9/pc for 100 pcs …)

3. Commodity, Merchandise, Cargo and Item
Commodity refers to anything sold for profit. Merchandise is goods bought and sold and always in singular number. Cargo is goods carried by a ship, plane, or vehicle. Item is a single thing on a list or in a catalogue; it is often used to stand for the goods previously mentioned in the letter.

4. Pamphlet, Brochure, Catalogue and Leaflet
Pamphlet is brochure or booklets. Brochure is a small book consisting of a few pages in a paper cover and advertising material is always in this form. Catalogue is a list, usually in the form of a book, of goods for sale with or without prices or pictures. Leaflet is a single sheet or printed paper, sometimes folded to form several pages, containing matter like advertising a product or giving directions on how to use it.

5. Capital, Capacity and Character
Capital means the overall financial worth or assets minus outstanding obligations. Capacity means the ability to promote its line of business as testified by the scope of its establishment and the volume of business actually done. Character means its record of honoring or dishonoring contracts and other obligations.

Useful Expressions

1. through the courtesy of, through the introduction of, on the recommendation of (the Commercial Counselor's Office, the chamber of commerce, banks, etc.)

(1) *Through the courtesy of the Paris Chamber of Commerce, we have your name as a firm who is interested in doing business with us.*

(2) *Through the courtesy of Mr. White, we are given to understand that you are one of the leading importers of silk in your area.*

(3) *On the recommendation of Messrs. Harvey & Co., we have learned with pleasure the name of your firm.*

(4) *On the recommendation of the Bank of China, we have got to know that you import Chinese textile and cotton piece goods.*

2. Your co. has been introduced to us by (Datex Trading Co., Messrs Johnson & Co. Ltd. of NY, etc.)

(1) *Your company has been introduced to us by ABC Trading Corporation.*

(2) *Your company has been introduced as leading exporter to us by John Smith.*

3. We learned your name and address (at the International Exhibition of Machinery and Equipment, in the *Times*, etc.)

(1) *We learned from the Commercial Counselor of our Embassy in Ottawa that you deal in general merchandise.*

(2) *We learned from <u>China Daily</u> that you are interested in electrical appliances and want to order immediately.*

4. to have one's name and address from

(1) *We have your name and address from China Council for the Promotion of International Trade.*

(2) *We are glad to have your name and address from <u>The Journal of Commerce</u>.*

5. to be transferred (forwarded) to ... for attention

(1) *Your letter of Sept. 8 has been transferred to us for attention from our Head Office in Beijing.*

(2) *Your inquiry has been forwarded to us for attention from the Commercial Counselor's Office of the Chinese Embassy in Rome.*

6. to be given/recommended by
You are recommended to our company by our sister corporation in Shanghai for the new product you are promoting.

7. to specialize in …
We specialize in chemical products (cotton piece goods, art and craft goods/arts and crafts/handicraft, straw and willow product, embroideries, porcelain wares, jade carvings, silk flowers, toys and gifts, fat-reducing tea, black tea, table-cloth and bath towels, imitation jewellery, etc.).

8. to handle in /deal (inclusively) in …
(1) *Messrs. Haruno & Bros. handles electronic products for export.*
(2) *We deal inclusively in textiles.*

9. We are …
(1) *We are a state-operated corporation, handling the export of animal by-products.*
(2) *We are China National Textile Import and Export Corporation, with its headquarters in Beijing.*

10. This is to introduce … as …/write to introduce/take the opportunity to introduce
(1) *This is to introduce the Pacific Corporation as exporters of light industrial products having business relations with more than 70 countries in the world.*
(2) *We write to introduce ourselves as exporters of fresh water pearls having many years' experience in this particular line of business.*
(3) *We take the opportunity to introduce our company as exporters dealing exclusively in leather goods.*

11. to inform somebody that …
(1) *We wish to inform you that we are specialized in the export of arts and crafts.*
(2) *We are pleased to inform you that we handle a wide range of electric fans.*

12. to establish business relations with/to enter into business relations with
(1) *We avail ourselves of this opportunity to write to you and see if we can establish business relations with you.*
(2) *We have come to know the name of your corporation and are pleased to write to you in the hope of establishing business relations with you.*
(3) *We are willing to enter into business relations with you on the basis of equality and mutual benefit.*
(4) *Your company has been introduced to us by Smith & Co. Ltd as prospective buyers of*

Chinese table-cloths. As we deal in the items, we shall be pleased to enter into direct business relations with you.

13. to fall/come /lie within the scope of ...

(1) *As the item falls within the scope of our business, we shall be pleased to enter into direct business with you.*

(2) *As the article lies within the scope of business of our branch in Nanjing, we have forwarded your letter to them for attention.*

14. to assure sb. of sth./assure sb. that ...

(1) *We assure you of the best quality and moderate prices of our goods.*

(2) *We assure you that we shall do our best to promote the business between us.*

15. look forward to/at your earliest convenience/as soon as possible

(1) *We look forward to your close cooperation in promoting this new product.*

(2) *Please send your catalogue and price list at your earliest convenience.*

I In each of the following sentences, choose the appropriate word or words in the parentheses and justify your choice.

1. We introduce ourselves (like, as, for) importers and exporters of light industrial (produce, products), having many years experience in this line of business.
2. We have been (bought, buy, buying) walnut meat from the local commission houses, who (are used to, used to, use to) send us quotations regularly.
3. We take the liberty (to, of, in) writing to you with a hope to get your best offers for Chinese bicycles.
4. It is (gratify, gratifying, grateful) to learn (in, from, through) your letter that you are in a position to supply us with Bitter Apricot Kernels.
5. The import and export business in China is (controlled, handled, done) by the state trading corporations.
6. We have concluded considerable business with Biddle and Sawyer Company (of, in, with, regarding) this line of business.
7. Your prompt (attention, reply, response) to this matter will be very much appreciated.
8. As (regarded, regards) machine tools, we regret to (say, inform) that we are not able to supply for the time being.

II. Arrange the following words and phrases in their proper order.

1. the leading exporters of textiles in Hangzhou
   to extend business to our market
   and that you wish
   we have been informed by
   Jameson Garments (Vancouver) Ltd.
   that you are one of

   _____
   _____
   _____

2. listed below
   we would like to
   have your lowest quotations
   for the captioned goods
   on the terms and conditions

   _____
   _____
   _____

3. which you recently advertised
   the Vernard line of ultrasonic equipment
   the features and costs of
   please send me
   in *Electronics* magazine
   some further information on

   _____
   _____
   _____

4. to receive
   a copy of your latest catalogue
   price list and export terms
   we are interested in
   and would be pleased
   importing Chinese furniture

   _____
   _____
   _____

5. If you would send us
   which you can supply
   a comprehensive price list
   we would be grateful
   of the goods
   together with some samples

   _____
   _____
   _____

III. Fill in the blanks with the appropriate words.

1. In _____ with our company's growth, to further expand our market, we have decided to establish an office in Dalian.
2. Please be good enough to provide the necessary information _____ us.
3. If your price is competitive, we shall be glad to place a substantial order _____ you.
4. This article is of particular interest _____ us.
5. Our Sales Contract _____ that the seller shall ship the goods within one month after

Looking for Potential Customers   **Chapter 6**   71

signing the contract.
6. Will you please provide Mr. Chadwick _____ a letter of recommendation, which you think would be useful?
7. We are gearing our production to your requirements and shall soon be _____ a position _____ offer you substantially.
8. If your price is _____ line _____ the market price, we can take large quantities.
9. There is nothing _____ at present.
10. Enclosed _____ _____ a copy of our price list.
11. He owes his success _____ chance.
12. Through the _____ of a Chamber of Commerce, we have learned that you are one of those representative importers of electric goods.

IV **Complete the following sentences in English.**
1. We are given to understand that
   a. 你公司是经营化工产品的国有公司。
   _____
   _____

   b. 你公司有意在平等互利的基础上与我公司建立业务关系。
   _____
   _____

2. We are desirous of
   a. 获得你方最近供应出口的商品目录。
   _____
   _____

   b. 把你方的新产品介绍给我方的客户。
   _____
   _____

3. Please do not hesitate to write us
   a. 关于推销中国水果和干果的任何建议。
   _____
   _____

   b. 你方需要订购手机的时候。
   _____
   _____

4. As you know,
   a. 许多外国商人渴望和我们进行贸易。
   _____
   _____

b. 我们已经和世界上100多家商号建立了贸易关系。
_____
_____

5. We are appreciative of
   a. 你方有和我公司建立贸易关系的意向。
   _____
   _____

   b. 你方愿意到广交会来洽谈业务。
   _____
   _____

V Give the English or Chinese equivalents of the following.

1. 建立贸易关系	
2. 扩大营业范围	
3. 最新价目单	
4. 主要出口商	
5. 生产日期	
6. 供参考	
7. to place volume orders	
8. in compliance with request	
9. trade discount	
10. irrevocable L/C	
11. Chamber of Commerce	
12. price scale	

VI Complete the following three letters with proper words.

Letter 1

March 1, 2014

Dear Sirs,

Your company has kindly been introduced to us _____ Messrs Freenan & Co. Ltd., Lagos, Nigeria, as prospective buyers of Chinese Cotton Piece Goods. As this _____ falls within the scope of our business activities, we shall be pleased to _____ into direct _____ relations with you at an early _____.

To give you a general idea of the various kinds of cotton piece goods now _____ for export, we _____ a brochure and a price list. Quotations and samples will be airmailed to you on _____ of your specific inquiry.

We are looking forward _____ your favorable reply.

Yours faithfully,

Letter 2

May 15, 2014

Dear Sirs,

Your name and address were _____ to us by the London Trade Board _____ a large exporter of fabrics of high quality.

We are importers of quality clothing materials, and have large annual _____ from our markets _____ Spain.

We should be obliged if you would _____ us your pattern books showing the complete _____ of these fabrics, _____ with your price list.
We look forward to the pleasure of hearing from you soon.

Yours faithfully,

Letter 3

May 18, 2014

Dear Mr. Jackson,

We were impressed by the _____ of sweaters that were displayed on your stand at the "Menswear Exhibition" that was held in NY last month.

We are a large chain of retailers and are looking for a manufacturer who could _____ us with a wide _____ of sweaters for the teenage market.

If you can _____ orders of over 1,500 garments at one time, please _____ us your current catalogue and price _____. We hope to _____ from you soon.

Yours sincerely,

VII. Translate the following letter.

Dear Sirs,

We have learned your name and address in the October issue of *Foreign Trade*. At present, we are interested in your bed-sheets and bath towels.

We take this opportunity to introduce ourselves as one of the largest importers of textiles in the area. We shall appreciate it very much if you will quote us your best CIF C5% London prices, indicating sizes and colors. Meanwhile, please send us some samples and catalogs. If your prices are reasonable and suitable for our market, we shall place a large order with you.

We have been handling textile for over 20 years and have a lot of clients. We would like to know if we could act as your sole agent in this area.

Your early reply will be highly appreciated.

Yours faithfully,

VIII Write a letter from the following particulars.

Letter One

Write to the Overseas Trading Co., Ltd. whose name and address you have learned on the recommendation of the National Bank of Bangladesh. Tell them that you hope to enter into business relations with them. The main line of your business is exporting Light Industrial Products. Samples and catalogues will be sent upon specific inquiries.

Letter Two

Write to Winter & Co., at 164 Royal Parade, Wellington, New Zealand. Acknowledge the receipt of their letter of September 9. Agree to their proposal of establishing relations with you. The Bureau concerned in Shanghai will handle the commodity inspection.

Chapter 7

Discussing Price

Lead-in: Case Study

Case One

Jo, sales manager in Excellent Chemical Co., has received an inquiry for PA80000-5AA chemical materials from Mr. Hansson in EVA Technology Co., and is making an offer to the inquiry to facilitate the business.

Case Two

Jeremy Lauwe from Tonton Electronics asks Ms. Anne Wang in Keyway Keyboard Co. who makes an offer to reduce the price of keytops with USA version by 10%, and if accepted intends to purchase 40,000 sets.

Case Three

After the offer and counter-offer, Mr. Jeff in Goodwill Computer Co. disagrees/agrees to the counter-offer from Jerrod in Union Co.

Section 1 Offer

An offer is actually a proposal of certain trade terms and an expression of willingness to make a contract according to the terms proposed. It is made either by a seller, called "selling offer", or by a buyer, called "buying offer" or "bid". In practice there are two popular types of offers. One is "firm offer" and the other "non-firm offer". In the case of the firm offer, the sellers promise to sell goods at a stated price within a stated period of time and can not take the offer back once it has been accepted. While a non-firm offer has no binding force upon the offerer or offeree and can be taken back at will.

When it comes to a firm offer, the information supplied should include name of commodities, quality, quantity and specifications and the details of prices, discounts, terms of payment, packing, insurance, date of delivery, etc. What is more, the period for which the offer is valid must be stated clearly.

When it comes to a letter of firm offer, the offerer should:

(1) express thanks for the enquiry or acknowledge the receipt of the inquiry;

(2) give favorable comments on the goods needed if possible;

(3) supply all the information requested, including name of commodities, quality, quantity and specifications, prices, discounts, terms of payment, packing, insurance, date of delivery, etc.;

(4) state clearly the period for which the offer is valid;

(5) express hope that the offer will be accepted and assure the customer of good service.

Sample 1   Firm Offer

Date: May 23
To: "Mr. Hansson" < EVA Technology Co.@earthlink.com>
From: "Jo" < Excellent Chemical Co.@hotmail.com>
Re: PA80000-5AA chemical material

Dear Mr. Hansson,

Thanks for your inquiry of May 21.

As requested, we will arrange to send you 2 kg of PA80000-5AA chemical materials by EMS post tomorrow for your approval.

As to the best price and delivery time, we would like to offer as follows:

FOB price: US$1.16/kg FOB Qingdao by sea
Shipment: within 20 days after order confirmed
Payment: by T/T before shipment
Packing: bulk packing in plastic keg
Validity: 30 days from the date quoted

Please advise your order position soon.

Best regards,

Jo Wang
Sales Manager

Sample 2 Non-firm Offer

Date: May 20
To: "Mr. Fung" < F&M Milk Powder, LTD.@earthlink.com>
From: "Xu Yulin" < Fair F&B Co. Ltd.@hotmail.com>
Re: Your inquiry for FB milk powder

Dear Mr. Fung,

Thank you for your interest in F&B milk powder. We are happy to make you a special offer, subject to our final confirmation, as follows:

The origin is Western Europe, and the quality is "Extra Grade" specifications as per the fax.

Packing: 4 layers paper bags with approx, 17/18 MT per 20' container

Price: US$2,000/MT CIF Lumpur

In case you have any further questions, Mr. Fung, please do not hesitate to contact me.

Sincerely yours,

Xu Yulin (Miss)
Overseas Sales Department

Section 2 Counter-offer

In a deal, on one hand, the seller with favorable or unfavorable profit will always claim that the profit is minimum, zero or even under the cost, and the buyer, on the other hand, will tend to lower the price as much as possible. Besides, the buyer is also likely to ask for a more favorable payment terms, a shorter delivery time or a free-give. Generally speaking, if an offeree partly agrees to or totally disagrees with the offer but puts forward the new suggestion, a "counter-offer" comes into being, which is actually a new offer from the original offeree.

When making a counter-offer, the buyer should express regret at inability to accept and state reasons, put forward amendments or new proposals, or suggest that there may be other opportunities to do business together.

To be more specific, in the counter-offer the buyer will:

(1) express the thanks for the offer or acknowledge the receipt of the offer;

(2) state the regret that the offer is on the high side or higher than that of the other suppliers;

(3) give reasons to make such a counter-offer, such as the slow market, severe market competition, a volume order or a limited budget, or directly put forward the target price or terms;

(4) require the seller to reconsider the offer and provide a better terms.

Sample 1   Counter-offer

Date: June 23
To: "Ms. Anne Wang" < Keyway Keyboard Co.@hotmail.com>
From: "Jeremy Lauwe" < Tonton Electronics @earthlink.com>
Re: Keytops with USA version

Dear Anne,

Thanks for your offer on June 21 for the keytops with USA version.

We find your price is 10% higher. Could you re-quote us a lower price as we are interested in buying 40,000 sets of keytops?

We are awaiting your answer by return.

Best regards,

Jeremy Lauwe

Sample 2   Counter-offer

Date: June 13
To: "Mr. Karl" < Messrs. Carlson & Maxwell @hotmail.com>
From: "Xu Yulin" < UNION COMPUTER CO. @earthlink.com>
Re: Your offer for computer case

Dear Mr. Karl,

Your FOB price of US$20/set is not good enough. We must have a price of US$18/set to get the business.

We suggest you re-examine the ESD Shield price, also study the alternative of using a wire for ESD protection or perhaps paint the underside of the frame to reduce the cost.

Please reply the above before next Monday.

Best regards

Xu Yulin (Miss)
Import Department

 Section 3 Acceptance and Refusal

After receiving the counter-offer from the buyer the seller needs to make a reply of acceptance or refusal, which is usually the case in the trade.

In the case of acceptance remember that harshness makes no perfect. Regardless of sufficient or insufficient profit margin, the seller will state that there is no profit margin or even under the cost and that the reason to accept is to intend to enter into business relationship with the client or maintain the relation with the regular custumer, which facilitates the transactions.

In the case of refusal the seller should:

(1) express the regret to know that the buyer is unsatisfied with offer;

(2) state that the offer is the best term almost with zero profit margin;

(3) give the reasons to make the refusal, such as good quality, costly materials, increased labor cost, appreciation or the fluctuation of the exchange rate;

(4) apologize for the refusal and express the hope for the next cooperation.

There are other cases in the seller's reply to the counter-offer besides the acceptance and refusal. For example, the seller may agree with counter-offer with some additional terms such as "to increase the quantity, change the terms of payment, deliver the goods in one lot instead of several lots, or replace the goods with the alternative"; sometimes to show the good faith the seller may also agree to reduce the price by half as the compromise. In both cases another counter-offer comes into being.

Sample 1   Acceptance

Dongbao Group

To: "Tom" <rxc@public.sta.net.cn>
From: "Clark Leony" <sawya@worldnet.uk>
Subject: Your counter-offer for backpack

Dear Tom,

Your counter-offer for backpack has been received, which actually leaves us almost no profit at the moment.

Considering that you are one of our regular customers and a large volume of 5,000 pieces, we are going to accept your price of US$9/piece CIF Basrah.

Please send the order as soon as possible for us to arrange the production.

Yours sincerely,

Clark Leony

Sample 2   Refusal

Date: June 15
To: "Xu Yulin" < UNION COMPUTER CO. @earthlink.com>
From: "Mr. Karl" < Messrs. Carlson & Maxwell @hotmail.com>
Re: Your counter-offer for computer case

We regret to hear that you can not accept the price we offered.

After we carefully checked your target price, we are really sorry to inform you that US$ 18/set is under our cost. To avoid the quality problem after shipment, we are not in a position to adopt any other alternative for the computer.

Sorry for our inability to help you in this case. However, we hope that we can cooperate with you in the future deals.

Best regards,

Karl
Export Department

Sample 3　Acceptance with Some Terms

Stephenson's Emporium

Date: July 17
To: Paul Lockwood <plockwood@jbs.com.cnd>
From: Francesco Marani <chtrooborg@tivoli.com>
Re: Real Brand Camera No. 900T

Your counter-offer for our Real Brand Camera No. 900T has reached us this morning.

After careful consideration we would be willing to accept your price offered. However in order to speed up the production with more cash flow, we would like to have payment by T/T instead of D/P.

Furthermore, the goods will be dispatched in one lot instead of several lots during a month, which actually saves both of us time and money.

If the terms acceptable, please inform us as soon as possible.

Best regards,

Francesco Marani

Supplementary Information

1. Incoterms

Incoterms (International Commercial Terms), developed by ICC in Paris, has been periodically revised to account for changing modes of transport and document delivery. The current versions include Incoterms 2000 and Incoterms 2010. Incoterms 2000 are grouped into 4 categories as follows:

Group E (departure)	EXW	Ex Works
Group F (main carriage unpaid)	FCA	Free Carrier
	FAS	Free Alongside Ship
	FOB	Free on Board
Group C (main carriage paid)	CFR	Cost and Freight
	CIF	Cost, Insurance and Freight
	CPT	Carriage Paid to
	CIP	Carriage and Insurance Paid to
Group D (arrival)	DAF	Delivered at Frontier
	DES	Delivered Ex Ship
	DEQ	Delivered Ex Quay
	DDU	Delivered Duty Unpaid
	DDP	Delivered Duty Paid

Incoterms 2010 rules define the responsibilities of buyers and sellers for the delivery of goods under sales contracts. Incoterms 2010 takes into account the latest developments in commercial practice, and updates and consolidates some of the former rules.

A new classification system divides the 11 Incoterms 2010 rules into two distinct groups.

(1) Rules for any mode of transport: EXW, FCA, CPT, CIP, DAT, DAP, DDP.

(2) Rules for waterway transport: FAS, FOB, CFR, CIF.

In addition to the 11 rules, Incoterms 2010 includes the following contents.

(1) Extensive guidance notes and illustrative graphics to help users efficiently choose the right rule for each transaction.

(2) New classification to help choosing the most suitable rule in relation to the mode of transport.

(3) Advice for the use of electronic procedures.

(4) Information on security-related clearances for shipments.

(5) Advice for the use of Incoterms 2010 in domestic trade.
Besides, it has the following changes.
(1) DAF, DES, DEQ & DDU were deleted;
(2) DAT (Delivered at Terminal) & DAP (Delivered at Place) have been added.

2. Expressions of Trade Terms

Trade terms are expressed in the unit price for goods. The expression of trade terms is illustrated as follows:

In FOB Shanghai FOB is the short form for "Free on Board". Shanghai is the port of shipment. However, if it is expressed as CIF Shanghai, Shanghai turns to be the port of destination.

It is popular to find unit price with commission, such as FOB C2.5% Shanghai, C is "commission", which refers to the money paid by the buyer to salesmen or agents. It is usually a percentage of the money received from the sales made.

The price term of a sales contract involves unit price and total price. Unit price includes the measuring unit, price, money of account and trade terms. For instance, a price term can be worded like this, "US$1,500 per MT CIF London including 3% commission" or "US$1,500 per MT CIF C3% London". The measuring unit includes six categories, which are weight (g — gram; kg — kilogram; oz — ounce; lb. — pound; MT — metric ton), unit (pc — piece; pr — pair; doz — dozen; gr — gross; set; ctn — carton; case; pkg — package), length (m — metre; ft — foot; yd — yard), square (sq.m, sq.ft, sq.yd), cubic (cu.m, cu.ft, cu.yd), volume (l — litre; gal — gallon; bu — bushel). The money of account includes US$, Pound, JY, EUR.

Discount/allowance, provided by the seller to the buyer, is the deduction in the money paid to the seller, and used as an encouragement to the buyer for various purposes. It is also indicated in a price term, for example, "$300 per MT FOB Shanghai including 2% discount" or "$300 per m/t FOB Shanghai less 2% discount".

3. Subject to Our Final Confirmation

This is a phrase used in a non-firm offer which indicates no definite validity period.
Similar phrases are as follows:
Offer is subject to change without notice;
Offer is subject to goods being unsold;
Offer is subject to prior sale.
While a firm offer is usually with a valid period, phrases commonly used are as follows:
Offer is valid for 5 days;
Subject to your confirmation reaching here on or before the 25th this month;
Subject to your acceptance before the end of this month;
Subject to your reply reaching here by August 15, Beijing time;
Subject to your reply reaching here within 5 days.

4. MT

MT is the short form of "metric ton".

1 metric ton = 2,204.6 lb = 1,000 kg (metric system)

1 short ton = 2,000 lb = 0.907 MT (US System)

1 long ton = 2,240 lb = 1.016 MT (British System)

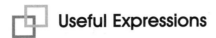

Useful Expressions

1. to thank for one's enquiry/offer

(1) *We thank you for your enquiry of Feb. 2 and are pleased to inform you we are in good connections with the best manufacturers in the country.*

(2) *Thank you for your letter of January 14.*

2. to have much pleasure in ...

(1) *We have much pleasure in enclosing a quotation sheet for our products and trust that their high quality will induce you to place a trial order.*

(2) *In accordance with the request of ... at the Guangzhou Fair, we have pleasure in sending you herewith the samples and a price list for ...*

(3) *We take pleasure in making you an offer as required by you, subject to our final confirmation.*

3. to be glad/pleased to ...

(1) *We are glad to learn from your enquiry of February 8 that you are interested in our ladies' blouses. As requested our catalogue and price list are enclosed together with details of our sale conditions.*

(2) *We were pleased to receive your enquiry of March 10 for our Portable Mixer Model PM-222.*

(3) *We are pleased to quote you the best price.*

4. We can ...

(1) *We can supply most items from stock and will have no trouble in meeting your delivery.*

(2) *We can allow you a special discount of 2% on the prices quoted for a quantity of 50 or more.*

5. We would like to ...

We would like to draw your attention to the trade and quantity discount we are offering in our publicity brochure pp.16-24, which may be of particular interest to you.

6. We regret that ...

(1) *We regret that it is impossible to accept your counter-offer, even to meet you half way; the*

price of raw material has advanced 20% and we shall shortly be issuing an advanced price list.

(2) Although we are anxious to open up business with you, we regret that it is impossible for us to allow the reduction asked for, because we have already cut our prices to the lowest point after examining our cost calculations.

7. to one's interest/in one's favor

(1) It would be greatly to your interest to make a trial of these goods.

(2) May we expect a trial order from you while prices are greatly in your favor?

8. Others

(1) As there is a heavy demand at this time of the year for heaters, you will have to allow at least 6 weeks for delivery.

(2) We do not see any advantage in your quotations, and would like to know whether you have any better value to offer.

(3) We desire to call your attention to our special offer. You will readily understand that this offer is good only for acceptance reaching us before the end of … In view of the heavy demand for this line, we advise you to send orders as soon as possible.

(4) Your competitors are offering considerably lower prices and unless you can reduce your quotations we shall have to buy elsewhere.

(5) We thank you for your offer, but we are buying at lower prices, are these best prices you can offer?

I Choose the appropriate word or words in the parentheses and then translate the sentences into Chinese.

1. We (offer, quote) you for 500 sets of Sewing Machines (at, on) $50 (on, at, of) CIF Lagos basis (for, in) June/July shipment.
2. There is (not, no) possibility (of doing, to do) business at this price.
3. We confirm (having sent, sending, to send) you a cable this morning, as per (confirmation copy, duplicate copy, carbon copy) enclosed.
4. Should you (prepared, be prepared) to (reduce, cut, cut down) the price by (5%, say 5%), we (will, would, shall) place our trial order (on, upon, with) you.
5. We write you today (with, in) the hope of entering into (business, business relations, business relation) with you.
6. We shall (try, do) our best to (meet, satisfy) your (requirement, requirements).
7. We need all the (necessary, needful) (informations, information) regarding your products

(exporting, exported, exportable) now.
8. We (often, always) (adhere, adhere to) the (principle, basis) of equality and mutual benefit (with, in, on) our trade (with, in, of) foreign countries.

II Arrange the following words and phrases in their proper order.

1. you will agree that
   when you see our samples
   and the high standard of craftsmanship
   the quality of the material used

   the most selective buyers
   will appeal to
   we think that

   _____
   _____

2. to meet your requirement
   we are at present unable
   though
   to revert to the matter

   once our supplies are replenished
   for the captioned articles
   we shall be only too pleased

   _____
   _____

3. and look forward to your first order
   details of which
   you will find in the catalogue
   draw your attention to

   we should like to
   such as stainless steel kitchenware
   our other products

   _____
   _____

4. steel tapes
   at your request
   we are now offering you

   CFR Lagos
   for 1,000 dozen
   at US$5 per doz

   _____
   _____

5. at considerably lower prices
   and therefore
   are obviously superior in quality
   but our products

   represent better value
   our competitors
   we are well aware that
   are quoting

   _____
   _____

III. Fill in the blanks with proper words or expressions.

1. As the market is _____ your price is _____ on the _____ side.
2. We _____ from your letter of March 20, that you are _____ the _____ for black tea.
3. We cannot _____ _____ _____ clear to reduce the price to the level you _____.
4. We hope to _____ business at something _____ our level.
5. You _____ _____ assured that the goods under Contract No. 4546 will be shipped _____ _____.
6. Since your price is _____ _____ _____ with the prevailing market, it is not _____ for the market at our _____.
7. While we appreciate your intention, we regret that we _____ entertain any fresh orders.
8. As soon as we are _____ a _____ to make an _____ for walnuts, we shall _____ you telegraphically.
9. We are enclosing a _____ of our new products for your _____.
10. We take _____ in informing you that we are _____ a _____ to accept new orders.
11. We have cut our price to the limit. We regret, therefore, being unable to comply _____ your request for further reduction.
12. As business has been done extensively _____ your market _____ this price, we regret that we can not accept your counter-offer. It is our hope that you would reconsider the matter and let us know _____ return.

IV. Translate the following letters.

Dear Mary,

Thank you for the information of the business card holder. I have not yet had a decision from the client. They have a number of layers of people to go through for final decisions. As soon as I have any information, I will advise you. I expect the decision will be made this week or as late as next week. I apologize for any inconvenience.

Kind regards,

Rose

敬启者：
　　感谢贵公司 8 月 1 日寄来的询价单，该函及所附的样品均已收悉。
　　鉴于该样品检验的结果，我们敢向贵公司保证，敝公司能够制造与该样品相同型号与品质的产品。
　　基于贵公司每年 100 000 双的需求量，我方报盘如下。
　　价格：CIF 大连每双 25 美元。
　　包装：塑料袋，外包装为纸板箱。
　　支付：即期的、不可撤销的、保兑的信用证。
　　交货：收到订单后的 90 天内，即 11 月、12 月船期。
　　我们可向贵公司保证，此价格是基于上述数量的最低价。其他技术性事项可参阅我公司的商品手册。
　　如有其他问题，请多多指点。

　　　　　　　　　　　　　　　　　　　　　　　　　　　　　你真诚的，

附件：商品手册一本

V　Please give the English or Chinese equivalents of the following.

1. 秋季目录	
2. 皮重	
3. 即期汇票	
4. 实盘	
5. 防辐射板	
6. T/T	
7. item number	
8. computer case	
9. alternative	
10. overseas department	

VI Complete the following two letters with proper words.

Letter 1

Dear Mike,

Re: Plush toys

Thank you for your _____ of November 13.

We would like to _____ as follows based on per 20' FCL.

Name of the commodity: KB5411 Bear in Ballet Costume
_____: 12 pcs/ctn, 162 cartons/20' FCL
Price: USD$9/pc CIFC3 Amsterdam
Shipment: to be _____ with 2 months from receipt of the relevant L/C
Payment: By sight L/C
Issuance: for 110% _____ value covering all risks and war risks

We will keep this offer _____ only for 7 days.

Yours truly,

Letter 2

Dear Sirs,

Re: Woolen Carpet

Thank you for your letter of October 12, _____ us woolen carpet.

However, we very much regret to state that we find the _____ is too high.

Information indicates that the same _____ made in China sold at much lower price. So if you should reduce your price _____ 3%, we might _____ to terms.

Considering our long-standing business relationship, we make you such a _____.

Hope you take our suggestion into consideration and give us your _____ as soon as possible.

Yours truly,

VII Write letters according to the following particulars.

Letter One

Write a letter to offer "Jade Rabbit" brand radios to the Oriental Trading Co. 488 Hotel Road, London, Britain at Stg. 40 per set CIF London, June shipment, commission 3%, and payment by L/C at sight.

Letter Two

Please read the following offer and then make a counter-offer as a buyer.

Dear Troy,

Re: our offer for sweater

Thank you for your fax of December 20 and your interest in our sweater.

As requested we would offer as follows:

Price: USD$35/dozen FOB Taiwan
Delivery: within 30 days after receipt of the L/C
Packing: standard export packing
Payment: by confirmed irrevocable sight L/C
Minimum order: 1,000 dozens
Validity: 30 days

Samples will be posted after the receipt of the charge.

Please don't hesitate to inform us the further information needed.

Looking forward to your order.

Yours truly,

Jean Wung

Chapter 8

Signing a Contract

Lead-in: Case Study

Huaxin Trading Co., Ltd. and James Brown and Sons have undergone a serial of correspondence and reached an agreement to the following price terms.

Art. No.	Commodity	Unit	Quantity	Unit Price (US$)	Amount (US$)
	Chinese Ceramic Dinner-ware				CIFC5 Toronto 12,737.00
HX1115	35 PCS Dinnerware and tea set	Set	542	23.5	16,320.00
HX2012	20 PCS Dinnerware set	Set	800	20.4	10,277.60
HX4405	47 PCS Dinnerware set	Set	443	23.2	7,645.40
HX4510	95 PCS Dinnerware set	Set	254	30.1	46,980.00

However, besides the price there are still some other essential terms to discuss before the signing of contract, such as terms of payment, packing, shipment and insurance. Please continue the correspondence until an order is placed and the contract is signed.

Section 1 Payment Terms

Payment plays a vital role in the international trade, which, if not ensured, will result in the total failure of the transaction. There are several commonly used terms of payment nowadays: remittance, L/C, collection, open account, installment, on consignment, cash on delivery and cash with order. As to the choice of the payment terms it depends.

In the first deal mostly both sides would prefer L/C because of its safety, but due to its expensive bank charges and a financial burden on the buyer resulting from the tie-up fund for over 30 days in usual practice only when the deal is over US$5,000 L/C will be applied. Letters regarding payment by L/C often fall into the following types: informing the open of L/C, urging establishment of L/C, amending L/C or asking for extension of L/C.

To inform the opening of the L/C, you should:

(1) acknowledge receipt of the message that the goods have been ready for shipment;

(2) inform the seller the effect of the payment, including the terms of payment, total amount,

and the quantity of the goods, etc.;

(3) ask for the confirmation of the shipment.

Messages urging establishment of L/C must be written with tact. The first message sent should be a polite note, which says that the goods ordered are ready but the relevant L/C has not yet come to hand. It is usually composed by:

(1) informing the buyer the goods are ready for shipment;

(2) emphasizing the closing date for shipment;

(3) urging the establishment of the L/C;

(4) giving a motivating ending.

When it comes to the deal between the regular customers, payment terms will vary a lot based on the usual practice.

Sample 1 Proposal for Payment by L/C from the Seller

CHINA NATIONAL IMPORT AND EXPORT CORPORATION

February 17, 2014
To: Mr. Woo < Messrs Aullivan & Son@gmail.com>
From: Tang Wanliang <CNIEC@qq.com>
Re: Payment by L/C

Dear Mr. Woo,

Thanks for your order #3325 and wish to say that we have adequate stocks of Type EM 127DN tapes in our warehouse, and that delivery date can be met.

Payment by irrevocable letter of credit is convenient for us, and we shall draw a 60 days bill on your bank.

We are now awaiting the arrival of your L/C, on receipt of which we shall make the necessary arrangements for the shipment of your order. Any request for further assistance or information will receive our immediate attention.

Sincerely yours,

Tang Wanliang
Overseas Sales Director

Sample 2   Proposal for Payment by L/C from the Buyer

October 27, 2014
To: Leon<Irina Office Equipment Co. Ltd.@hotmail. com>
From: Hamzza<Niger Trading@google.com>
Re: L/C payment

Dear Leon,

We would like to place an order for 500 Irina 272 microphones at your price of US$50 each CIF Logos, for shipment during November/December.

We would like to pay for this order by a 30-day L/C. This is an order involving US$25,000 and since we have only moderate cash reserves, tying up funds for 1 or 2 months would be inconvenient for us.

We much appreciate the support you have given us in the past and would be most grateful if you could extend this favor to us. If you are agree to the terms, please send us your contract. On receipt, we will establish the relevant L/C immediately.

Yours faithfully,

Hamzza A. Sesay
Managing Director

Sample 3   Asking to Ship an Order Cash on Delivery

Huangshan Tea Exporting Co., Ltd.

June 6, 2014
To: Mr. Spiros Augustatos
From: Geng Shuying
Re: Cash on delivery

Dear Mr. Augustatos,

Thank you for your order No. 5656 of 30 May for 500 cases of black tea.

We would like to arrange immediate shipment. Unfortunately, we do not have sufficient credit information to offer you open account terms at this time.

Would it be acceptable to ship this order cash on delivery?

If you wish to receive open account terms for your next order, please provide us with the standard financial statement and bank reference. This information will be held in strictest confidence.

We look forward to hearing from you.

Yours sincerely,

Geng Shuying
Export Manager

Sample 4   Informing the Establishment of the L/C

Burgeon International Trading Co., Ltd.

July 15, 2014
To: Mike
From: Bill D. H.

Dear Mike,

Please be informed that we have opened L/C No. 302155 on July 10 through "Bank of China, New York Branch" to your bank.

Please check and send us shipping details ASAP.

Thanks.

Sincerely,

Bill D. H.
Manager
Import Department

Sample 5 Urging the Establishment of L/C

GENTPACE INTERNATIONAL TRADING CO., LTD.
38 Da'an Street, Harbin, Heilongjiang, China
Phone: (0451) 400 0000   Fax: (0451) 400 0001   Zip Code: 150000

May 5, 2014
To: Mr. Amin
ATT: General Manager
From: Wang Ju

Dear Mr. Amin,

We refer to your order for 500 dozen pairs of Apple jeans and our sales confirmation No. 225.

We would like to remind you that the delivery date is approaching and we have not yet received the covering letter of credit.

We would be grateful if you would expedite establishment of the L/C so that we can ship the order on time.

In order to avoid any further delay, please make sure that the L/C instructions are in precise accordance with the terms of the contract.

We look forward to receiving your response at an early date.

Sincerely yours,

Wang Ju
Department Three

Sample 6 Amending L/C

June 15, 2014
To: Mr. Boosh
ATT: Financial Department
From: Picker
Re: L/C 800918 for Towball Shipment

Dear Mr. Boosh,

We regret to inform you that we can only ship above goods at the end of June if we can receive your following amendments by cable before this week.

(1) Please change the price term to CIF Shanghai, China.
(2) Transshipment is to be allowed.
(3) Extend the latest shipping date to July 25, 2014 and the validity of the L/C to August 10, 2014.

We will proceed the packing and inspection only upon receipt of your above amendment. To show our sincerity, we will pay for the amendment charge and will return you the freight cost form Shanghai to HK after shipment is made.

Please move faster on this amendment to avoid the delay in shipment. Please understand that our bank can only make the payment to us upon receipt of your correction.

We are really sorry for the trouble caused and appreciate your great help on the matter.

Yours sincerely,

Picker
General Manager

Section 2 Packing

The goods will have to travel a long distance to reach the clients abroad. A good handle of the packing will earn you not only the profits but also the clients. The general principle in packing is to make sure that the goods are secured for the long journey and kept as small and light as possible.

There are 3 main packing methods: bulk packing/outer packing, small packing/inner packing and individual packing. When writing a packing instruction, you should write as explicitly as possible, not only outer packing but also inner packing. Outer packing is used for the convenience of protection and transportation of the goods while inner packing is designed for the promotion of sales. The goods should be packed in a way according to the importer's instruction or the trade custom without violating the importing country's regulations on outer packing material, length and weight, or going against the importing country's social customs and national preference for inner packing colors and designs, etc. To facilitate the identification of goods, the outer packing must be marked clearly with identifying symbols and numbers which should be the same as indicated in the commercial invoice, the bill of lading and the other shipping documents. The packing list should be provided in the foreign trade.

Marks include main mark, which must indicate the destination, carton number and country of origin (sometimes the receiver's name also indicated for easy reorganization), and side mark, which must clearly show the quantity, net weight and gross weight (specifications occasionally appear).

Marks can be generally divided into two kinds, shipping mark or simply known as mark, and indicative and warning mark. Shipping mark is usually a symbol consisting of the name or initials of the consignee or shipper, destination and packaging number, etc. Indicative and warning mark gives handling instructions in words or by internationally recognized symbols, such as "Do Not Drop", "This Side Up", "Keep Dry", "Handle with Care" and so on. Apart from these two kinds of marks, there may be some other marks to indicate dimensions and weight.

The nowadays packing containers are: plastic bag, box, carton, wooden case, crate, pallet, foamed polystyrene, air bubbles plastic sheet, and container.

In a letter about packing, the instructions must be given in a very specific way so that the other party can fully comprehend and follow the instructions. At the same time letters regarding packing will cover the packing methods, quantity, size, weight, as well as whether the packing meets the needs or there are any improvements.

Sample 1 Stating Packing Requirements

Forward Hardware Co., Ltd.
987 Jiangnan Road, Kunshan, Jiangsu, China
Tel: (0520) 5000000   Fax: (0520) 5000001   Zip Code: 215300

May 20, 2014
To: Mr. Folk
From: Tang Wanliang

Dear Mr. Folk,

On May 20, we received your consignment of 40 cardboard cartons of steel screws.

We regret to inform you that 10 cartons were delivered damaged and the contents had spilled, leading to some losses.

We accept that the damage was not your fault but feel that we must modify our packing requirements to avoid future losses.

We require that future packing be in wooden boxes of 20 kilos net, each wooden box containing 40 cardboard packs of 500 grams net.

Please let us know whether you can meet these specifications and whether they will lead to an increase in your prices.

We look forward to your early confirmation.

Sincerely yours,

Tang Wanliang
Overseas Sales Director

Sample 2 Stating Marking Requirements

October 27, 2014
To: James Sen
From: Hamzza A. Sesay

Dear James,

The countersigned copy of contract No. 250 of October 3, 2014 for 300 pairs of shoes is enclosed.

The letter of credit is on its way to you.

Please mark the cartons in diamond with our initials, the destination and contract number are as follows:

SSD
Tokyo
250

The mark will apply to all shipments unless otherwise instructed.

Please advise us by fax as soon as shipment is effected.

Yours faithfully,

Hamzza A. Sesay
Managing Director

Sample 3 Buyer's Response to Packing

BURGEON International Trading Co., Ltd.
Telex: 478309 Burgeon USA   Fax: (1)320-816

July 15, 2014
To: Mike
From: Bill
Re: Packing for ready-made blouse

Dear Mike,

We have approached our clients about packing after receiving your letter of July 10. After our repeated explanation they accept your packing of the blouse in cartons if you guarantee that you will pay compensation in all cases wherein they cannot indemnify from the insurance company for the reason that the cartons used are not seaworthy.

We must remind you that should the insurance company refuse compensation, you would hold yourselves responsible for the losses. Our clients might sustain on account of your use of such cartons.

We hope you can understand our candid statement is made for our mutual benefits, as packing is a sensitive subject, which often leads to trade dispute.

We appreciate your cooperation.

Sincerely,

Bill D. H.
Manager
Import Department

Sample 4 Packing Proposal from the Buyer

Dear Mr. Wang,

We refer to our order for 500 dozen pairs of Apple jeans and your sales confirmation No. 225.

Particular care should be taken to the packing of the goods to be delivered in the first order. It is the usual practice here that 10 shirts are packed to a carton and 10 cartons to a strong seaworthy wooden case. There will be a flow of orders if this initial order proves to be satisfactory.

We are enclosing our confirmation of purchase.

We trust this order will be the first of a series of deals between us.

Sincerely yours,

Leonardo
Department Three

Sample 5 Amending for Packing and Marking

Dear Mr. Fang,

Re: S/C No. 800918 for Packing

We have received the above S/C and find that the packing clause is not so clear. The relative clause reads as, "Packing: seaworthy export packing, suitable for long distance ocean transportation."

In order to eliminate possible future trouble, we should like to make clear beforehand our packing requirements as follows:

The tea under the captioned contract should be packed in international standard tin boxes, 24 boxes to a pallet, 10 pallets in a FCL container. On the outer packing please make our initials JGT in a diamond, under which the port of destination and our order number should be stenciled. In addition, warning marks like KEEP DRY, USE NO HOOK etc. should also be indicated.

We look forward to your reply.

Yours sincerely,

Picker
General Manager

Sample 6 Informing the Details of the Packing

Dear Mr. Augustatos,

The consignment you ordered per Indent 9613 was dispatched today, and should arrive within three weeks.

The engine parts have been wrapped in waterproofed material and packed into crates measuring $6' \times 3' \times 3'$. Carburetor units have been packed separately into boxes attached into crates to the side of each crate. Lifting hooks are provided at four points. These crates are non-returnable.

The generator has been bolted into specially made crates and surrounded by hard padding. These have lifting hooks at two points. A charge of US$120 has been made on each of these crates, which is repayable if you return them in reasonable condition.

Yours sincerely,

Geng Shuying
Export Manager

Section 3 Shipment

In shipping goods abroad, the dealer has various alternative methods which include ship, truck, rail, air and parcel post.

The choice will depend on the nature of the product (light or heavy, fragile or sturdy, perishable or durable, high or low in value per cubic meter, etc); the distance to be shipped; available means of transportation; and relative freight costs.

Goods having high weight or cubic capacity or value ratio, the usual method of shipping overseas is by ocean cargo vessel. However, when speed is essential, air cargo may be preferred, although more expensive. For example, ski jackets are shipped from Germany to Japan by sea but towards the end of the ski season, air cargo is used.

Shipment is mostly made by ocean vessels, which is the most economical means compared with other forms of transport such as overland transport, and air transport and usually involves tramp, liner or container. The contract between the ship-owner and shipper may take the form of either a Charter Party or a B/L. When goods are shipped by road, rail or air, the contract of carriage takes the form of Consignment Note or Air Way Bill. To ensure the prompt delivery of the ordered goods in satisfactory manner, the parties concerned, including the consignor, the carrier, and the consignee should stay in frequent contact.

Shipment is a complicated process. Before shipment, the buyer generally sends the shipping requirement to the seller, informing the way of packing and the relevant information, known as the shipping instructions. As to the shipping advice, it is usually sent from the seller to the buyer immediately after the goods are loaded on the vehicle to advise the shipment.

Letters regarding shipment are usually written for the following purposes: to urge an early shipment, to amend shipping terms, to give shipping advice, to dispatch shipping documents and so on.

Sample 1　Asking for the Transportation Method

Dear Mr. Esses,

I am pleased to receive your order for our livestock and I will be pleased to send these to you in 5 weeks' time as arranged.

It would help us to know how you would like the current order of small tropical fish to be transported. As explained in our catalog the fish are packed in special insulated plastic containers which should keep them in good condition for up to thirty days after leaving here. We can send them by air or by sea — as you wish, but by air the cost of carriage, which we will invoice to you, will be increased by 50% — from £80 to 120.

As you know you have also ordered some pythons later in the year. These will travel much more easily in the large reinforced crates we provide. They simply go to sleep if the temperature falls. Unlike the fish.

Please let us know the method of transport you prefer for both consignments.

Sincerely,

Picker
Export Manager

Sample 2　Informing the Transportation Method

SGSA　AAA
E-mail address: train@SGSAAAA.com

August 16, 2014

To: Ms. Lee

Dear Ms. Lee,

Re: P/O 10003

Please note that the packing we request is 6 pcs in an inner box and 6 boxes in an export carton.

Also, please ship this order the same as previous shipments by direct air to us, and use air authorized code #6785.

Please follow above packing instruction and advise shipping details soon.

Sincerely,

Train Tata

Sample 3   Advising Partial Shipment

Wolf Machine Exporting Co., Ltd.
E-mail address: Geng Shuying@WME.com

June 6, 2014

To: Mr. Augustatos

Our telex of today refers hereto.

We have shipped, in partial fulfillment of your order No. 685, five sets of NY565 milling machines per S.S. "Five Star" which sailed today.

We enclosed all the copy documents.

As for the remaining 6 sets, we will endeavor to advance shipment and will advise you as soon as it is affected.

We appreciate the business you have secured for us. All further inquires and orders will continue to receive our prompt and careful attention.

Yours sincerely,

Geng Shuying

Sample 4   Urging an Early Shipment

SOMO COMPANY LIMITED
E-mail address: Tang wan-liang@SOMO.com

March 20, 2014

To: Helen

Re: our purchase contract No. 885.

We wish to remind you that we have had no news from you about shipment of the goods.

As mentioned in our last letter, we are in urgent need of the goods and we may be compelled to seek an alternative source of supply.

Under the circumstances, it is not possible for us to extend further our letter of credit No. 562 which will expire on May 21. Please understand how serious and urgent it is for us to resolve this matter.

We look forward to receiving your shipping advice.

Sincerely yours,

Tang Wanliang
Overseas Sales Director

Sample 5   Giving Shipping Advice

Burgeon International Trading Co., Ltd.

July 15, 2014

Dear Mike,

We are please to inform you that the Teddy Bear you ordered on May 25 will be shipped by S.S. "Maria", which is scheduled to leave for Guangzhou on July 30.

We enclose our invoice and shall present shipping documents and our draft for acceptance through the Citi-bank, Guangzhou Office, as agreed.

When the goods reach you we trust you will be completely satisfied with them.

We look forward to further orders from you.

Sincerely,

Bill D. H.
Manager
Export Department

Sample 6   Amending Shipping Terms

LOGO Trading
44 Long Street Lagos, Laos
Tel: 46374   Fax: 64653

October 27, 2014

Dear Sirs,

Re: Shipment of L/C No. 2324N02

We are sorry for the delay in the shipment under the above L/C, as there is no vessel available this week. The soonest vessel will be early next week. So, please kindly amend/extend the latest shipping date to November 11 and the expiry date of the L/C to November 30, 2014

Also, please e-mail us your inspection standard and confirm if every piece packed in a blister is OK.

Yours faithfully,

Hamzza A. Sesay
Managing Director

Section 4 Insurance

Insurance is closely related to foreign trade. In international business, the transportation of the goods from the seller to the buyer is usually over a long distance and has to go through the procedures of loading, unloading and storing. This process involves various risks, which may result in the damage or loss of the goods, and thus the inconveniences or even financial losses to both the seller and the buyer. To protect the goods against possible losses, before shipment, the buyer or the seller usually applies to an insurance company for insurance covering the goods to be transported. Then where can you get the cargo insurance?

A specialist cargo insurance broker will find you a good price, ensure the cover suits your needs and help you with claims; some banks offer cargo insurance as part of a finance package. You can also ask your freight forwarder for a quote, but research suggests that their costs and service don't match those offered by specialist brokers. You need to be aware that carriers, freight forwarders or third-party service suppliers will not automatically insure goods that are under their care or control. They can only do so if instructed in writing.

The party who bears the obligation of insuring the goods under the sales contract, who is the exporter or the importer, arranges cargo insurance. Many exporters would like to arrange insurance and freight but pass on the cost to the buyer. However, the experts believe that which is better depends.

The exporter has greater control over the risk and could win business from competitors who do not offer insurance if he offers. Besides, if you leave your buyer to arrange insurance, they will do so before paying for the goods. You may not be paid in full if there's a problem and they're not adequately insured. In addition, if the goods are rejected when they get to the port of entry or to the customer's premises, they won't be covered by insurance, and the responsibility will be back with you.

The importer will minimize the risks if he arranges insurance of goods that imported. He'll know how much he is paying and what's included. His supplier might not be able to give him full details of insurance cover they arrange, or if they do, the information may not be entirely reliable.

There are three sets of standard clauses published by the Institute of London Underwriters which set the scope of coverage the latter having wider scope.

(1) Institute Cargo Clauses I (Free of Particular Average, FPA).
(2) Institute Cargo Clauses II (With Particular Average, WPA).
(3) Institute Cargo Clauses III (All Risks).

In addition, three new sets of clauses dated 1/1/1982 drafted by the Institute are also used.

(1) Institute Cargo Clauses (C) =almost equivalent to I above.
(2) Institute Cargo Clauses (B) =almost equivalent to II above.
(3) Institute Cargo Clauses (A) =almost equivalent to III above.

When you write a letter of covering insurance, see to it that you should write down clearly the following information: subject matter, duration of coverage, insurance amount and premium, scope of cover, etc.

Signing a Contract Chapter 8 109

Sample 1 Asking the Buyer to Cover Insurance

Overseas Trading Co., Ltd.

March 20, 2014
To: Mark
From: Tang Wanliang

Dear Mark,

Refer to our purchase order No. 885 for 1,000 sets of TCL Color Television.

We have booked shipping space for the consignment on S.S. "Ocean Trader" which sails for your port on or about June 1.

We would be grateful if you could arrange insurance cover for the consignment at your end.

Please telex your confirmation as soon as possible.

Sincerely yours,

Tang Wanliang
Overseas Sales Director

Sample 2 Asking the Seller to Cover the Insurance

LOGO Trading
44 Long Street Lagos, Laos
Tel: 46374   Fax: 64653

October 27, 2014
To: Mr. Kum
From: Hamzza A. Sesay
Re: Our order No. 321 for 30 cases of assorted canned food

Dear Mr. Kum,

We wish to refer you to our order No. 321 for 30 cases of assorted canned food, from which you will see that this order is placed on CFR basis.

In order to save time and simplify procedures, we now desire to have the shipment insured at your end. We shall be pleased if you will arrange to insure the goods on our behalf against All Risks for 110% of the full invoice value, i.e. US$3,000. May we suggest that you follow our proposal?

We shall, of course, refund you the premium upon receipt of your debit note, or, if you like, you may draw on us at sight for the amount required.

We sincerely hope that our request will meet with your proposal.

Yours faithfully,

Hamzza A. Sesay
Managing Director

Sample 3 Response of Having Covered Insurance

Dear Sesay,

Re: Your order No. 321 for 30 cases of assorted canned food

We have received your letter requesting us to effect insurance on the captioned shipment for your account.

We are pleased to inform you that we have covered the above shipment against All Risks for US$3,000 with Insurance Company of Seoul. The policy is being prepared accordingly and will be forwarded to you by the end of this week together with our debit note for the premium.

For your reference, we are making arrangements to ship the 30 cases of assorted canned food by

S.S. "Princess", sailing on or about November 10.

Sincerely,

Bill D. H.
Manager

Sample 4   Answering a Request for Excessive Insurance

GENTPACE INTERNATIONAL TRADING CO., LTD.

May 5, 2014
To: Mr. Wang
From: Leonardo

Dear Mr. Wang,

Thank you for your letter of May 1 referring to your order No. 811 for 5,000 sets of "Sea Gull" Cameras.

Firstly, your request for insurance coverage up to the inland city is acceptable on condition that such extra premium is for your account.

Secondly, we cannot grant you insurance coverage for 125% of the invoice value, because the contract stipulates that insurance is to be covered for 110% of invoice value.

We trust that you will find this arrangement acceptable.

Sincerely yours,

Leonardo

Sample 5   Stating Type of Insurance Coverage

Unitech Livestock Co., Ltd.
963 Tianmu Road, 14th Floor, Birmingham 200070, Britain

March 3, 2014
To: Mr. Green
From: Picker

Dear Mr. Green,

We refer to your order No. 339 for 200 CL500 VCRs.

We shall be shipping your order by S.S. "Spring", due to leave here at the end of this week.

Unless you give contrary instructions, we will arrange an all-risk insurance policy for the shipment. In our opinion, this type of cover is necessary for a cargo of this nature.

We look forward to your early reply.

Sincerely,

Picker

Sample 6   Informing the Insurance Rate

June 6, 2014
To: Mr. Augustatos
From: Geng Shuying

Dear Mr. Augustatos,

Thank you for your fax of May 25.

I am pleased to let you know that we can arrange an all-risk open cover policy for jeans shipments to South Europe.

As you propose to ship regularly, we offer you a rate of 0.0045 for a total cover of US$110,000.00. I am enclosing a block of declaration forms, and you would be required to submit one for each shipment, giving full details.

I look forward to receiving your confirmation.

Yours sincerely,

Geng Shuying
Export Manager

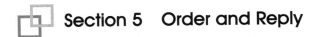

Section 5 Order and Reply

After a serial of discussion about the terms of goods, an order will be placed if both parties reach an agreement. An order is a formal request for a certain quantity of specific goods at a certain price to be fulfilled within a certain period of time. An order must keep the important principal of clarity and accuracy so as to avoid misunderstandings and troubles in future. For this reason an order usually includes such details as:

(1) quality descriptions;
(2) quantity statement;
(3) all documents required;
(4) price and mode of payment;
(5) packing and marking requirements;
(6) shipping or forwarding instructions;
(7) other necessary details.

When placing an order the writer may express the hope of being given prompt and careful attention to the order besides the details mentioned above.

An order may take the form of a letter, a telegram, a telex message, a fax, E-mail message or a printed order form. Most ordering today is done on standardized order forms, purchase forms, and requisition forms, and is handled by means of standardized procedures.

After the receipt of the order a seller should lose no time to state the acknowledgment either by a printed acknowledgment form or a letter, or both. The following are what should be done for acknowledgment.

(1) Acknowledge the order with expression of thanks.
(2) Give the seller's reference number.

(3) Restate the contents of the order and where possible add a few favorable comments on the goods ordered.

(4) Restate the shipping instructions, such as the date of shipment and the port of destination.

(5) Restate the terms of payment.

(6) Draw attention to other products likely to be of interest.

(7) Assure the buyer of prompt and careful execution of order and express your desire for future orders and enclose S/C in duplicate for counter-signature.

If turning down an order, the seller should explain the reason, show appreciation of the buyer's confidence in the seller's company and goods, express regret of inability to be helpful and the wish for further contacts, i.e., be polite and generalize the terms so that the buyer does not think the refusal only applies to him.

Sample 1   Initial Order

November 11, 2014
To: Jones Wou
From: Ann

Dear Mr. Wou,

Re: Initial order No. 101

Thank you for your letter of November 9. We find both quality and prices satisfactory and would like to place an order with you the following items on the understanding that they will be supplied from current stock.

Cargo: Cotton prints
Unit price: 40 cents/y CIF Liverpool
Quantity: 700 yards
Payment terms: by confirmed irrevocable L/C
Shipment: Dec. shipment
Insurance: All risks

Please send us your S/C in duplicate.

Best regards,

Ann

Sample 2 Acknowledgement of the Initial Order

November 2, 2014
To: Ann
From: Jones Wou

Dear Mr. Ann,

Re: Your initial order No. 101

Thank you for your order for our cotton prints and welcome you as one of our customers.

We confirm our acceptance of your order No. 101 and will supply the goods in due course. The S/C has been signed and sent to you under separate cover.

We are enclosing a copy of our latest catalogue and price list and hope that our handling of this initial order will lead to further business between us and mark the beginning of a happy relationship.

Best regards,

Jones Wou

Sample 3 Order from the Buyer

DDC Computers, Inc.

February 17, 2014
To: Eunice Chang
From: Lester Bemstein

Dear Mr. Chang,

New Order No. MA-123

Thanks for your yesterday's e-mail and the fine price you made us for iPad 5.

We accept your price and terms and would like to confirm our firm order No. MA-123 as per the copy enclosed.

Please do 100% test before shipment to make sure the quality and ship the goods on time as instructed. Please confirm your acceptance by return fax and send us a Pro Forma Invoice as soon as possible for opening L/C.

Best regards,

Lester Bemstein

Sample 4 Acknowledgement of the Order

Apple Group

February 18, 2014
To: Lester Bemstein
From: Eunice Chang

Dear Mr. Bemstein,

Your Order No. MA-123

Our Ref. P/I 103-B

Many thanks for your order of February 17 and we confirm the acceptance of your order No. MA-123. We also confirm that we will do 100% test before shipment and will proceed as stipulated in the order.

The duly singed P.O. is appended. Enclosed please find our Pro Forma Invoice P/I 103-B as requested for opening L/C.

We look forward to fostering and strengthening our future business cooperation.

Best regards,

Eunice Chang

Signing a Contract **Chapter 8** 117

Sample 5   Reply to Delay the Supply of the Order

Apple Group

February 18, 2014
To: Lester Bemstein
From: Eunice Chang

Dear Mr. Bemstein,

Your Order No. MA-123

Many thanks for your order of February 17 but we regret that we are unable to execute the order from our stocks, owing to the heavy demand recently.

We have undertaken to replenish our inventory in 2 months and hope that it will not be inconvenient for you to allow us one month extension.

We shall be grateful if you could confirm your order on the revised conditions.

Best regards,

Eunice Chang

Sample 6   Refusal of the Order

July 25, 2014
To: Mr. Augustatos
From: Helen

Dear Mr. Augustatos,

We received your order, P.O. #1852 today, in which you confirmed us the quantity of 2 containers only.

As offered in our last correspondence, we would give you 1.5% discount only on the basis of the order for total 3 containers. So, please reconfirm if you want to increase the quantity to 3 containers to get the 1.5% discount, or only order 2 containers without any discount.

We are looking forward to receiving your order soon.

Best regards,

Helen

Supplementary Information

- **Regarding Payment Terms**

   1. Remittance

   Remittance includes Telegraphic Transfer/Cable Transfer (T/T), Mail Transfer (M/T). The simple expression of "Payment: by T/T" will lead to dispute. Usually it should be stated as "Payment: by T/T before shipment" or "Payment: by T/T within 30 days after shipment".

   2. Cash with Order

   Cash with order requires the buyer place the funds at the disposal of the seller prior to shipment of the goods or provision of services. It is used when the buyer's credit is doubtful, when there is an unstable political or economic environment in the buyer's country, and/or if there is a potential delay in the receipt of funds from the buyer, perhaps due to events beyond his control. Advantage to the seller is immediate use of funds. Disadvantages to the buyer are that he pays in advance tying up his capital prior to receipt of the goods or services, that he has no assurance that what he has contracted for will be supplied, received in a timely fashion, and received in the quality or quantity ordered.

   3. Open Account

   Open account is used in the long-term purchase or several transactions per month. Usually the exporter delivers the goods first and then importer pays to him. We can have mail transfer (M/T), telegraphic transfer (T/T), and demand draft (D/D) in such payment term.

4. Collection

Collection is an arrangement whereby the goods are shipped and the relevant bill of exchange (Draft) is drawn by the seller on the buyer, and/or document(s) is sent to the seller's bank with clear instructions for collection through one of its correspondent bank located in the domicile of the buyer. Collection is of two types: collection on clean bill of exchange and collection on bill of exchange with document (or called documentary collection). The later can also be divided into D/P (D/P at sight and D/P at XX days after sight) and D/A. Collection on clean bill is seldom used in foreign trade except a balance of payment or some extra charges involved in the trade are to be collected.

• Regarding Packing

1. Mark Samples

Main Mark	Side Mark
BM NEW YORK C/NO. 1-100 MADE IN THAILAND	586 Notebook Computer QTY: 2 set NW: 20 kgs GW: 24 kgs

Indicative and Warning Marks: THIS SIDE UP, TOP, FRAGILE, KEEP DRY, STOW AWAY FROM HEAT, ACID — WITH CARE, USE NO HOOKS, OPEN THIS END, TO BE KEPT COOL, DO NOT STOW ON DECK, DO NOT DROP, INFLAMMABLE, GLASS — WITH CARE, LIFT HERE, PERISHABLE, HANDLE WITH CARE.

2. Packing Materials

(1) Bale: a package of soft goods (cotton, wool, sheepskin) tightly pressed together and wrapped in a protective material. Usual size 30×15×15 inch may be strengthened by metal bands.

(2) Carton: made of light but strong cardboard, or fiberboard with double lids and bottoms, fixed by glue, adhesive tapes, metal bands or wire staples. Sometimes a bundle of several cartons is made up into one package, held by metal bands.

(3) Container: There are 3 types of container, general cargo container, specific cargo container, air freight container. Usually there are twenty-foot container (20' GP) and forty-foot container (40' GP). The container service has the following advantages: Containers can be loaded and locked at factory premises or at nearby container bases, making pilferage impossible; There is no risk of goods getting lost or mislaid in transit; Manpower in handling is reduced, with lower costs and less risk of damage; Mechanical handling enables cargoes to be loaded in a matter of hours rather than days, thus reducing the time ships spend in port and greatly increasing the number of sailings; Temperature controlled containers are provided for the types of cargo that need them. The popular used term of FCL is a short form for Full Container Load and LCL for Less than

Container Load.

(4) Crate: a case not fully enclosed. It has a bottom and a frame, sometimes open at the top. Crates are built for the particular thing they have to carry. Machinery packed in a crate needs a special bottom to facilitate handling.

3. Commonly Used Packing Documents
PACKING LIST (NOTE)　装箱单
WEIGHT LIST (NOTE)　重量单
MEASUREMENT LIST　尺码单
PACKING LIST AND WEIGHT LIST　装箱单/重量单
PACKING NOTE AND WEIGHT NOTE　装箱单/重量单
PACKING LIST AND WEIGHT LIST AND MEASUREMENT　装箱单/重量单/尺码单
PACKING NOTE AND WEIGHT NOTE AND MEASUREMENT　装箱单/重量单/尺码单
WEIGHT AND MEASUREMENT LIST　重量单/尺码单
WEIGHT AND MEASUREMENT NOTE　重量单/尺码单
PACKING AND MEASUREMENT LIST　装箱单/尺码单
PACKING AND MEASUREMENT NOTE　装箱单/尺码单

● Regarding Shipment

1. Four Main Methods of Transporting Goods
(1) ROAD TRANSPORT tends to be comparatively cheaper and more direct than rail, and in the past few years haulage has doubled in many countries. The reasons for this include the increased capacity for lorries to carry goods, particularly with the introduction of containers, faster services, road improvements, and ferries offering rolling-on and rolling-off facilities.

(2) RAIL TRANSPORT is faster than road, which is necessary especially when transporting perishable goods, i.e. fish, fruit, meat, etc., and can haul bulk commodities in greater volume than road transport. Nevertheless, rail transport tends to be comparatively more expensive than road haulage.

(3) AIR TRANSPORT has the advantages of saving time, particularly over long distances. Insurance also tends to be cheaper as consignments spend less time in transit. However, with bulky, cumbersome equipment and bulk commodities, air transport is much more expensive.

(4) SEA TRANSPORT is the most widely used of the four forms of transportation in international trade. It is generally considered to be a cheap mode of transport for delivering large quantities of goods over long distances.

2. Shipping Procedure
The following steps are involved in a typical overseas shipping procedure.
(1) The Freight Forwarder is advised of the export order.

(2) The terms of sale are examined to determine the exporter's shipping responsibility and ability to fill the order.

(3) If letter of credit is involved, it must also be carefully examined to insure that any shipping conditions (such as shipping date, no partial shipments, discharge port, transshipment restrictions, etc.) are met or, if impossible to meet, arrangements should be made for the letter of credit to be amended.

(4) Quotations on freight rates sought from different shipping agents.

(5) A shipping line and vessel are selected.

(6) Space is booked as early as possible (as shipping space is not easily available to all destinations) through a shipping agent. The space should be on a ship with an acceptable loading port and acceptable estimated time of arrival (or ETA) at the required port of destination.

3. Some Knowledge of Shipment

The choice of loading port must be balanced against the preferred date of sailing. Information about sailing schedules is available in specialized shipping publications and in the business sections of the major newspapers.

The agent that represents the shipping line will, in booking the space, requires full details of the shipment, including weight, size, contents value, ports of shipment and destination. This is recorded by the exporter onto a shipping note that is sent to the steamship office.

The shipping agent then sends the exporter a contract number and an engagement note showing the details of the shipment, including name of the ship, destination, loading port, loading date, arrival date, and the shipping rate.

The exporter may cancel the space that has been reserved if the export order falls through. However, it should let the shipping company know as soon as possible so that the space can be allocated to someone else. Otherwise the shipping company will invoice the exporter for the unused space.

(1) Customs forms are filled out for the country of destination.

(2) The shipment is appropriately packaged and marked.

(3) Wait for the "calling forward" notice from the shipping company.

(4) The shipment is dispatched to the port with a consignment note.

(5) A bill of lading is obtained from the shipping company and freight charges are paid.

(6) The bill of lading and other required documents are delivered to the bank for collection.

4. Tramp and Liner

A tramp is a freight-carrying vessel, which has no regular route or schedule of sailings. It is first in one trade and then in another, always seeking those ports where there is demand at the moment for shipping space.

A liner is a vessel with regular sailings and arrivals on a stated schedule between specified ports.

5. Bill of Lading

(1) Definition: in Hamburg Rules, B/L means a document which evidences a contract of carriage by sea and the taking over or loading of the goods by the carrier, and by which the carrier undertakes to deliver the goods against surrender of the documents. A provision in the document that the goods are to be delivered to the order of a named person, or to order, or to bearer, constitutes such an undertaking.

(2) Function: a receipt for the goods, an evidence of the contract of carriage, a document of title.

(3) Classification: shipped on board B/L and received for shipment B/L; clean B/L and unclean B/L; "In apparent good order"; direct/with transshipment/through B/L.

6. Services Offered by the Freight Forwarder

Freight forwarder can offer a variety of services: advising on the best routes and relative shipping costs; booking the necessary space with the shipping or airline; arranging with the exporter for packing and marking of the goods; consolidating shipments from different exporters; handling Customs clearance abroad; arranging marine insurance for the shipment; preparing the export documentation; translating foreign language correspondence; scrutinizing and advising on ability to comply with letters of credit.

7. Manufacturers' Certificate of Quality

Manufacturers' Certificate of Quality is one of the quality certificates acceptable. The rest are Quality Certificate issued by Bureau of Commodity Inspection and Quarantine, Quality Certificate issued by an independent public survey, and Quality Certificate issued by our agent. It is best that the manufacturer will be able to issue the certificate since it can fulfill the 100% testing experiment, or it has been awarded by ISO, UL, CE, FCC and etc.. The goods tested by Bureau of Commodity Inspection and Quarantine, an independent public survey, or agent will adhere to AQL (acceptable quality level), which can not be guaranteed with 100% approved quality.

8. S.S.

S.S. is the abbreviation of "steam ship". We also have M.V., which is the abbreviation of "motor vessel". There are several modes of shipment, which are direct shipment, indirect shipment, partial shipment, and transshipment.

• Regarding Insurance

1. Insurance Stages

The stages of arranging insurance cover are as follows:

(1) The party seeking cover completes a proposal form;

(2) The insurance company assesses the risk and fixed a premium to be paid;

(3) The premium is paid and cover starts;

(4) If a loss is suffered, the insured makes a claim for compensation;
(5) The claim is investigated, and if found to be valid the compensation is paid.

2. Insurance Documents

The insurance policy is the principle document and is in fact a contract of indemnity. As the insurance may cover a certain period of time, or many shipments of goods, another document-the insurance certificate-is used. This is issued for each shipment that is made.

There is also a procedure of insurance often used now, known as open cover, by which there is a rather general arrangement between the insurer and the insured that the latter will have all consignments insured by the former.

A cover note is a small document issued by the insurance agents to their customers and tell them that there are insured, and to give proof of this until the policy is ready.

The insurance policy is the principle document and is in fact a contract of indemnity. As the insurance may cover a certain period of time, or many shipments of goods, another document-the insurance certificate-is used. This is issued for each shipment that is made.

3. Duration of Cover

The period covered by a marine cargo policy is defined as "Warehouse to Warehouse" in the Transit Clause of the Institute Cargo Clauses. Under this clause, the insurance attaches from the time when the goods leave the warehouse for the commencement of transit, continues during the ordinary course of transit, and terminates either on delivery to the final warehouse at destination or on the expiry of 60 days after completion of discharge, whichever shall first occur. It further provides to the effect that the insurance shall terminate on delivery to any other warehouse or place of storage, whether prior to or at the destination named in the policy, which the assured elects to use either for storage other than in the ordinary course of transit, or for allocation or distribution.

However, the duration of cover against War risk is limited to "Waterborne", which means that the goods are covered against War risks only when they are on board the ocean going Vessel.

4. Insured Value and Insured Amount

Since it is impracticable to assess the market value of the insured goods at the time and place when and where the loss of or damage to them takes place during the course of transit, an agreement on the valuation of the goods is made beforehand between the insurer and the assured when the contract of marine cargo insurance is concluded. Such value is called "Agreed Insured Value" and the marine cargo insurance policy is called a "Valued Policy".

The insured amount is the limit of the amount, for which the insurer is liable in respect of one accident, and insurance premiums are calculated upon this amount. Although the Insured Value and Insured Amount are different terminologies, the insured amount is normally fixed at the same as the insured value.

5. CIF Terms and Cargo Insurance

Insurance conditions are normally specified in the sales contract and/or Letter of Credit, but in cases where there are no specific instructions therein, it is usual to follow the practice of the trade. Of course, it is desirable to make the insurance conditions clear in the sales contract.

Normally the insured amount is shown in the sales contract and/or Letter of Credit. Current Incoterms provide that the insured amount should be not less than the amount of 110% of the CIF value.

Under CIF terms, the exporter is bound to provide marine insurance covering the whole voyage up to the final destination and to furnish the importer with shipping documents including the insurance policy.

There is another type of contract called C&I contract which is considered to be a variation of the CIF contract. Under C&I contracts, ocean freight is excluded from the price of sales contract since it is payable at the destination by the buyer. However, the obligation of the exporter relating to insurance is identical to that of CIF contract.

6. FOB and C&F Contracts

Under FOB terms, the exporter is bound to load the goods onto the carrying vessel at his own cost and risk, but he does not need to arrange insurance to protect the interests of the importer, which will be insured by the importer. In the case of C&F contract, the position of the exporter relating to insurance is quite the same as FOB contract, since the insurance premium covering the ocean voyage is excluded from the price of sales contract. The difference between FOB and C&F contracts relates to whom the ocean freight is paid by. Under FOB and C&F contracts, the exporter has an obligation of sending a shipping advice to the importer immediately on completion of loading the cargo at the port of shipment, so that the importer may effect insurance without delay. On the other hand, the exporter bears the risk before loading for which he will have to arrange insurance on his own behalf.

The importer's position regarding insurance protection under various trade terms is the reverse of the exporter's. The importer on CIF terms must rely upon the insurance arranged by the exporter, and on FOB or C&F terms he has to effect insurance by himself.

● Regarding Order and Reply

1. Pro Forma Invoice

Pro forma invoice is an invoice sent for form's sake and does not bind either the seller or the buyer. A pro forma invoice is not necessarily involved in every transaction. It is generally used a) to serve as a formal quotation or as a price reference; b) to enable the buyer to make the necessary preliminary arrangements, such as obtaining an import license for the goods he would like to order. Contained in a pro forma invoice are usually the descriptions of the goods, quantity, price, terms of payment, time of shipment, etc., but these do not involve the seller in any contractual obligations. Its contents are to a great extend similar to a commercial one. It will be a good policy to indicate in a pro forma invoice a prescribed period for which the price and conditions mentioned therein will remain good.

2. Commercial Invoice

Commercial invoice is a document prepared by the seller and addressed to the buyer, describing the goods, price and the shipping terms. It serves to provide the complete information on a transaction between the buyer and the seller. Its primary function is to indicate to the buyer the sale of goods at its price terms on the part of the seller and to check the price and the goods bought on the part of the buyer. It's usually made out in triplicate or quadruplicate. The commercial invoice generally bears the seller's own heading in its top. It contains the following information.

(1) "Invoice" or "Commercial Invoice".

(2) Name and address of the buyer and the seller and the date of invoice.

(3) Complete description of the goods and its packing. If the payment is to be effected by means of a documentary credit this description must exactly conform to that given in the credit.

(4) Unit price where applicable and price terms.

(5) Terms of settlement such as by documentary L/C. In the case of settlement by L/C the name of the issuing bank and L/C number should be shown thereon.

(6) Shipping marks and numbers, weight and/ or quantity of goods, and the name of the vessel if known.

(7) Seller's signature.

(8) Port of loading and discharge or place of receipt and delivery.

(9) Number of the contract and the invoice.

It should be reiterated that all invoices must be correct, include all details required by the buyer, and conform to those regulations governing import licenses, customs duties and exchange controls in the buyer's country.

3. Other Invoice

Other invoice includes customs invoice, shipping invoice, sample invoice, consular invoice, and visaed invoice.

4. Order

Order from the buyer usually carries the name as "purchase order, order sheet, indent, purchase contract, purchase agreement, purchase confirmation, purchase note". Different types of the order are: trial order, sample order, initial order, small order, formal order, large order (= big order), repeat order, minimum order, regular order.

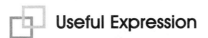

Useful Expression

● **Regarding Payment Terms**

1. Payment by the Usual Methods

(1) *D/P is applicable only if the amount involved for each transaction is less than US$1,000.*

(2) *Please expedite the L/C so that we may execute the order smoothly.*

(3) *The shipment date is approaching. It would be advisable for you to open the L/C covering your order No. 751 as early as possible so as to enable us to effect shipment within the stipulated time limit.*

(4) *Please see to it that payment is made by confirmed, irrevocable L/C in our favor, available by draft at sight, and allowing transshipment and partial shipment.*

(5) *We have instructed the Bank of Toronto to open L/C for US$20,000/ order No. 25/1,000 casks of iron nails in your favor.*

(6) *We have instructed our bankers, the Standard Chartered Bank, Hong Kong to telegraph the sum of HK$20,000 for the credit of your account at the BOC, Shanghai.*

(7) *We have extended the shipment and validity dates of the L/C to October 15 and 31 respectively.*

(8) *The buyer shall pay the total value to the seller in advance by T/T not later than May 15.*

(9) *It has been our usual practice to do business with payment by D/P at sight instead of by L/C. we should, therefore, like you to accept D/P terms for this transaction and future ones.*

(10) *Your proposal for payment by time draft for Order No. 1156 is acceptable to us, and we shall draw on you at 60 days' sight after the goods have been shipped. Please honor our draft when it falls due.*

(11) *In order to pave the way for your pushing the sale of our products in your market, we will accept payment by D/P at sight as a special accommodation.*

(12) *Your request for payment by D/P has been taken into consideration. In view of the small amount of this transaction, we are prepared to effect shipment on this basis.*

(13) *On the examination of the ... we found the following discrepancies/mistakes/points do not conform to the terms contracted. Therefore please instruct your bank to make the necessary amendment.*

2. Payment by L/C

(1) *To cover the value of goods ordered under our P/C No. ... an irrevocable L/C No. ... for USD ... has been established by the BOC in ... on ... in your favor.*

(2) *In accordance with the terms of our Contract No. ... for ..., we prepare to open the covering L/C within this week, and shall advise you by cable as soon as it is opened. We expect your best cooperation in the execution of this order.*

(3) *Just a line (a few lines) to inform you that we have today opened an L/C to cover our purchase of Surgical Instruments.*

(4) *We have opened an L/C in your favor for the amount of USD ...*

(5) *Application has been made to the bank for the establishment of L/C covering ... mts of rice.*

(6) *We have instructed our bank to issue a confirmed, irrevocable L/C in your favor.*

(7) *As soon as I hear from you that the goods are ready for shipment, I shall ask the buyer to establish an L/C.*

(8) *In compliance with your cable request of ..., we have amended the relative L/C to allow*

shipment not later than ... We look forward to your advice of shipment in due course.

(9) *Reference is made to the prepayment of USD ... called for in our Contract No. ... The BOC in this city has advised us of the arrival of your Banker's Letter of Guarantee. We are remitting the money to you by mail transfer through (said) Bank.*

(10) *Referring to the goods ordered under our Contract No. ... in the value of USD ... to be collected by D/A, we wish to advise that we have accepted your draft D/A ... days after sight on presentation by BOC, and we will make payment at its maturity.*

(11) *Please note that payment is to be made by confirmed, irrevocable L/C allowing partial shipments and transshipment, available by draft at sight.*

(12) *Our usual mode of payment is by confirmed, irrevocable L/C, available by draft at sight for the full amount of the invoice value to be established in our favor through a bank acceptable to us.*

(13) *In order to cover this order we have established an irrevocable and confirmed L/C in your favor through Barclays Bank, London for Stg. 45,000.*

(14) *We have opened an irrevocable L/C No. GB418 through the Citibank, NY.*

• Regarding Packing

1. to be packed/wrapped/supplied in ...

(1) *The 0.5 litre tins of paint will be supplied in strong cardboard cartons, each containing 48 tins, with a gross weigh of 50 kg.*

(2) *All export bicycles are wrapped in strong waterproof material at the port and packed in pairs in lightweight crates.*

2. to pack ... in

(1) *We will pack the material in bales of approximate 2 metres in length and 3 metres in girth. The protective canvas will be provided with ears to facilitate lifting.*

(2) *We pack our shirts in plastic-lined, waterproof cartons, reinforced with metal traps.*

3. to be needed for ...

A special crate with reinforced bottom will be needed for the transport of such a large machine, and both padding and bolting down will be essential.

4. to object to ...

We object to packing in cartons unless the flaps are glued down and the cartons secured by metal bands.

5. usual packing for ...

(1) *Our usual packing for dyed poplin is in bales lined with water proof paper, each containing 500 yards in single color.*

(2) *Our usual packing for tea has proven successful for a long time in many export shipment.*

6. care/consideration … given to/taken into packing

(1) *The great care must be given to packing as any damage in transit would result in a great loss.*

(2) *The careful consideration has been taken into packing. We have improved it so as to avoid damage to the goods.*

7. to limit/cut … to ...

(1) *Please limit the weight of any one carton to 10 kg and metal-strap all cartons in stacks of 4.*

(2) *Please cut vent-holes in the cases to minimize condensation.*

8. Others

(1) *Please note that the packing we require is 6pcs in an inner box and 6 boxes in an export carton.*

(2) *We require that future packing be in wooden boxes of 20 kilos net, each wooden box containing 40 cardboard packs of 500 grams net.*

(3) *We provide both 20 and 40 foot containers. They open at both ends, thus facilitating loading and unloading.*

(4) *For goods liable to be spoiled by damp or water, our containers have the advantage of being watertight and airtight.*

• Regarding Shipment

1. Informing the Shipping Time

(1) *The shipment is stated with a fixed date, for examples, shipment during January, shipment at/before the end of March, shipment on/before May 15th, shipment during April/May.*

(2) *An indefinite date of shipment is stipulated depending on certain conditions such as shipment within 30 days after receipt of L/C, shipment subject to shipping space available, shipment by first available steamer.*

(3) *The shipment is indicated with a date in the near future usually in such terms as immediate shipment, prompt shipment, and shipment as soon as possible, but without unified interpretation as to their definite time limit. It is advisable to avoid using these ambiguous terms.*

(4) *We will ship by the first steamer available next month.*

(5) *We are able to effect shipment within one month after your order has been confirmed.*

(6) *To repack the goods would involve a delay of about 2 weeks in shipment.*

(7) *The goods have long been ready for shipment, but owing to the late arrival of your L/C shipment can hardly be effected as anticipated.*

(8) *We regret that we are unable to meet your need for advancing the shipment to November.*

(9) *We inform you with pleasure that we have booked freight for our Order No. on the S.S. ... ETD (ETA) ... Please make sure to deliver the goods in time. For delivery instructions, please contact ... at ...*

(10) *We look forward to your prompt shipment./The shipment shall be effected as soon as possible./Immediate delivery would be required.*

(11) *We should be glad/please let us know when you could manage to ship the goods.*

(12) *Shipment is to be made in May/within 3 days/in the first half of March.*

(13) *It has to be stressed that shipment must be made within the prescribed time limit, as a further extension will not be considered by our end-user.*

(14) *It is fixed that shipment to be made before the end of this month and, if possible, we should appreciate your arranging to ship the goods at an earlier date.*

2. Advising Shipment

(1) *Your order No. ... will be shipped by S.S. "Manchester".*

(2) *We are pleased to inform you that we have booked shipping space for our Order No. ... of Chemical Fertilizers on S.S. "Daching", ETA ... For delivery instruction please contact ...*

(3) *We advise/wish to advise you that ...*

(4) *As per your request we have shipped all your orders by ...*

(5) *We have pleasure in advising that we have completed the above shipment according to the stipulations set forth in L/C No. ...*

(6) *All your orders booked up to date have been executed.*

(7) *The furs ordered have been dispatched by ...*

3. Others Sentence Pattern Regarding Shipping

(1) *We are unable to effect shipment according to the price and other terms originally agreed upon owing to the delay of your L/C, and therefore the responsibility for any loss arising subsequently will wholly rest with you.*

(2) *We wish to draw your attention to the fact that the goods have been ready for shipment for a long time and the covering L/C, due to arrive here before March 13, has not been received up to now. Please let us know the reason for the delay.*

(3) *As there is no direct sailing from Shanghai to your port during April/May, it is imperative for you to delete the clause "by direct steamer" and insert the wording "partial shipment and transshipment are allowed".*

(4) *As the cargo is to be transshipped at HK, we shall require through Bs/L.*

(5) *Your instructions as to marking have been accurately carried out and the goods packed with all the care of our experienced dispatch staff.*

(6) *In view of the fragile nature of the goods, we require them to be forwarded by air, and we would therefore be glad to know the lowest rates.*

● Regarding Insurance

1. 说明保险情况时，insurance 后接介词的一般用法

（1）表示所保的货物，后接 on，如 insurance on the 100 tons of wool。

（2）表示投保的险别，后接 against，如 insurance against all risks。

（3）表示保额，后接 for，如 insurance for 110% of the invoice value。

（4）表示保险费或保险费率，后接 at，如 insurance at a slightly higher premium, insurance at the rate of 5‰。

（5）表示向某保险公司投保，后接 with，如 insurance with the People's Insurance Company of China。

2. to cover insurance …

(1) *We have covered insurance on the 100 metric tons of wool for 110% of the invoice value against all risks.*

(2) *In the absence of definite instructions from our clients, we generally cover insurance against WPA and War Risk; if you desire to cover FPA (Free from Particular Average), please let us know in advance.*

(3) *For transactions concluded on CIF basis, we usually cover the insurance against All Risks at invoice value plus 10% with the People's Insurance Company of China as per CIC of January 1.*

(4) *We can cover all basic risks as required as long as they are stipulated in the Ocean Marine Cargo Clauses of the Lloyd Insurance Company, London.*

(5) *Please see that the above mentioned goods should be covered for 150% of invoice value against All Risks. We know that according to your usual practice, you insure the goods only for 10% above invoice value, therefore the extra premium will be for our account.*

3. to effect insurance …

(1) *We will effect insurance against the usual risks, for the value of the goods plus freight.*

(2) *We will effect insurance against all risks, charging premium and freight to the consignments.*

4. owing to …

(1) *Owing to the fact that these bags have occasionally been dropped into the water during loading and unloading, the insurers have raised the premium to …%. We are therefore of the opinion that it would be to your advantage to have WA (With Average/With Particular Average) cover instead of FPA.*

(2) *Owing to the risk of war, we cannot accept the insurance at the ordinary rate. At the same time, it would be to your advantage to have particular average cover.*

5. Please insure/cover for us

Please insure/cover us on the cargo listed on the attached sheet.

6. Others

(1) *As you will be placing regular orders with us, we suggest that we take out an open policy approximately $1,500,000 annually. The rate for insurance would be 46 per cent, and would cover all risks except war, warehouse to warehouse, on scheduled sailings.*

(2) *As you hold the policy, we should be grateful if you would take the matter up for us with the underwriters to ensure indemnification.*

(3) *I regret to report the loss of ... insured with you under the above policy.*

(4) *Will you please quote us a rate for the insurance against all risks of a shipment of ... from ... to ... by S.S. ... The invoice value is ...*

(5) *We are making regular shipments from ... to ... and should be glad to hear whether you would be prepared to issue an open policy.*

● Regarding Order and Reply

1. to place an order with somebody for something

(1) *We are pleased to place the following orders with you if you can guarantee shipment from Shanghai to Singapore by October 9.*

(2) *We shall place a large order with you provided the quantity of the goods and shipping period meet our requirements.*

(3) *If this first order is satisfactorily executed, we shall place further orders with you.*

(4) *The material supplied must be absolutely waterproof, and we place our order subject to this guarantee.*

2. to send/give somebody one's order for something

(1) *We are pleased to find that your materials appear to be of fine quality. As a trial, we are delighted to send you a small order for 2,500 dozen Rubber Shoes.*

(2) *We have the pleasure of sending you an order for 1,000 dozen umbrellas, at US$ 45 per dozen CIF New York, based on your catalog No. 51 of July 1. We trust the prices mentioned therein are still in force.*

3. to order something at a price

We order 100 units of Italian furniture No. TS11 at $300 per unit FOB Genoa. If this order is acceptable, please let us know by SWIFT.

4. to enclose an order

(1) *We enclosed a trial order. If the quality is up to our expectation we shall send further orders in the near future. Your prompt attention to this order will be appreciated.*

(2) *We are pleased to enclose an order we have received from Messrs Grayson Bros for 300 dozen pairs of "Moonlight" Rubber Shoes.*

(3) *We enclosed our order, but must point out that the falling market here will leave us little or*

no margin of profit. We must ask you for a better price in respect of future supplies.

(4) Your samples of Red Leaf Brand Health Tea have received favorable reaction from our clients, and we are pleased to enclose our order for 400 cartons.

(5) Thanks for your letter of November 2 with catalogue and price list. We have selected four qualities and take pleasures in enclosing our order sheet No. 26.

5. to be pleased to …

We are pleased to place you an order for 100,000 sets of MP3 players.

6. to be sorry to …

(1) We are sorry to ask you to reduce 1,000 pcs from order No. … due to economic depression (wrong calculation).

(2) We are sorry we cannot accept your quantity increase because we have completed the production and it is difficult to prepare the material for the increased small quantity.

7. to regret that …

We regret that we cannot at present entertain/fill any new orders for … owing to heavy orders.

● Regarding Payment Terms

I Choose the appropriate words to complete the sentences.

1. Mr. Smith will make a note (of, for, to, against) Mr. Sanchez's request for consular invoice.
2. Payments should be made (at, upon, by, after) sight draft.
3. Payment by L/C is our method of (negotiating, settling, financing, assisting) trade in chemicals.
4. If D/A is possible, it will help ease the (license, licensing, to license, licensed) problem.
5. Mr. Yin could agree (with, to, in, over) D/P terms.
6. 90% of the credit amount must be paid (at, by, against, when) the presentation of documents.
7. You don't say whether you wish the transaction to be (at, by, on, in) cash or (at, by, on, in) credit.
8. We have opened an L/C in your favor (at, by, on, in) the amount of HKD20,000.
9. The deal will be done on the basis that payment is made (with, to, in, over) advance, (at, by, on, in) installment or (on, of, for, to) delivery.
10. The check will soon fall (due, short, out, in).

Signing a Contract Chapter 8

II Fill in the missing words.

1. As usual, for the value of the goods we are _____ on you at 60 days in favor of the Bank of China and trust you will _____ our draft upon _____.
2. We regret to learn from our bankers that you refuse to _____ our draft without giving any reasons.
3. We are drawing _____ you at sight and sending the documents _____ the Bank of China for _____.
4. _____ is made in your letter of December 15 and ours of November 30.
5. We consider it _____ to make it _____ in the first place.
6. We hope that this trial shipment will _____ to your entire satisfaction and will lead to _____.
7. It appears that the stipulations in the L/C are not _____ agreement _____ the contract.
8. Please advise us whether your buyers approve _____ the design.
9. We are agreeable _____ your suggestion.
10. We shall _____ delivery of the goods as soon as they are released from the Customs.

III Please give the English or Chinese equivalents of the following.

1. 开立信用证	_____
2. 信用证指示	_____
3. 托收	_____
4. 货到付款	_____
5. 预付货款	_____
6. 赊销	_____
7. D/P	_____
8. sight draft	_____
9. installment	_____
10. down payment	_____
11. cash reserves	_____
12. to extend the L/C	_____

IV Arrange the following words and phrases in their proper order.

1. at 60 days' sight   with regard to terms of payment

being unable	for D/A
to consider your request	we regret

2.
what difficulties	upon receipt of this letter
in opening the L/C	you actually have
please let us know	

3.
during this sales-pushing stage	we are pleased
to accept	as a special accommodation
payment by D/P	to inform you
that we are ready	

4.
on the basis of D/A	to have you
as one of our customers	to do business
we would like	but
we regret our inability	

5.
we are unable	any extension of import license
of our L/C No.789	much to our regret
do not permit	to comply with your request
because the present import regulations	for an extension

V **Translate the following sentences.**

1. The check for USD1,000 was returned by Chase Manhattan Bank for the reason of "Non-Sufficient Funds".

2. In the event of our acceptance of your offer we shall open an irrevocable L/C in your favor, payable in China against shipping documents.

3. The L/C procedure is being preceded by BOC.

4. As requested in your fax of December 15, shipment of 500 mts of soybeans will be effected under guarantee in the absence of the L/C amendment. Please, therefore, honor the draft accordingly.

5. It will interest you to know that as a special sign of encouragement, we shall consider accepting payment by D/P during this sales-pushing stage.

6. 请注意，付款是以保兑的、不可撤销的、允许分装和转船的、见票即付的信用证支付。

7. 你方以付款交单方式付款的要求，我方以予以考虑。鉴于这笔交易金额甚微，我们准备以此方式办理装运。

8. 你方可能记得，按照我方第321号售货确认书规定，有关信用证应不迟于11月15日到达我处。因此，希望你方及时开证，以免耽误装运。

9. 请注意第268号合约项下的800辆自行车备妥待运以久，但至今我们尚未收到你方有关的信用证。请速开来，以便装运。

10. 现寄上邮政汇票1 000美元结清欠款。

VI Complete the following letters with proper words.

Letter 1

Dear Sirs,

We _____ an application form for documentary _____ and shall be glad if you will arrange to _____ for our account with your office in London an _____ letter of credit for $ 1 000 in _____ of the Urban Trading Company, the credit to be _____ until November 30.

The credit which _____ shipment of 2,000 tons of Steel may be used _____ presentation of the following _____: Bills of _____ in _____, one copy of Commercial _____, Packing List, _____ of Insurance and Certificate of _____. The company may _____ on your London office at 60 days' _____ for each shipment.

Yours faithfully,

Letter 2

Dear Sirs,

Thank you for your letter of 10 November, 2014.

We have _____ your request for a _____ delivery of silver cutlery on documents against _____ terms, but _____ to say that we cannot _____ to your proposal.

As an _____, the best we can do for the trial is to _____ you direct payment at sight terms.

If you _____ our proposal you run very little risk, since our silver cutlery is well _____ for its quality, attractive design and reasonable _____. Our lines sell very well all over the world and have done so for the last 100 years. We do not think you will have any difficulty in _____ a satisfactory volume of _____.

If you find our proposal _____, please let us know and we can then expedite the transaction.

Sincerely yours,

Letter 3

Dear Ms. Ni,

Order No. 9953

Thank you for your order which has been _____ and is being sent to you today.

As _____ we have forwarded our bill, No. 2782 for DM1,720.00 with _____ to your bank, Industrial & Commercial Bank of China, Caohejing Branch, Shanghai. The draft has been _____ out for payment 30 days after _____, and the documents will be handed to you on _____.

Yours sincerely,

VII Writing.

1. 根据下列提示写一封完整的买方回复函。

> 主题：有关 L/C No. 78967 上的错误（N2 的 N1）
> 说明：由于这是一批紧急出货，我方将不修改信用证，但会指示银行接受你方瑕疵押汇文件。
> 结论：请确认并告知出货明细。

2. 根据下列提示写一封信用证修改函。

> 主题：感谢收到 L/C No. 880128，但有下列错误。
> （1）价格条件应该是 FOB HK。
> （2）应该允许转运。
> （3）最后出货期应该是 10 月 3 日。
> 请尽快修改，并回电确认。

3. A foreign buyer whom you do not want to loss has purchased 2,000 pieces of cotton piece goods from you for delivery in September. As the goods are ready for shipment, write a letter to the buyer urging them to open the covering L/C immediately.

● **Regarding Packing**

I Choose the appropriate words to complete the sentences.

1. We regret that we have suffered heavy loss (resulted in, resulted from, resulting in,

resulting from) your improper packing.

2. We would suggest that you (secure, will secure, securing, are secured) the carton with double straps.
3. Metal handles should be fixed to the boxes to (make, convenience, easy, facilitate) carrying.
4. We give you on the attached sheet full details regarding packing and marking, which must be strictly (observed, abide by, signified, submitted).
5. Your comments on packing will (be passed, passed, be passing, passing) on to our manufactures for their reference.
6. This container can be easily opened (on, at, in, by) both ends.
7. We give you on the attached full details (regarded, regarding, be regarded, regard) packing and marking,
8. Taking into consideration the transport condition (in, on, with, at) your end, we have improved our packing so as to avoid damage to the goods.

II Fill in the missing words.

1. Packing _____ sturdy wooden cases is essential. Cases must be nailed, battered and cured by overall, mental strapping.
2. The greatest care must be _____ to packing and crating as any damage in transit would cause us heavy losses.
3. As the goods will probably be _____ to a thorough examination, the cases should be of a type which can be easily made fast again after opening.
4. Our cartons for canned food are not only seaworthy but also strong enough to protect the goods from possible _____.
5. Each jar is wrapped in tissue paper before being _____ into its individual decorative cardboard box.
6. We understand your concern about packing, and can assure you that we take every possible precaution to ensure that our products _____ our customers in prime condition.
7. The boxes are packed in strong cardboard cartons, 12 _____ a carton, separated form each other by paper dividers.
8. Since the crates are specially made to _____ 24 cartons, there is no danger of movements inside them.
9. The crates are lined with waterproof, airtight material. The lids are secured by nailing, and the crates are _____ with metal bands.
10. Since cartons are comparatively light and compact, they are more convenient to handle in the _____ of loading and unloading.

Signing a Contract **Chapter 8** 139

III Please give the English or Chinese equivalents of the following.

1. 修改包装指令	_____
2. 包装条款	_____
3. 包装不妥	_____
4. 适合海运的包装	_____
5. 防水防潮	_____
6. to coat with antirust grease	_____
7. to pack in spear/in block/in slice/in bulk	_____
8. padding	_____
9. carton label	_____
10. to line with craft paper	_____

IV Arrange the following words and phrases in their proper order.

1. please
   if cartons are used
   ensure to
   protection from damp
   in strong polythene bags
   each chemical
   supply

   _____
   _____

2. reinforced by battens
   a light case
   and be much cheaper
   would meet your requirements
   as the former
   would be non-returnable
   than a solid wooden case

   _____
   _____

3. when
   the various items
   into handles
   for shipment
   we will pack them
   of suitable size
   of your order
   in our warehouse
   are complete

   _____
   _____

4. covered with waterproof fabric   please make our order up

and strapped into bales   of about 200kg each
with metal bands   horizontally
and vertically

5. of the machine   against the container
   and generously padded   to avoid
   are to be wrapped   all polished parts
   knocking and scratching

V Translate the following sentences.

1. The packing of our Men's shirt is each in a poly bag, 5 dozens to a carton lined with waterproof paper and bound with two iron straps outside.

2. Our cotton prints are packed in cases lined with draft paper and waterproof paper, each consisting of 30 pieces in one design with 5 colourways equally assorted.

3. Glass wares are fragile goods. They need special packing precautions against jotting.

4. Please note the packing is 5pcs in an inner box, 10 boxes in an export carton, 6 cartons in a pallet.

5. 我们高兴地通知贵公司，现可以接受按买方指定的图纸和包装的订单。

6. 雪茄烟每5支装一包，20包装一条，144条装一纸箱。

7. 集装箱的防水和密封设计能够避免货物受潮或沾水而导致损坏。

VI Writing.

1. Write a letter to your customer telling him that you have improved your packing and that from now on all garments are to be packed in cartons instead of wooden cases.
2. 根据下列提示写出货包装函。

> 先生：
> 　　请注意我们要求的包装是 10 个装一个内盒，10 盒装一个外箱。
> 　　此外请和以前出货一样用直飞方式空运给我们，并使用空运授权编号 82028。
> 　　请按以上述包装方式包装并尽快告知出货明细。

VII Complete the following letters with proper words.

Letter 1

Dear Sirs,

The 12,000 cycles you ordered will be _____ for dispatch by February 17. Since you require them for onward _____ to Bahrain, Kuwait, Oman and Qatar, we are arranging for them to be _____ in seaworthy containers.

Each bicycle is enclosed in a corrugated cardboard pack, and 20 are banded together and _____ in sheet plastic. A container holds 240 cycles; the whole cargo would therefore comprise 50 containers, each weighing 8 tons. _____ can be made from our works by rail to be forwarded from Shanghai harbor. The freight _____ from works to Shanghai are US$80 per container, totally US$4,000 for this _____, excluding container hire, which will be charged to your account.

Please let us have your delivery _____.

Yours faithfully,

Letter 2

Dear Sirs,

We would refer to our order No. 120 of August 15 for machine tools.

Please now _____ the first part of this order (items 1-8) by air, as these are urgently _____ by customers. We suggest the use of cartons with hinged lids to _____ opening for Customs examination.

You will no doubt _____ with your arrangements for transport by sea for the reminder of the consignment, and we would ask you to be particularly careful to seal each box _____ a watertight bag — we recommend plastic — before packing into cases. In your last consignment we were obliged to remove a certain amount of rust, which we presume had formed during the _____.

Yours sincerely,

Letter 3

Dear Sirs,

Your consignment of chemicals is now _____ for dispatch, and we are arranging _____ by S.S. "Yamagawa Maru", sailing from Shanghai on May 24.

The sulphuric acid is supplied in thirty 4-gallon carboy, doubled-packaged for extra safety, and with a protective lid to _____ breakage of the mouth. The ammonia is in forty 5-cwt steel drums.

Please _____ safe arrival of the consignment.

Yours sincerely,

- **Regarding Shipment**

I   Correct the inappropriate words and expressions.

1. Only by the end of the next month the goods can be packed ready for delivery.
2. Having no direct steamer to your port from Dalian, the goods have to be transshipped at Hong Kong.
3. Please send us full instructions for the ten cases for London such as contents, value, consignee and who pays all the charges.
4. All powders are wrapped in plastic bags and packed in tins, which the lids are sealed with adhesive tape.

5. As requested, we are already carried out making and numbering on all cases.
6. For the boxes are possible to receive rough handling at this end, you must see to it that packing is strong enough to protect goods.
7. In order that we facilitate to sell, it would be better to pack the goods in cases of 50 dozen each equally.
8. We would ask you to do everything probable ensuring punctual shipment.

II Fill in the missing words.
1. We regret our _____ to comply with your request for shipping the goods in early May.
2. We have the pleasure of informing you that the _____ has gone per S.S. "East Wind" and hope it will arrive at the destination in perfect condition.
3. Shipping shall be _____ within 40 days.
4. Before deciding which form of transport to use, a _____ will take into account the factors of cost, speed and safety.
5. Some parts of the machine susceptible to shock must be packed in seaworthy cases capable of withstanding rough _____.
6. In order to ensure the earlier shipment we would like to make this an _____ and agree to transshipment.
7. Goods sold shall be guaranteed by the seller to _____ to the sample arrival at destinations.
8. The consignment will be sent _____ to reach the final destination by the end of March.
9. This is to certify that the goods _____ by this invoice are neither of Taiwan nor of Singapore origin.
10. Even though the goods are ready, we don't know whether we can _____ the shipping space immediately.

III Please give the English or Chinese equivalents of the following.

1. 提前装运	
2. 搬运不当	
3. 包机	
4. 装载日期	
5. 舱位	
6. weight memo	
7. forwarding agent	
8. to reach in good order	
9. initial shipment	
10. dead freight	

IV. Arrange the following words and phrases in their proper order.

1. in accordance with your instructions
   to inform you that
   packed in twelve 100 kg cases
   your order No. 32
   we are pleased
   has been dispatched

   _____

2. the order
   today
   in view of the urgency of
   by air
   it should reach you tomorrow
   so that
   we have dispatched
   the goods

   _____

3. in the case of
   without prior notice
   except
   alteration
   are subject to
   our rates
   special contract

   _____

4. and method of transport
   for any country
   and as a result of
   our wide experience
   you wish to export
   on suitable packing
   we can advise you

   _____

5. in one of our previous letters
   for an early delivery
   the users
   of the machines contracted
   are in urgent need
   as you have been informed
   and in fact are pressing us

   _____

V. Complete the following sentences.

1. Please send us your shipping instructions
   a. 以便我们备货装船。

   _____

   b. 以便我们租订舱位。

   _____

   c. 以便我们办理海关手续。

   _____

2. According to the contract stipulations
   a. 唛头由买方选定。
   _____

   b. 买方必须在九月份内完成货物的装运工作。
   _____

3. We would rather ... than .../We prefer ...
   a. 装直达轮，而不在新加坡转船。
   _____

   b. 货物用木箱包装，箱净重 100 公斤，不用双层麻袋包装。
   _____

   c. 采用付款交单方式，而不采用 60 天期汇票支付。
   _____

4. It is expressly stated that
   a. 货物必须于 10 月底以前装船。
   _____

   b. 500 公吨花生应于 9 月装运，其余 500 公吨于 10 月装运。
   _____

   c. 1 000 公吨花生必须一次装船。
   _____

VI Complete the following letters with proper words.

Letter 1

Dear Sirs,

We are p_____ to confirm that the 100 COMPASS power switches under your order No. JY-120 are now ready for s_____. When p_____ your order stressed the importance of p_____ delivery and we are g_____ to say that by m_____ a special effort we have been able to improve o_____ the delivery a few days a_____ of the time agreed upon.

We now await your shipping instructions and immediately we receive them we shall send you our shipping a_____.

We look forward to your e_____ reply.

Yours faithfully,

Letter 2

Dear Sirs,

We feel it n_____ to invite your a_____ to the subject order concluded with you last September and accepted by you in your letter of October 2, 2014, with w_____ a countersigned copy of the contract was enclosed.

According to the s_____ schedule in the contract, two thirds of the order was to be shipped by the end of December, the b_____ to follow in February this year. We are, however, very much d_____ to have received no news f_____ your about the first shipment. And, w_____ is more, you haven't even r_____ to our fax of October 10, 2014.

We anxiously await your reply soon.

Yours sincerely,

Letter 3

Dear Sirs,

_____: Contract No. 123456

Referring _____ our previous letters, we wish to call your _____ to the fact that _____ to the present moment no _____ has come from you about the _____ under the contract.

As you have been _____ in one of our previous letters, the users are in urgent _____ of the machines _____ and are in fact pressing us for assurance of an _____ delivery.

Under the circumstances, it is obviously impossible for us to again _____ L/C No. 123456, which _____ on August 24, and we feel it is our duty to remind you _____ this matter again.

As your prompt attention to shipment is most _____ to all parties _____, we hope you will fax us your shipping _____ without further delay.

Yours truly,

Signing a Contract **Chapter 8** 147

VII Writing.
1. Write to a firm of shipping agents asking them to arrange for consignment to be collected from your factory and make all arrangements for transportation on Dares Slam. Include imaginary particulars as to nature of consignment, names and addresses of consignors and consignee, and say who will take delivery of the consignment upon arrival.
2. As secretary of Harding & Co. of Hull, write to Scandinavian Liners Ltd. for details of their sailings to Norway and Sweden and for quotations of their rates for manufactured woolen goods.

● **Regarding Insurance**

I Correct the inappropriate words and expressions.
1. The cargo is to be insured from warehouse to warehouse by All Risks.
2. As requested, we have covered insurance with 20,000 transistor radios at 10% above the invoice value for All Risks.
3. Unless we hear from you on the contrary before the end of this month, we shall arrange to cover the goods against FPA for the value of the goods plus freight.
4. As concerned foreign trade, the following three risks cover an insurance policy, namely, FPA, WPA and All Risks.
5. If you wish to insure the cargo for 130% at the invoice value, the premium for the difference among 130% and 110% should be in your account.
6. For goods sold on CIF basis insurance is to effect by us for 110% of the invoice value against All Risks based from warehouse to warehouse clause.
7. The insurance covers only WA and War Risks. If extra additional insurance coverage is required, the buyer is borne the extra premium.
8. Please effect insurance in our account of RMB 13,200 on the goods against All Risks, from Shanghai to Los Angeles.

II Fill in the missing words.
1. WPA coverage is too narrow for a shipment of this nature, please extend _____ to include TPND.
2. Insurance is to be covered _____ buyers.
3. We note that you wish us to insure shipment to you _____ 10% invoice value.
4. Please insure _____ invoice value _____ 10%.
5. We shall provide such coverage _____ your cost.
6. Our clients request their order to be insured _____ all risks and war risk. Please arrange for the insurance cover accordingly.
7. Please arrange to supply these and charge _____ our account.
8. Regarding insurance, the coverage is _____ 110% of invoice value up to the port of destination only.

9. Buyer's request for insurance to covered up to the inland city can be accepted on condition that such extra premium is for _____ account.
10. Since the premium varies with the extend of _____, extra premium is for buyer's account, should additional risks be _____.
11. The insurance _____ varies with the nature of the goods, the degree of "cover" desired and the place of destination.

III Please give the English or Chinese equivalents of the following.

1. 水渍险	
2. 保单	
3. 投保人	
4. 投保金额	
5. 保费	
6. particular average	
7. additional coverage	
8. salvage charges	
9. underwriter	
10. constructive total loss	

IV Arrange the following words and phrases in their proper order.

1. which we intend to export
   all risk
   an open cover policy
   for our chinaware shipment
   we would like you
   over the next three months
   to arrange

   _____

2. further policies
   on other shipments
   if you can
   competitive rates
   offer us
   with you
   we will consider

   _____

3. the shipment
   if you will arrange
   on our behalf
   against All Risks
   for 110% of the invoice value
   as we now desire to have
   insured
   we shall be pleased

to insure the goods   at your end

4. and the insurance policy   as required
   will be sent to you   with PICC
   together with the other shipping documents   we have covered your order
   through the bank

5. of the shipping company's agent   we had
   examined by   opened the case
   in the presence   and the contents
   a local insurance surveyor

V Translate the following Chinese sentences into English.

1. 请将装运给我们的货物投保水渍险和战争险。

2. 请按发票价的110%投保。

3. 至于第345号合约项下的300部相机，我们将自行办理保险。

4. 至于索赔，我们的保险公司只接受超过实际损失5%的部分。

5. 请告知我们价格是否包括偷窃及提货不着险。

6. 如果没有你们的明确指示，我们将按一般惯例投保水渍险和战争险。

7. 很遗憾，我们不能接受这一索赔，因为你们的保险没有包括"破碎险"。

8. 根据你们惯常用的 CIF 价格条件，所保的是哪些险别？

_____

_____

VI **Translate the following passage.**

> 关于第×××号 3 000 桶铁钉的售货合约，兹通知你方，我们已由伦敦中国银行开立了第×××号保兑的、不可撤销的信用证，共计金额×××英镑，有效期至 5 月 15 日为止。
>
> 请注意（做到）上述货物必须在 5 月 15 日前装出，保险必须按发票价的 150%投保综合险（All Risks）。我们知道，按照一般惯例，你们只按发票价另加 10%投保，因此额外的保险由我们负责。
>
> 请按我们的要求办理保险，同时我们等候你方的装运通知。

VII **Complete the following letters with proper words.**

Letter 1

Dear Sir,

Re: Insurance

Answering your _____ of June 25 in _____ to insurance, we would like to _____ you of the following.

All Risks. Generally we cover insurance WPA & War Risk in the _____ of definite instructions from our_____. If you desire to _____ All Risks, we can provide such coverage at a slightly higher premium.

Breakage. Breakage is a _____ risk, for which an extra _____ will have to be_____. The present rate is about …%. Claims are payable only for that of the _____, that is over 5%.

Value to be insured. We note that you wish to insure _____ to you for 10% above _____ value, which is having our _____ attention.

We trust the above information will _____ your purpose and _____ your further news.

Yours truly,

Letter 2

Dear Sirs,

We will be _____ a consignment of 100 photocopiers to Daehan Trading Company, Limited, Pusan, the Republic of Korea. The consignment is to be _____ on to the S.S. "Dashun", which sails from Shanghai on December 16 and is _____ in Pushan on December 19.

Details with _____ to packing and value are _____, and we would be grateful if you could quote a _____ covering all risks from port to port.

As the matter is urgent, we would _____ a prompt reply. Thank you.

Very truly yours,

● Regarding Order and Reply

I Correct the inappropriate words and expressions.

1. Please send us as soon as possible the following goods, which listed in your current spring catalogue.
2. The enclosed order is given strictly on the condition which shipment must be made not later than the first day of May.
3. We reserve the right to cancel this order except the goods are in our hands at the end of June.
4. We are handling your order with great care and you can depend on us effecting delivery well within your time limit.
5. You may rest assured that fresh supplies are due to arriving early next month.
6. If the quality of your goods is satisfied, we will place a large order with you.
7. Very much we would like to supply you the product, we are unable to fill your order owing to the heavy backlog of commitments.
8. We cannot make you an offer, as the goods are not in stock.

II Fill in the missing words.

1. Our offer is _____ subject to your _____ _____ one week.
2. We have established _____ irrevocable letter of credit _____ the Bank of China, Shanghai.
3. Please keep us _____ _____ the response to our new product Kunlun Brand TV set in your market.

4. Please _____ one copy of Purchase Confirmation completed _____ your counter-signature.
5. We confirm telegrams exchanged resulting _____ the sale to you of 100 tons Grounding.
6. We are sending you our Sales Contract No. 175 _____ duplicate.
7. We expect to put _____ the deal.
8. We trust that you will give special care to the goods, _____ they _____ be damaged.
9. Your price was rather _____ the high side, so we are afraid we can not _____ your offer.
10. You will be advised _____ time when the machines are ready _____ shipment.
11. The relative L/C will be airmailed soon and you are requested to ship the above lot _____ the first available steamer upon receipt _____ our L/C.
12. We have pleasure _____ sending you the attached Orders Confirmation No. 350, _____ our recent purchase _____ you of 1,500 cowhides.

III Please give the English or Chinese equivalents of the following.

1. 确认订单	
2. 下订单	
3. 取消订单	
4. 续订	
5. 库存	
6. to adjust the price	
7. to hold to the contract	
8. discrepancy	
9. current stock	
10. trial order	

IV Arrange the following words and phrases in their proper order.

1. at the named prices   to give you an order
   they will be supplied   for the following items
   we are pleased   on the understanding that
   from current stock

   _____
   _____

2. and please sign and return   for the Order No. GD34
   to us   in duplicate
   thank you very much   we are pleased
   for our file   to enclose
   one copy of which   our Sales Confirmation No. 9975

3. can be delivered well   our immediate attention
   within your time limit   is receiving
   your order   and

4. by 5%   while
   in the prices of raw materials   we have to explain that
   thank you for your order   owing to a corresponding rise
   our price has increased

5. we are ready   in order to finalize
   a 5% discount   however
   to allow you   the first transaction between us
   if you can increase   the quantity to 1,000

V. Translate the following passages.

> 　　接到你公司 9 月 5 日印花细布（printing shirting）订单，非常高兴，并欢迎你公司成为我公司的客户之一。
> 　　确认按你方来信列明价格供应印花细布，并已安排下周由"公主号"轮装出。
> 　　深信你公司收到货物后，定会感到完全满意。你公司也许不甚知道我公司的经营范围，现附上目录一份。希望这首批订单将导致彼此更多的业务往来，展开愉快的工作关系。

Re: O/No.16620 Resistors

We have found that we are overstocked on some items. Please advise if you will accept the following reductions/cancellations:

Zero ohm 1/4W 500 Kpcs-Cancel
120 ohm 1/4W-reduce from 100K to 75K pcs

Please review and advise by return.

If you cannot accept to cancel the quantity listed above, could you accept a partial reduction?

Please advise.

VI. Complete the following letters with proper words.

Letter 1

Dear Sirs,

We thank you _____ your quotation of the 13th April and for the _____ tin so kindly sent us.

As your _____ are quite up to our expectations, we are pleased to _____ our Order Form for 5,000 1b. of the "Rainbow" tea. You will observe that delivery is to be _____ by the 19th April.

We have every reason to believe that this _____ will be successful, and we hope to entrust you with further _____ in the near future.

Yours faithfully,

Smith & Sons

Signing a Contract **Chapter 8** 155

Letter 2

Dear Sirs,

Thank you for your order of December 10 for 300 pairs of children shoes. But we very much regret to say that we are now unable to supply the goods you _____ immediately because of the heavy _____ for the goods.

The manufacturer has promised us a further _____ at the end of this year. And we will notify you as soon as the goods are _____.

Meanwhile, we are enclosing a booklet of our other models for your _____. We believe that they will meet your _____.

Please _____ us if we can be of any help to you.

Yours sincerely,

Letter 3

Dear Sirs,

Order No. LT463-Baletto Ladies' Tights

We have _____ the _____ shipment ex S.S. "Blue Seas" and are _____ to inform you that we _____ the goods quite _____.

_____ we believe we can sell additional _____ in this market, we wish to place with you a _____ order for 500 dozens of the _____ style and sizes.

We would be _____ if you could _____ early shipment of this repeat order as we are in _____ need of the goods.

If the goods are not available from _____, we would be grateful if you could _____ us, with full particulars of the replacement goods which can be shipped from stock.

Yours faithfully,

Letter 4

Dear Ms. Green,

We are please to _____ your letter of 14th March in _____ us that you are satisfied with our ladies' tights _____ to you per S.S. "Blue Seas". We also _____ that you wish to _____ a repeat order.

We _____ that we cannot at present _____ any new orders for Baletto ladies' tights _____ to heavy orders.

We are, however, _____ your order before us. As soon as we are in a _____ to accept new orders, we will _____ you by e-mail.

With _____ to stock lines, we _____ a list for your _____. Should you be _____ in any of these, please let us know you _____, stating _____, style and _____.

Very truly yours,

VII Writing.

1. Write a letter to an Essential Balm manufactured ordering 1,200 cartons of Jade Rabbit brand Essential Balm for delivery during the following month at the price and on the terms quoted by the manufacturer. As this is an initial order, give reference.
2. The Western Trading Co. has ordered 30,000 pairs of household slippers of your manufacture. You cannot fulfill the order by the date mentioned. Give an imagined reason for this and state clearly when you could make delivery.

Chapter 9

Dealing with Complaints

Lead-in: Case Study

Fortune Goods has placed an order with Everlong Batteries Ltd. for 12,000 ultra super long-life batteries on May 17. However, after the arrival of the goods, Fortune Goods has found a shortage of the goods, which are 1,200 batteries only. To correct the mistakes, the company lodges a complaint against Everlong Batteries Ltd. and asks them to make up the shortage.

Section 1 Complaints

Complaint in international trade is an expression of dissatisfaction with a product or service, either in oral or in writing, from the customer. The party may have a genuine cause for complaint, although some complaints may be made as a result of a misunderstanding or an unreasonable expectation of a product or service. How a customer's complaint is handled will affect the overall level of customer satisfaction and may affect long-term customer loyalty. It is important for providers to have clear procedures for dealing rapidly with any customer complaints, to come to a fair conclusion, and to explain the reasons for what may be perceived by the customer as a negative response.

Usually there are several reasons for complaints: wrong shipment, wrong ordering, wrong destination, shortage, package damage, quality problem, delay in shipment, market claim and others. The purpose of writing a letter of complaint or claim is to get better service or reasonable compensation instead of accusing the others. Accusations do not help either company. They often make it more difficult to correct the errors and to work together in the future. Thus, a complaint letter to a supplier, customer, or other businessperson about their work must be written in a restrained and tactful way. Effective complaint letters (and any other way of complaining) should be concise, authoritative, factual, constructive and friendly.

Three elements are usually presented in a complaint or claim letter.

(1) Detailed presentation of facts to explain what is wrong. This explanation should give exact dates, name and quantity of goods, contract number or any other specific information that will make a recheck easier for the reader.

(2) A statement of the inconvenience or loss that has resulted from this error. This strengthens

your argument for redress.

(3) A statement of how you want the reader to act. The writer who doesn't know what adjustment is proper should try to stimulate prompt investigation and action.

In general, letters of complaint usually include the following stages.

(1) Background.
(2) Problem, cause and effect.
(3) Solution.
(4) Warning (optional).
(5) Closing.

Sample 1　Complaint on the Shortage of the Goods

Fortune Goods
317 Orchard Road
Singapore

July 24, 2014
From: J. Wong
Attn: Mr. David Choi <Everlong Batteries HK@gmail.com>

Sales Manager,

Re: Order No. 768197

I am writing to inform you that the goods we ordered from your company have not been supplied correctly.

On May 17, 2014 we placed an order with your firm for 12,000 ultra super long-life batteries. The consignment arrived yesterday but contained only 1,200 batteries.

This error put our firm in a difficult position, as we had to make some emergency purchases to fulfill our commitments to all our customers. This caused us considerable inconvenience.

I am writing to ask you to make up the shortfall immediately and to ensure that such errors do not happen again. Otherwise, we may have to look elsewhere for our supplies.

I look forward to hearing from you.

Yours sincerely,

J. Wong

J. Wong
Purchasing Officer

Sample 2   Complaint on Delivery of Wrong Goods

INTEGRATED Textile CO., LTD.
34 Regent Street, London, UK

May 20, 2014
To: Mr. George

From: Tony

Dear George,

Re: Our Order No. BT-6098

We are writing to complain about the shipment of our Order No. BT-6098 for all-cotton, men's golf shirts of various sizes received this morning. These were ordered on September 13 from the Winter Catalogue, page 35, and confirmed by telephone and fax on May 15, 2014 (copy enclosed). However, upon unpacking the boxes, we found that they contained 350 women's shirts, all size extra large.

Since this shipment does not conform to our order and cannot be sold through our golf shops, we cannot accept it as delivered. We do, however, have firm orders for the men's shirts requested. Thus, we suggest that you send someone to pick up the wrongly delivered shirts, and reship the correct order within the next week.

Thank you for your prompt attention to this matter.

Yours faithfully,

Tony Smith
Chief Buyer

Sample 3 Complain on the Quality of the Sample

B&B Machinery Trade Co.
P.O. Box 41440, Houston, USA

August 5, 2014
To: Joana
From: Lily

Dear Joana,

Please be advised that the samples you sent to us are not what we want. For your better understanding, we airmailed the relevant samples showing you the exact parts which we need for replacement.

Our customer complained a lot about the poor design and workmanship of the product. Please correct the problems mentioned and provide all parts we need before August 13, or ask someone to bring them here to make the replacement and correction right away.

Looking forward to your early reply.

Sincerely yours,

Lily Hu

Sample 4 Complaint on the Quality of the Goods

Sanshin Cotton Co.
P.O. Box 100, Keelung Taipei

June 27, 2014
To: Sherlock Ham
From: Fred Johns

Dear Ham,

We would refer to your consignment of cotton (Order No. 120-05), which arrived this morning.

On opening the cases we found that the goods are severely damaged and much inferior in quality to your previous samples.

Please advise us when we can expect to receive our order, as some of our customers have been waiting for up to six weeks.

Please also let us know what we are to do with the cotton now in our possession.

Sincerely yours,

Fred Johns

Fred Johns

 Section 2   Adjustment to the Complaints

    Every complaint or claim, no matter how trivial it seems, is important to person who makes it. It, therefore, requires a prompt answer or acknowledgment. The answer should be factual, courteous and fair.

    If you admit that your company is in error or is willing to take responsibility for the claim, you should writer a letter to the customer, expressing apologies and indicating what steps the company is taking to set the matter right.

    There are also some times when a customer's request for an adjustment has to be denied. You may not grant the original claim or only agree to partial adjustment. In that case, your letter must be written carefully. The key is not to make the customer feel that he is considered over demanding in making his request, but to assure him that his complaint has been seriously considered and use facts to convince him of your position. Refusal of compensation tests your diplomacy and tact as a writer.

    There is no need for the sellers to go into a long story of how the mistake was made. A short explanation may be useful but, generally speaking, the buyers are not interested in hearing how or why the error occurred but only in having the matter put right, in receiving the goods they ordered — or at least value for the money they have paid — or in knowing when they may expect to receive the delayed consignment. Here are the tips for an adjustment letter to a complaint.

    (1) Begin with a reference to the date of the original letter of complaint and to the purpose of your letter. If you deny the request, don't state the refusal right away unless you can do so tactfully.

    (2) Express your concern over the writer's troubles and your appreciation that he has written you.

    (3) If you deny the request, explain the reasons why the request cannot be granted in as cordial

and non-combative manner as possible. If you grant the request, don't sound as if you are doing so in a begrudging way.

(4) If you deny the request, try to offer some partial or substitute compensation or offer some friendly advice (to take the sting out of the denial).

(5) Conclude the letter cordially, perhaps expressing confidence that you and the writer will continue doing business.

In case the sellers are the first to discover that a mistake has been made, they should not wait for a complaint, but should write, telex or fax at once to let the buyers know, and either put the matter right or offer some compensation.

Sample 1   Reply to the Shortages

July 24, 2014
From: Mr. David Choi
Attn: J. Wong

Dear Mr. Wong,

Re: Order No. 2639/L

Please accept our apologies for the error made by our company in filling your order No. 2639/L dated July 23, 2014.

You ordered 12,000 Ultra super-long-life premium batteries, but our dispatch office sent 1,200. This was due to a typing error.

The balance of 10,800 batteries was dispatched by express courier to your store this morning and will arrive by Monday, August 5, 2014.

Since we value your business, we would like to offer you a 10% discount off for your next order with us.

We look forward to receiving your further orders and assure you that they will be filled correctly.

Yours sincerely,

David Choi

David Choi
Distributions Manager

Sample 2 Reply to Complaint on Delivery of Wrong Goods

New Times Trading Company Limited
13-14/F., Industry Building, 35 Harbour Road, Wanchai Hong Kong

May 27, 2014
To: Mr. Smith
From: George

Dear Smith,

Thank you for your letter of May 20, 2014 informing us of the shipment of your Order No. BT-6098 for golf shirts. Your complaint was immediately sent to our Customer Relations Representative for investigation.

We have confirmed through our inventory and shipping documents that a mistake was indeed made on your September 13 order. The slip-up occurred in our new, automated inventory control system, which is causing some problems during the data entry stage. Your order number was unfortunately confused with another one (BT-6998), and the error was not caught before the shirts were sent out.

We are very sorry for this mistake and the inconvenience caused and we want to do everything possible to help you satisfy your customers promptly. We offer to redeliver the correct shirts under BT-6098 by DHL Express Mail upon receiving your directions. As to the non-conforming shirts, we suggest that you send them back to us, carriage forward.

You are a valuable customer and we sincerely regret this mistake. We assure you that every possible action will be taken by our management to prevent a repetition of same mistake in future orders.

Yours sincerely,

George

Sample 3 Reply to the Quality Complaint

Merry Best Inc.
2868 Hunan Street, jining 93215, China

August 7, 2014
To: Lily
From: Joana

Dear Lily,

After further conversations regarding the problems you have addressed in the letter of August 5, we have decided as below:

- To save time, we will airmail the parts you need tomorrow.
- Our Representative in USA tonight will contact you to make arrangement to go to the job site and correct all problems you have addressed.

We sincerely apologize for the inconvenience we caused to you and hope all problems will be solved very soon.

Yours sincerely,

Joana

Sample 4 Reject the Complaint

B&B Contton Trade Co.
P.O. Box 41440, Wulumuqi, Xinjiang, China

June 27, 2014
To: Fred Johns
From: Sherlock Ham

Dear Johns,

Thank you for your letter of May 15 referring to the consignment of cotton goods sent to you per S.S. "Ocean Prince". We regret to note your complaint.

We have investigated the matter thoroughly. As far as we can ascertain, the goods were in first class condition when they left here. The bill of lading is evidence for this.

It is obvious that the damage you complain of must have taken place during transit. It follows, therefore, that we cannot be held responsible for the damage.

We therefore advise you to make a claim on the shipping company, Prince Line, who should be held responsible.

We are grateful that you have brought the matter to our attention. If you wish, we would be happy to take issue with the shipping company on your behalf.

We look forward to resolving this matter as soon as possible.

Yours sincerely,

Larry Chen

Sample 5 Refund of the Damaged Goods

Lake Covarde Supplies
B.S. Sound 25 Cromwell St, Glen Iris, Victoria, 3146

April 26, 2014

Mr. Adeilaide Johnson
Care2Care Pvt. Ltd.
2 Holt Street, Surry Hills
Address GPO Box 4245,
Sydney, NSW

Dear Mr. Johnson,

Sub: Refund of Damaged Goods

I have just received your letter regarding the shipment of damaged goods you received through Lake Covarde Supplies. I regret for the inconvenience that it has caused you.

As per your claim and details regarding the matter, it has been found that your claim of $2,000 for the broken furniture stands legitimate. We have already dispatched the cheque through registered mail at the address provided by you. It will reach at your doorsteps within 2 working days. The damage to your items was a result of a mishap whilst transporting it. It was an unfortunate accident and a big mistake that the items were not checked before delivery. We take all the responsibility of the damage and are sorry for the inconvenience caused to you.

I must remind you to keep the damaged items in the same condition in which you received them until our representatives can inspect them. The inspection should take place within 2 weeks. You will be informed beforehand so that you can provide us the timings which suit you the most.

I am sure that this unfortunate accident will not hamper our relationship in the future.

Sincerely,

Nikilesh Ahujha
Customer Relations
Lake Covarde Supplies

Supplementary Information

1. Discrepancy and Claim Clause

In practice, it is strongly recommended that a discrepancy and claim clause be included in a contract. In case the goods delivered are inconsistent with the contract stipulations, the buyer should make a claim against the seller within the validity under the support of a re-inspection certificate or survey report issued by a nominated surveyor.

2. Penalty Clause

A penalty clause sometimes should be included in the contract in case one party fails to implement the contract such as non-delivery, delayed delivery, delayed opening of L/C. Under such clause, the party failing to fulfill the contract must pay a fine, a certain percentage of the total contract value.

3. Points for Attention in Complaining

There are some points for attention in complaining.

(1) For international shipment, any claim by Buyer shall reach Seller within 21 days after arrival of the goods at the destination stated in B/L accompanied with satisfactory evidence thereof.

(2) For domestic shipment, any claim by Buyer shall be posted within 30 days after arrival of the goods at the place of the end user.

(3) Seller shall not be responsible for damages that may result from the use of goods.

(4) Seller shall not be responsible for any amount in excess of the invoice value of the defective goods.

4. Broker

Broker is a person hired to act as an agent or intermediary in making contracts or sales.

5. Underwriter

Underwriter is an agent who underwrites insurance; an employee of an insurance company who determines the acceptability of risks, and the premiums that should be charged.

Useful Expressions

● To Raise a Complaint

1. Paragraph One: Background

This section describes the situation.

(1) *I am writing to inform you that the goods we ordered from your company have not been supplied correctly.*

(2) *I attended your exhibition Sound Systems 2013 at the Fortune Hotel (22-25 January) and found it informative and interesting. Unfortunately, my enjoyment of the event was spoiled by a number of organizational problems.*

(3) *I am a shareholder of Sunshine Bank and I am very concerned regarding recent newspaper reports on the financial situation of the bank. Your company is listed as the auditor in the latest annual report of the bank, so I am writing to you to ask for an explanation of the following issues.*

(4) *I am writing to inform you of my dissatisfaction with the food and drinks at the "European Restaurant" on 18 January this year.*

2. Paragraph Two: Problem

1) Cause

(1) *On July, 17 2014 we placed an order with your firm for 12,000 ultra super long-life batteries. The consignment arrived yesterday but contained only 1,200 batteries.*

(2) Firstly, I had difficulty in registering to attend the event. You set up an on-line registration facility, but I found the facility totally unworkable.

(3) You sent us an invoice for $10,532, but did not deduct our usual 10% discount.

(4) We have found 16 spelling errors and 2 mislabeled diagrams in the sample book.

2) Effect

(1) This error put our firm in a difficult position, as we had to make some emergency purchases to fulfill our commitments to all our customers. This caused us considerable inconvenience.

(2) Even after spending several wasted hours trying to register in this way, the computer would not accept my application.

(3) I am therefore returning the invoice to you for correction.

(4) This large number of errors is unacceptable to our customers, and we are therefore unable to sell these books.

3) Solution

(1) I am writing to ask you to please make up the shortfall immediately and to ensure that such errors do not happen again.

(2) Could I please ask you to look into these matters?

(3) Please send us a corrected invoice for $9,479.

(4) I enclose a copy of the book with the errors highlighted. Please re-print the book and send it to us by next Friday.

3. Paragraph Three: Warning (Optional)

(1) Otherwise, we may have to look elsewhere for our supplies.

(2) I'm afraid that if these conditions are not met, we may be forced to take legal action.

(3) If the outstanding fees are not paid by Friday, August 2, 2014, you will incur a 10% late payment fee.

4. Paragraph Four: Closing

(1) I look forward to receiving your explanation of these matters.

(2) I look forward to receiving your payment.

(3) I look forward to hearing from you shortly.

• To Make an Adjustment

1. Paragraph One: Acknowledging Receipt of a Complaint Letter

(1) Thank you for your letter of ... regarding/concerning/in connection with ...

(2) I refer to your letter of ... about/relating to ...

(3) Apology for the error or fault ...

(4) We must apologize for ...

(5) We sincerely apologize for ...

(6) *Please accept our apologies for ...*
(7) *I would like to apologize for the error made by our company in ... (verb+ing)*

2. Paragraph Two: Accepting the Complaint
We agree that the usual high standards of our products/services were not met in this instance.

3. Paragraph Three: A Short Explanation of the Fault
1) Introductory phrase
As a result of our investigation, we found that ... (Not: After our investigation ...)
2) Causes
(1) *The error was caused by .../was due to ...*
(2) *Apparently, the problem was the result of .../resulted from ...*
(3) *The cause of/reason for the mistake was ...*
3) Effects
(1) *As a result ...*
(2) *This led to ...*
(3) *Consequently ...*
4) Solutions
(1) *We have modified/changed our ...*
(2) *We have implemented a system to ...*
(3) *To prevent re-occurrences we have set up a verification procedure.*
5) Assurances
We assure you that this will not happen again.
6) Investigation to be made
(1) *We are currently investigating the cause of ...*
(2) *We will investigate the cause of ...*
7) Proposal to settle the difficulty
(1) *As a gesture of our regret, we are prepared to .../we are willing to .../we would like to ...*
(2) *To show goodwill, we will ...*
(3) *We have dispatched the new items by express courier. They should arrive by Monday, July 29, 2014.*
(4) *To show our goodwill, we would like to offer you a 5% discount on your next order with us.*

4. Optional: Declining the Complaint
1) Regret at dissatisfaction
(1) *While we can understand your frustration, ...*
(2) *We understand how disappointing it can be when your expectations are not met.*
2) Rejecting responsibility for the problem leading to the complaint
(1) *I regret to inform you that ...*
(2) *I am afraid that ...*

(3) *Unfortunately, I must point out that ...*

3) Reasons for the rejection

(1) *This is because the guarantee period has expired.*

(2) *This is due to the fact that the guarantee period has expired.*

(3) *If a third party (another person or organization) is to blame, direct the complainer to that party.*

(4) *We therefore suggest that you contact ...*

4) A concluding paragraph aiming at retaining the goodwill of the customer

We look forward to receiving your further orders, and assure you that they will be filled correctly/promptly.

I. Multiple choice.

1. The goods under Contract No. 15408 left here _____.
   A. in a good condition
   B. in good conditions
   C. in good condition
   D. in the good condition

2. We have lodged a claim _____ ABC & Co. _____ the quality of the goods shipped _____ m.v. "Peace".
   A. against, for, by
   B. with, for, under
   C. on, against, as per
   D. to, for, per

3. As the goods are ready for shipment, we _____ your L/C to be opened immediately.
   A. hope
   B. anticipate
   C. await
   D. expect

4. As arranged, we have effected insurance _____ the goods _____ 110% of the invoice value _____ all risks.
   A. of, at, with
   B. for, in, against
   C. on, for, against
   D. to, at over

5. It is important that your client _____ the relevant L/C not later than April 15, 2014.
   A. must open
   B. has to open
   C. open
   D. opens

6. The goods _____ shipped already if your L/C had arrived by the end of December.
   A. would be
   B. must have been
   C. had been
   D. would have been

7. The buyer suggested that the packing of this article _____ improved.
   A. be
   B. was to be
   C. would be
   D. had to be

8. If we had a sample in hand, we _____ to negotiate business with our end-users now.
   A. would be able
   B. should have
   C. had been able
   D. should have been able

II. Fill in the missing words.

1. We are lodging a claim _____ the shipment _____ S.S. "Red Star" _____ short delivery.
2. We hope you will _____ our analysis acceptable.
3. _____ examinations we found that the goods do not agree the original.
4. Please give our claim your _____ attention and _____ us have your reply _____.
5. We confirm _____ received your remittance _____ $789 _____ settlement _____ our claim.
6. We regret _____ bear that several bags of the last _____ were broken _____ transit.
7. The shipment was _____ by insurance _____ All Risks.
8. _____ the time of loading, the goods _____ in good condition.
9. We regret your claim could hardly _____ _____ as the goods were damaged _____ transit.
10. Your claim has been passed on _____ our insurance company, who will get _____ touch _____ you soon.
11. We are very sorry to hear that the goods you received are not _____ _____ the quality expected.
12. Please _____ _____ the matter as one of urgency and let us have your cable reply by earliest opportunity.

III. Give the English or Chinese equivalents of the following.

1. 投诉	
2. 客服	
3. 发货不到	
4. 不可抗力	
5. 检验报告	
6. faulty goods	
7. replacement	
8. complete refund	
9. wrong delivery	
10. shortage of goods	

IV. Translate the following sentences into English.

1. 鉴于原料价格近日上涨，我们不得不调整部分价格。

2. 很遗憾地通知你方，三号箱及六号箱破损，箱内货物因包装不良严重损坏。

3. 如果你们退回机器，我们将进行修理并完好地送还你方。

4. 对于所遭受的损失，我们不得不要求你方负责。

5. 无论如何，我们要求你方采取措施以防止类似事件再次发生。

6. 我们已彻底查询，但所得到的唯一解释是标签混乱了。

7. 货号有误，导致你方收到错货，我们对此深表歉意。

8. 请完全按照我们所订的货物立即补发一批。

V Complete the following letter with proper words.

Letter 1

Dear Sir,

We have received your _____ of 30 May and very much regret that some of your customers are _____ with our serges supplied to your Order No. AD-190.

We have been manufacturing serges for many years and can _____ to produce a material that _____ competitor has yet succeeded in producing at the price _____. The reputation _____ by our serges on international markets _____ to their high _____. From what you say it would seem that some of the materials escaped the _____ we normally give to all materials in our _____ department.

We can understand your problem, but regret that we cannot accept your suggestion to take _____ all the _____ serges from the batch about which you _____. Indeed, there should be no need for this since it is unlikely that the number of _____ serges can be very large. We will of course _____ any piece of serge found not to be _____ and on this particular _____ we are _____ to allow you a special _____ of 5% to _____ for your trouble.

Yours truly,

Letter 2

Dear Sir,

We _____ your consignment of toys this morning (our order No. Sl106). However, on _____ the contents we found that the electric trains _____ on one side of case No. 8 were badly dented, and are unsellable. This case had obviously been stuck by a heavy object or dropped, and we _____ this out to your local agents, who _____ the receipt "one case side damaged".

No doubt you will take the matter up _____ your insurers; however for the present we should be obliged if you would send us 12 replacement trains, Catalogue No. 248T. The _____ report will be forwarded immediately it has been prepared.

Yours sincerely,

Letter 3

Dear Sir,

We have received your fax of 2nd March, and very much _____ the delay in delivering the above. We are now making the necessary _____ for immediate delivery, which means you will have both excavators by 20th March at the latest.

The HERCULES JBM is the most successful excavator we have so far produced. It was an instant success at its first appearance last year at the Hong Kong Building Exhibition and we were soon _____ with orders. Your own order was received in November and according to the waiting list we had then was not _____ for delivery until April. Nevertheless, we put the delivery date _____ so that you would have the machines in March. In February production was slightly set back by the late arrival of some special parts and this has been _____ for the delay in the present case.

We trust that you will not be unduly inconvenienced _____ having to wait a few more days. The performance of the HERCULES JBM excavators will amply compensate you.

Yours sincerely,

VI. Writing.

Write to your suppliers explaining that in a delivery of mental wastepaper bins twenty-seven were either slightly dented or badly scratched and that you have had to sell them at a price considerably below the recommended retail selling price. Submit a claim for the difference between the recommended retail price and the price at which the damaged bins were actually sold.

Chapter 10

Other Business Partnership

Lead-in: Case Study

Case One

DDC Clothes Inc. is a well-developed sales organization in USA. It reads about a Chinese company, Charm Textile Export Corporation from a magazine International Trade; thus, DDC takes the opportunity to write to Charm Textile Export Corporation, hoping to obtain sales agency business from Charm, to develop market for Charm's textiles in America.

Case Two

Shenzhen Citex Electronics Technology Co., Ltd. advertises on alibaba.com, looking for distributors in Europe and America to distribute their electronic products. Vi & Kee Co., Ltd is writing a letter, with the hope of obtaining the opportunity to be such a role.

Case Three

Syfaa Textiles Trading Inc. is expecting to be granted franchise license from a famous brand garments company. The market manager of Syfaa searches the internet and finds the relative information and then writes a letter, introducing Syfaa, expressing the intention of being franchisee.

Case Four

Wal-Mart Stores Inc. makes an advertisement for a company to open another chain store in South Africa. Good Neighbor Inc. reads the information and is very interested in it. It sends a letter to Wal-Mart Stores Inc., describing itself as a most relevant promotional and distribution channel.

Section 1   Agency

A vast amount of international trade is handled not by direct negotiation between importer and exporter but by agencies. Internationally, agency can simply indicate such a relation that the exporter empowers a foreign businessman to conduct business performance abroad. An international trade agent acts as a representative for companies that want to do business in other countries. Such agents can facilitate every step of the deal, from locating a supplier to verifying shipment. This type of agent has representatives and offices in many foreign countries and is familiar with the pertinent laws, including trade restrictions, tariffs, and so forth. Working with an international trade agent may allow a company to avoid some common trading pitfalls.

Agency is a common practice in the international trade, especially in marketing, transportation, insurance and advertisement etc. According to the degree of authority that the agents were invested, they could always be classified into three types: general agent, sole agent and commission agent.

There are mainly four steps in writing an application letter of being an agent.

(1) Briefly describe the source of information through which you got to know that they want an agent.

(2) State your past experience of being any kind of agent and introduce yourself or your company as well as the marketing plan.

(3) Show your interest in acting as an agent and provide some related companies for them to refer to.

(4) List some general terms for them to consider if you want to and then express your eager willingness as a closing.

Sample 1   Importer Offering Sole Agency Service

DDC Clothes Inc.
1881 Long Beach Street, Los Angles, CA 90025
Tel:1-213-686-0000   Fax: 1-213-686-0001

February 17, 2014

Dear Mr. Woo,

We have a well-developed sales organization in USA and are represented by a large staff in various parts of the country. From their reports, it seems clear that there is a good demand for your textiles and as we believe you are not directly represented in USA, we are writing to offer our service as your sole agent.

In view of the wide connections which we are fortunate enough to possess, we think you will agree that a 5% commission on net sales is quite reasonable. We are also prepared to guarantee payment of all accounts, for which we should require a commission of 2.5%.

You will naturally wish to have information about us. For this we refer you to the CITI Bank who is consented to answer your inquiries as to our financial standing and so on.

We are looking forward to your favorable reply.

Yours sincerely,

Lester Bemstein
Overseas Sales Director

Sample 2   Declining a Request for Offering Sole Agent Service

Cathay Textile Import & Export Corporation
2000 Central Boulevard, Pudong, Shanghai, China
Tel: 86 020-33445566   Fax: 86 020-33445567

February 27, 2014

Dear Mr. Bemstein,

Thank you for your inquiry regarding the sole agency for the sale of our textile products in USA.

After serious consideration, we think that it would be premature to commit ourselves at this stage when the record of transactions shows only a moderate volume of business.

Please do not misinterpret the above remark, which in no way implies dissatisfaction. As a matter of fact, we are quite satisfied with the amount of business you have brought us. However, we are of the opinion that a bigger turnover must be reached to justify establishing the agency.

In view of the above, we think it advisable to postpone this matter until your future sales warrant such a step. We hope that you will agree with us on this point and continue to give us your cooperation.

Yours faithfully,

Catherine Wang

Sample 3 Entrusting Customer with Sole Agent

Cathay Textile Import & Export Corporation
2000 Central Boulevard, Pudong, Shanghai, China
Tel: 86 020-33445566   Fax: 86 020-33445567

February 27, 2014

Dear Mr. Bemstein,

We have received your letter of February 17, and, after careful consideration, have decided to entrust you with the sole agency for our textile products in USA.

The agency agreement has been drawn up for the duration of 1 year, automatically renewable on expiration for a similar period unless notice is given to the contrary; the terms and conditions are set forth in details.

Enclosed is a copy of the draft. Please go over the previsions and advise us whether they meet with your approval.

We shall do all our power to assist you in establishing a mutually beneficial trade.

Sincerely yours,

Catherine Wang
Manager
Export Department

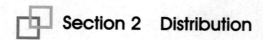

Section 2 Distribution

Distribution is the process of making a product or service available for a consumer or business user, using direct means, or using indirect means with intermediaries.

Distribution of products takes place by means of channels. Channels are sets of interdependent organizations (called intermediaries) involved in making the product available for consumption. Merchants are intermediaries that buy and resell products. Agents and brokers are intermediaries that act on behalf of the producer but do not take title to the products.

Distributor is an entity that buys noncompeting products or product lines, warehouses them, and resells them to retailers or direct to the end users or customers. Most distributors provide strong manpower and cash support to the supplier or manufacturer's promotional efforts. They usually also provide a range of services (such as product information, estimates, technical support, after-sales services, credit) to their customers.

No matter how wonderful a product is, it can't benefit your business if you don't own the rights to it. Items that are patented copyrighted or trademarked have a limited distribution, and you won't be able to sell or otherwise distribute them in your business without getting permission from the person or entity that owns the rights, and that is not always the manufacturer. A well-written business letter can be your first step toward getting distribution rights to the product.

Sample 1   Manufacturer Looking for Distributors

Shangduo (Guangzhou) Leather Goods Co., Ltd.
A4 Zone, No. 2 Industrial Park, Changhong Village, Junhe Street,
Baiyun District, Guangzhou, Guangdong
Tel: 0086-20-22054111   Fax: 0086-20-22054099

January 12, 2014

Dear Sirs,

We are Shangduo (Guangzhou) Leather Goods Co., Ltd., established in 1999 in Guangzhou, China, specializing in all kinds of customized leather premiums, unique leather accessories, corporate leather gifts, office/hotel supplies and more, with floor space of more than 10,000 sqm, more than 400 employees and 3 production lines. With so many years of development, we now have had 2 branch companies, one in Beijing and the other in Shanghai.

Our products are receiving warm welcome, and we are expending our business into North America, expecting a reliable Canadian or American organization to be our distributor. If it is of your interest, we can come to further contact for the matters concerning distribution contract.

For more information, please reach us by shangduo@163.com, or visit our website: http://www.shangduo.com. We are looking forward to your early reply.

Sincerely yours,

Lukas Feng
General Manager

Sample 2　Asking for Distribution Right

To: "Lukas Feng" <shangduo@163.com>
From: Brighttrade@hotmail.com
Date: April 12
Subject: Establishing Distribution Relationship

Dear Sirs,

We understand from your online message released on April 7 that you are seeking a distributor for the range of your leather products. We have been distributor for years, dealing with leather products for 12 years, and have wide connections in this area.

Also, market statistics show that the demand for goods of this line has increased in recent years at our end, and we believe that there is a profitable market waiting to be developed.

Our details, including our business and financial status, are attached. If we can meet your requirements, could you please forward catalogue and pricing information? We are glad to enter into distributor contract with you.

We look forward to receiving your early reply and assure you of a mutually beneficial cooperation between us.

Yours sincerely,

Leanne Menegaz
Sales Director

Sample 3 Reply to Accept the Requirement for Distribution Right

To: "Leanne Menegaz"<Brighttrade@hotmail.com>
From: "Lukas Feng" <shangduo@163.com>
Date: April 15
Re: Establishing distribution relationship

Dear Leanne Menegaz,

Thank you very much for your letter of April 12, expressing your interest in distribution-ship with us. After immediate and overall consideration, we accept you being our executive distributor in Canada on the understanding that you countersigned the contract attached. Of course, we can come to further discussion, if there is anything that can't be agreed upon.

We are attaching our catalogue and price list for your information, and also some samples are airmailed to you at no charge.

If you have any questions, please do not hesitate to contact us at 001-780-329-6279. We're looking forward to receiving our early countersigned contract.

Yours sincerely,

Lukas Feng
General Manager

Sample 4 Informing Distributor Information

From: Mr. Dean Wilson
Sales Manager
Ferguson Pharmaceuticals
52, Aaron Place,
Greenway Dr., New York – 45216

To: Mr. Greg Jackson
General Manager
G. Fields Supplies
25, Oak Park, IL-45125

February 14, 2014

Dear Mr. Jackson,

I am writing to inform you that recently we have extended our distributorship in your city, Oak Park.

We have authorized "Wayne Chemists" as our local distributor in Oak Park. They will be selling our products. They have many stores in other parts of the Illinois state and we are expanding our business through them. They also have proper arrangements or marketing and it will benefit us.

So, in future please approach them for our products for your business needs. "Wayne Chemists" are known for timely delivery and efficient work. You can contact us if you need any other information about them.

Contact details of our distributor:
Wayne Chemists
152, Miguel's Place
Luis St, Oak park-41253

Regards,

Mr. Dean Wilson
Sales Manager
Ferguson Pharmaceuticals

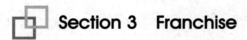

Section 3 Franchise

Franchise is a license to operate an individually owned business as though it were part of a chain of outlets or stores. It concerns businesses that use a Franchise Model: Usually, there are three types of business concepts using the franchise model.

(1) Distributorship, such as car dealership.

(2) Brand Name Licensing. Sports franchises fall into this category.

(3) Business Format, where a franchisee purchases the right to operate a unique business system (retail, home-based, fast food concept etc.).

Some of these ventures are difficult to launch because of the costs involved, whereas others are more easily attainable.

Sample 1 Asking for Franchise License

To: Franchisesubway@subway.com
From: Shanghaisimenki@126.com
Subject: Establishing Franchise relationship

Dear Sirs,

Through the courtesy of the Chamber of Commerce in America, we have learned that you are an American fast food restaurant franchisor and have been supplying the best quality fast food all over the world, and we are sure there is a large demand for various exotic fast foods in our city. We are writing to you in the hope of obtaining franchising right from you.

We are Shanghai Simenki Restaurant Co., Ltd, one of the largest fast food restaurants in China, with more than 40 chain restaurants in all major cities in China. We have been dealing with a large variety of foods from Italy, the USA and the Chinese Taipei, and consider that we have considerable experience in this field. If we can meet your standard, we are glad to enter into franchise agreement with you.

A bright prospect for your products in our market is foreseeable. We look forward to receiving your favorable reply and assure you of our best achievements at all times.

Yours sincerely,

Annie Huang
Market Manager

Sample 2 Reply to Accept the Requirement for Franchise License

To: "Market department" < simenki@126.com >
From: "Cathy" < Franchisesubway@subway.com>
Re: Establishing Franchise relationship

Dear Miss Huang,

Thank you very much for your letter of May 20, showing your interest in our business. After careful consideration, we accept your requirement to be one of our franchisee in your territory on condition that you can meet the basic requirements in the FDD we are attaching here.

As you've read about, we are one of the fastest growing franchises and the largest single-brand restaurant chain and the largest restaurant operator in the world, with 40,855 restaurants in 105 countries and territories. Our Subway's menu varies between countries, most significantly in places where there are religious requirements relating to the meats served. We always bear the slogan "Eat Fresh".

Please refer to the attachment for our catalogue and company profile and your latest details, especially the banker's reference showing your net worth and your liquid assets, are highly appreciated, which will be an essential factor for further consideration to enter into the franchise agreement.

With various franchise opportunities available, we can ensure we will help you make the right decisions so you can hit the ground running and grow your business, quickly and easily. If you have any questions, please do not hesitate to contact us at 1-860-270-8689. We're looking forward to your early reply.

Yours sincerely,

Cathy Stephen
Market Manager

Sample 3 Reply to Refuse the Requirement for Franchise License

To: "Market department" < simenki@126.com >
From: "Cathy" < Franchisesubway@subway.com>
Re: Establishing Franchise relationship

Dear Miss Huang,

Thank you very much for your letter of May 20. As you know, we primarily sell submarine sandwiches (subs) and salads as well as breakfast sandwiches, English muffins and flatbreads, which we can't be sure whether there is a ready market in your territory.

I regret to say that, at this stage, an arrangement to grant you franchise would be rather premature. We would, however, be willing to be engaged in trial cooperation with your company to see how the arrangement works. It would be necessary for you to test the market for our products at your end.

Please click the attachment to get our menu and our company profile for your reference and our representative will be sent to your market soon to discuss details concerning the trial business.

If you have any questions, please do not hesitate to contact us at 1-860-270-8689. We're looking forward to your early reply.

Yours sincerely,

Cathy Stephen
Market Manager

Section 4　Chain Store

Chain stores are retail outlets that share a brand and central management, and usually have standardized business methods and practices. Before considered a chain, stores must meet a litmus test; it must have more than 10 units under the same brand and have a central headquarters, otherwise it offers franchise contracts or is publicly traded. These characteristics also apply to chain restaurants and some service-oriented chain businesses. In retail, dining, and many service categories, chain businesses have come to dominate the market in many parts of the world. A franchise retail establishment is one form of chain store.

Chain stores are usually group of retail outlets owned by one firm and spread nationwide or worldwide, such as Body Shop, K-Mart, Wal-Mart. Chain stores, usually have (1) similar architecture, (2) store design and layout, and (3) choice of products.

Sample 1　Applying to Join in Chain Store Business

> **Date:** January 13, 2014
> **To:** "Mr.Karl" < kroger.ir@kroger.com.>
> **From:** "Hu Yuheng" < Dalian Hongyun Trade Co.@163.com>
> **Subject:** Chain Store Business

Dear Mr. Karl,

Through your online message, we have learned with pleasure that you are granting established relevant company chain store business. We are writing to apply for such right.

We are a leading trade company, specializing in grocery stores, which, we think, falls within your business line. We have very large numbers of permanent customers in our 36 chain stores in China, and with considerable sales volume.

Attached please find our profile and detailed information about our business.

We are looking forward to your favorable reply early.

Sincerely yours,

Zhu Yuheng
Import Department

Sample 2 Accepting the Application for Chain Store Business

Date: January 19, 2014
To: "Zhu Yuheng" < Dalian Hongyun Trade Co.@163.com>
From: "Mr.Karl" < kroger.ir@kroger.com.>
Re: Your Application for Chain Store Business

Dear Mr. Zhu,

We are pleased to receive your letter of January 13, applying for being granted chain store business permission. We are writing to offer you such right.

From the material attached, we find with pleasure that you are handling in grocery stores, and have 36 chain stores in your country, which is really of interest to us.

As you may have acknowledged, We, the Kroger Co., a supermarket retail chain, have been around since 1883 and owned over 2,400 supermarkets all over the United States. We are implementing new marketing strategy and expanding our business globally.

We are sending you, under separate cover, our proposal and terms and conditions for cooperation.

For any problems or further information, please do not hesitate to contact us at 1-866-221-4141. Your early reply will be appreciated.

Sincerely yours,

Karl Black
Market Manager

Sample 3 Reply to Refuse the Application for Chain Store Business

Date: January 19, 2014
To: "Zhu Yuheng" < Dalian Hongyun Trade Co.@163.com>
From: "Mr. Karl" < kroger.ir@kroger.com.>
Re: Your Application for Chain Store Business

Dear Mr. Zhu,

Thank you very much for your letter of January 13, expressing your interest in our chain store business cooperation. As described on our website, we, Kroger, own mall jewellery stores, hypermarkets, convenience stores and department stores all over the United States. And today, we rank as one of the world's largest retailers.

However, after careful consideration, we regret to say that, in view of sales volume, a company headquartered in Shanghai or Beijing will be appreciated to being granted chain store business service.

Since this is our first step into Chinese market, we should take turnover into the foremost consideration. However, we don't know if you are so kind enough to recommend chain stores in the cities mentioned above.

Thank you again for your kind consideration and favor to us. Wish you prosperous business.

Yours sincerely,

Karl Black
Market Manager

Supplementary Information

1. Agency and Agent

An agency arises when one person (the Principal) authorizes another person(the agent) to make contracts on his behalf with third parties. It follows that there will usually be an actual appointment to confer the necessary authority on the agent. Once appointed, he shall act for the principal within the agreed authority to make contracts on the principal's behalf.

According to the degree of authority that the agents were invested, agents are classified into three basic types: General Agents, Ordinary agents, and Exclusive Agent/Sole Agent.

2. General Agent

A general agent, a firm or a person, is appointed by the principal to transact all business of a specific kind in a specific place on behalf of the principal for some rate of commission during a specific period of time under the general agency agreement or contract.

3. Ordinary Agent

An ordinary agent is appointed by the principal to carry out certain activities on behalf of the principal within a specific area for a specific period. A principal may appoint several ordinary agents in one area under the ordinary agency agreement or contract.

4. Exclusive Agent

An exclusive agent is the only one that is authorized by the principal to exclusively transact the business of his principal of a specific kind within a specific period of time under the exclusive agency agreement or contract.

5. Intermediary

An intermediary (or go-between) is a third party that offers intermediation services between two trading parties. The intermediary acts as a conduit for goods or services offered by a supplier to a consumer. Typically the intermediary offers some added value to the transaction that may not be possible by direct trading.

6. Franchise

Franchise is a license to operate an individually owned business as though it were part of a chain of outlets or stores. It concerns Businesses that use a Franchise Model. Some of these ventures are difficult to launch because of the costs involved, whereas others are more easily attainable.

7. Distributorship

It means to grant the right to sell their parent company's products such as car dealership, i.e. General Motors, Ford, Toyota etc. or vending machine routes.

8. Brand Name Licensing

This gives the licensee the right to use the parent company's brand in conjunction with the operation of their own business. Here, the product or service is franchised (or licensed) and not the business itself. For example, a sports store in a small town is granted the exclusive rights in that town to sell Nike products. Sports franchises fall into this category as well.

9. Business Format

It is the most common franchise format where a franchisee purchases the right to operate a unique business system (retail, home-based, fast food concept etc.) that has an established history and track record created by the franchisor. In exchange for a pre-determined royalty structure, the Franchisor provides initial and ongoing training, sales and marketing support, and many other services and assistance to aid in the franchisee's business success.

10. Financial Status

Financial status, also referred to as financial standing or financial condition, is the status of the assets, liabilities, and owners' equity (and their interrelationships) of an organization or a person, as reflected in its financial statements. It is mostly used to determine borrowing qualification.

11. Franchising Royalties

Franchising royalties are fees that franchisees pay to the franchiser in exchange for the existing structure and brand rather than incurring the expense and time of structuring and creating a business model independently. Franchising royalties can vary from a monthly percentage of profits to a per annum profit split to a monthly flat rate, depending upon the stipulations of the Franchise Agreement. Franchising royalties are usually used to support the overhead of the franchise operation itself. Frequently, royalties are paid as a percentage of monthly profits for the life of the Franchise Agreement, and are non-negotiable.

12. FDD

FDD, the short form of Franchise Disclosure Document, is a legal document which is presented to prospective buyers of franchises in the pre-sale disclosure process in the United States. It was originally known as the Uniform Franchise Offering Circular (UFOC) (or uniform franchise disclosure document), prior to revisions made by the Federal Trade Commission in July 2007.

13. Bank Reference

Bank reference, also known as Banker's reference, is information released by a bank about a customer, to another bank or lending institution. Bank references generally include:

(1) number of years of a customer's relationship with the bank;
(2) number of loans and the amounts of their balances;
(3) type and quality of collaterals provided;
(4) a copy of the customer's latest statement of financial affairs on file with the bank.

Banks usually are under no obligation to seek the customer's approval (or to reveal the identity of the recipient) for releasing such information.

14. To Customize

To customize means producing, manufacturing or modifying something according to a customer's individual or special requirements

15. Retail Outlet

A retail outlet is a store that simply sells merchandise purchased by the store from a wholesaler, or manufactured by the company that owns the store directly to the consumer, or a store that is opened by the manufacturer, often near the factory, for the purposes of selling over-produced or irregular merchandise at discount prices. Some retail outlets, generally in a fixed location, are large stores with a wide variety of merchandise, while others are small specialty boutiques.

Useful Expressions

1. ... the wide connections/a good (wide) connection

(1) *We have many connections in your country.*
(2) *He set up in business and soon had a good connection.*
(3) *We have received a number of enquires from our trade connections here for your bicycles.*
(4) *We have established business connection with them.*

2. to represent (sb.)

(1) *Please let us know whether you now represent any other suppliers in the same line.*
(2) *We ask if you wish to be represented in this market.*
(3) *Regarding the sale of Chinese bicycles in your district, we have already been represented by Messrs. Smith & Co.*

3. to entrust ... with

(1) *The volume of business done does not warrant entrusting you with sole agency in your*

area.

(2) *In view of the fact that the rate of premium you quoted is quite reasonable, we have decided to entrust your company with the insurance of this shipment.*

(3) *The local bank issues a trust deed for payment, then sends it to a correspondent bank at the seller's end by means of mail and entrusts him to pay the money to the sellers.*

(4) *We have entrusted this matter to our representative, who will have a discussion with you.*

4. to appoint ... as ...

(1) *They appointed him as General Manager of the new company.*

(2) *Mr. Smith was appointed to be the sole agent for the sale of our product in your market.*

(3) *Regarding the sale of Hisense color TV sets in European market, we have appointed ABC Co. as our agent.*

(4) *If you were to appoint us as your agent, we should be prepared to discuss the rate of commission with you.*

5. a wide range of

(1) *Our business covers a wide range of light industrial products.*

(2) *We can supply woolen blankets in a wide range of designs.*

(3) *The goods enquired for are out of line with our range of activities.*

(4) *We are sending you a full range of samples.*

6. Commission

(1) *The above price includes your commission of 2%.*

(2) *We do not pay any commission on our traditional products.*

(3) *Considering your sustained efforts to cooperate with us, we agree to raise your commission to 3%.*

(4) *For large sales volume, we can grant you a 5% commission/a commission of 5%.*

(5) *We can give/allow/grant you a commission of 5% on large sales volume.*

Exercises

I Choose the appropriate word or words in the parentheses and then translate the sentences into Chinese.

1. Considering your sustained efforts to cooperate (between, with, to) us, we agree to raise your commission to 3%.
2. We have entrusted this matter (to, for, with) our distributor, who will have a discussion with you for an acceptable resolution.
3. We have received a number of enquires from our trade connections for your bicycles, and

we are confident to achieve the sales (amount, figure, turnover) requirement for a sole agent.

4. The demand for fast food has increased in recent years in our area and we believe that there is a profitable market of such chain restaurant waiting to be (occupied, developed, opened).

5. Regarding the sale of Hisense color TV sets in European market, we have appointed ABC Co. (for, as, become) our agent.

6. We have very large numbers of permanent customers in our 30 chain stores in China, with (considerable, considerate, considering) sales volume.

7. If you were to appoint us as your agent, we should be prepared to discuss the (amount, rate, figure) of commission.

8. I've got your business information online and learned that you are applying for franchise business. Please refer to the attachments for our franchise agreement. Maybe we can come (into, for, to) terms.

9. We currently have the sole agency for another computer company. Under the terms of the contract, we are barred (from, against, for) selling any other company's products.

10. Having had experience in dealing with similar products, we have wide (connections, relationship, ways) in this market and a number of long-standing customers.

II Arrange the following words and phrases in their proper order.

1. 10 per cent on orders placed
   would be heavy,
   we feel that
   the early work on development
   as
   during the first 12 months
   would be a reasonable figure
   however

_____

_____

2. the best quality fast food
   to find
   from the online message
   that
   you are
   fast food restaurant franchise
   and have been supplying
   we are pleased
   an American

_____

_____

3. due to
   the increasing demand
   we are reforming
   for goods of this line
   a profitable market
   and
   expanding into Europe
   at our end

Other Business Partnership　Chapter 10　193

in recent years　　　　　　　　our marketing strategies
there is　　　　　　　　　　　　we believe

_____
_____

4. the grant for　　　　　　　　immediate and overall consideration
　 a sole agency　　　　　　　　a much larger turnover
　 I regret　　　　　　　　　　　you
　 after　　　　　　　　　　　　should first meet
　 so　　　　　　　　　　　　　at this stage
　 to say that　　　　　　　　　would have
　 to build up　　　　　　　　　the sales volume requirement

_____
_____

5. should be offered　　　　　　the wide connections
　 in view of　　　　　　　　　　your sales figure
　 on net sales　　　　　　　　　to meet
　 on the condition that　　　　we possess
　 a 5% commission　　　　　　　we are confident

_____
_____
_____

III　Fill in the blanks with the appropriate words or expressions.

1. From your _____ message, we understand that you are seeking a distributor for _____ your leather products.
2. We are a leading trade company, specializing in grocery stores, which, we think, _____ your business line.
3. We have a well-developed sales organization in USA and are _____ by a large staff in various parts of the country.
4. Enclosed is a copy of the agreement. Please go over _____ and advise us whether they meet with your approval.
5. We would, however, be willing to _____ trial cooperation with your company to see how the arrangement works.
6. We look forward to receiving your _____ and assure you of our best achievements at all times.
7. In view of _____ we possess, we think you will agree that a 5% commission on net sales is quite reasonable.

8. If it is of your interest, we can _____ further contact for the matters concerning distribution contract.
9. After serious consideration, we think that it would be _____ to commit ourselves at this stage.
10. Your latest details are highly appreciated, which will be an essential factor for further consideration to _____ the franchise agreement.
11. We have been distributor for years, _____ leather products for 12 years, and have wide connections in this area.
12. We are _____ our business _____ North America, expecting a reliable Canadian or American organization to be our distributor.

IV Please give the English or Chinese equivalents of the following.

1. 现金流	
2. 营业额	
3. 独家代理商	
4. 净销售额	
5. 经销商	
6. 零售商	
7. 代理佣金	
8. 门店	
9. 启动成本	
10. 销售量	
11. after-sales services	
12. franchise royalty	
13. customized leather premiums	
14. banker's reference	
15. the terms and conditions	
16. a mutually beneficial trade	
17. business format	
18. agent's territory	
19. wide connections	
20. liquid assets	

Other Business Partnership **Chapter 10** 195

V Complete the following letters with proper words.

Letter 1

Dear Anson,

Thank you very much for your kind _____ for distribution ship with us. As _____ required in your last letter, I'd like to _____ you some fast sale items in South Africa for your easy _____ first. The details are as attached. We are also inviting you to visit our _____ at www.shvfurniture.com to know more about us.

Regarding the _____ contract, normally we only accept terms and conditions based on executive distributor agreement. In view of our wide _____ popular and competitive products, we are sure you can make _____ sales at your end easily. If needed, some free _____ can be airmailed to you for further _____.

We would also like to get some _____ information concerning your sales figure and your _____ standing, which can help us to _____ some agreements and facilitate our cooperation.
We are looking forward to the mutually beneficial _____ between us.

Best regards,

John

Letter 2

Dear Sirs,

We would like to offer our services as agents for the _____ of your products in Australia.

As agents of the highest standing, our company was _____ in 1926. We have been agents in several West European countries, including France, Germany and Italy.

There is a growing _____ in Australia for Chinese textiles, especially for fancy worsted suiting and printed cotton and nylon fabrics. There are great prospects for good quality fabrics at _____ prices, and according to a recent Chamber of Commerce survey the demand for Chinese textiles is likely to grow _____ during the next 2 or 3 years.

If you would send us details of your _____, with samples and prices, we could inform you of their _____ for the Australian market, and also indicate the patterns and _____ for which sales are likely to be _____. We would then arrange to call on our customers with your collection.

You will naturally wish to have _____ and may write to Barclays Bank Ltd., 99 Piccadilly, Manchester, or to any of our _____, whose names we will be glad to send you.

We feel sure we should have no difficulty in arranging _____ to suit us both. We are looking forward to hearing from you soon.

Yours faithfully,

Cedric Jones

VI Translate the following letter.

Dear Sirs,

Statistics from Canadian Cosmetics, Toiletry and Fragrance Association show a marked increasing demand for cosmetics toiletries in Canada in recent years. So, we are convinced that there is a considerable market here for your products.

There is every sign that an advertising campaign, even on a modest scale, would produce very good results if it were backed by an efficient system of distribution.

We are well-known distributors of over 15 years' standing, with branches in most of the principal cities in Canada. With knowledge of the local conditions, we feel we have the experience and the resources necessary to bring about a market development of your trade in this country. Reference to the Canadian Cosmetics, Toiletry and Fragrance Association and the Canadian Chamber of Commerce would enable you to verify our statement.

If you were to appoint us as your distributor, we should be prepared to discuss the terms and conditions of the contract.

We hope you will see a worthwhile opportunity in our proposal, and that we may look forward to your early decision.

Yours faithfully,

VII Write letters according to the following particulars.

Letter 1

Guangzhou Cityclothing Business Co., Ltd. made an advertisement on alibaba.com to look for a Canadian executive agent. A Canadian company read the advertisement and wrote a letter to apply for the role.

Letter 2

Sandhu Importer/Distributors Inc. is seeking opportunities to be distributor of lights. You, sales manager of Foshan Electrical And Lighting Co., Ltd., got the information on alibaba.com. So, you are writing a letter to consult for cooperation of establishing distributionship.

Letter 3

You, market advisor of Burger King Corporation (BKC), received an e-mail inquiring of franchising license, including the minimum financial requirements to qualify as a franchisee, the start-up cost, a monthly royalty fee and the franchise fee for a 20-year Franchise Agreement, place for in-restaurant training. Now you are replying favorably to answer all the questions and you also make a brief self-introduction.

Letter 4

Lowe's Companies Inc., getting the information about Shanghai Bailian Group from www.bailiangroup.cn, writes a letter to the number one commercial chain group in China, Bailian Group, expressing the willingness to conclude chain store business. In the letter Lowe's introduces itself: Founded in 1946, the world's 2nd largest home improvement retailer, more than 1,825 stores in the United States, Canada and Mexico, wide range from appliances and tools, to paint, lumber and nursery products, committed to offering high-quality home improvement products at everyday low prices, while delivering superior customer service.

Part 3

Simulation Training in Major Documents

Chapter 11

Official and Organizational Documents

Section 1 Export License

进出口许可证制度是我国实行对外贸易管理的一种行政保护手段,是根据我国的对外贸易政策对进出口货物和物品实行全面管理的制度,是根据国家的法律、政策、对外贸易计划和国内外市场的需求,以及承担的有关国际公约义务,对进出口经营权、经营范围、贸易国别、进出口商品品种及数量等实行的制度。进口经济贸易主管部门或者由其会同国务院有关部门,根据《中华人民共和国对外贸易法》关于对限制进口货物实行配额或许可证管理的规定,制定公布实行进口许可证管理的商品。出口许可证是由国家对外经贸行政管理部门代表国家统一签发的、批准某项商品出口的、具有法律效力的证明文件,也是海关查验放行出口货物和银行办理结汇的依据。根据国家规定,凡是国家宣布实行出口许可证管理的商品,不管任何单位或个人,也不分任何贸易方式(对外加工装配方式按有关规定办理),出口前均须申领出口许可证;非外贸经营单位或个人运往国外的货物,不论该商品是否实行出口许可证管理,价值在人民币 1 000 元以上的,一律须申领出口许可证;属于个人随身携带出境或邮寄出境的商品,除符合海关规定自用、合理数量范围外,也都应申领出口许可证。

手工填写出口许可证的注意事项如下。

(1)"出口商"与"发货人"的名称及代码必须一致,并应确保代码正确无误。

(2)"合同号"的填写必须清晰可辨,应特别注意区别字母大小写、数字及其他符号。

(3)"报关口岸"栏内应填写口岸名称及其代码。

(4)"进口国(地区)"栏内应填写中文国名(地区名)及其代码。

(5)"付款方式"栏内应填写付款方式的中文名称。

(6)"商品编码"一般为 10 位数字代码,请确保代码正确无误,并与"商品名称"相一致。

(7)"规格、等级"栏内应按不同商品的相应要求填写,字数不宜过多。

(8)"单位"、"数量"、"单价"的填写应确保正确无误,并与合同一致。

(9)外资企业出口、来料加工等贸易方式应在备注栏内注明"非一批一证"。

(10)"出口许可证号"、"出口许可证有效截止日期"应由发证机关填写,企业请勿填写。

中华人民共和国出口许可证
EXPORT LICENCE OF THE PEOPLE'S REPUBLIC OF CHINA

No. 0177985

1. 出口商： Exporter 亮光玩具有限公司	2. 出口许可证号： Export licence No. 0999985
3. 发货人： Consigner 亮光玩具有限公司	4. 出口许可证有效截止日期： Export licence expiry date 2014-7-20
5. 贸易方式： Terms of trade 一般贸易	6. 进口国（地区）： Country/Region of purchase USA
7. 合同号： Contract No. HY05CS007	8. 付款方式： Payment conditions Irrevocable Sight L/C
9. 报关口岸： Place of clearance 广州海关	10. 运输方式： Mode of transport 海运
11. 商品名称： Description of goods three items of plush toy	商品编码： Code of goods 6911.1010

12. 规格、等级 Specification	13. 单位 Unit	14. 数量 Quantity	15. 单价（USD） Unit price	16. 总值（USD） Amount	17. 总值折美元 Amount in USD
BG2046 DALMATION DOG	PCS	1,000	US$20.00	US$20,000	
BG2053 TEDDY BEAR	PCS	2,500	US$9.00	US$22,500	
BG 2054 TEDDY BEAR IN SWEATER	PCS	1,800	US$15.00	US$27,000	

18. 总计 Total	US$ 69,500
19. 备注 Supplementary details	20. 发证机关签章 Issuing authority's stamp & signature 21. 发证日期 License date 01 JUNE, 2014

Section 2　Certificate of Origin

原产地证书（Certificate of Origin）是出口商应进口商要求而提供的、由公证机构或政府或出口商出具的证明货物原产地或制造地的一种证明文件。原产地证书是贸易关系人交接货物、结算货款、索赔理赔、进口国通关验收、征收关税的有效凭证，它还是出口国享受配额待遇、进口国对不同出口国实行不同贸易政策的凭证。本书以 CO 为例介绍其填写要求。

第1栏：出口方。填写出口方名称、详细地址及国家（地区），此栏不得留空。出口方名称是指出口申报方名称，一般填有效合同的卖方或发票的出票人。若经其他国家或地区转口需要填写转口商时，应在出口商后面加填英文"VIA"，然后再填写转口商名称，不能直接写转口商。

第2栏：收货方。应填写最终收货方的名称、详细地址及国家（地区），通常是外贸合同的买方或提单的通知人。如果信用证需要，可不显示收货人，则第二栏应加注"TO ORDER"或"TO WHOM IT MAY CONCERN"，但不能留空。有转口商的同上。

第3栏：运输方式和路线。填写从装运港到目的港的运输路线，如经转运，应注明转运地。企业申报另外的信息，例如装运日期等内容，应符合实际情况并在不影响证书签发质量的前提下接受。因船运或空运等客观原因造成的第2、第3栏不一致，可以接受。如果提单上只显示到转运港信息，则建议加上"then to XXXX（最终目的国）"。

第4栏：目的国家/地区。一般与最终收货人国别、最终目的港国别一致，不一定与第3栏显示的港口国别一致（提单显示的卸货港不一定是最终目的地港口）。

第5栏：签证机构使用栏。企业申报时留空。

第6栏：唛头及包装号。按照出口发票上所列唛头填写完整，不可简单地填写为："AS PER INVOICE NO. …."或者"AS PER B/L NO. …."。包装无唛头，应填写"N/M"或者"NO MARK"。此栏不得留空，内容多可用附页。

第7栏：商品名称、包装数量及种类。应填写具体商品名称（能明确归类到 H.S.品目4位数），不得用概括性表述。例如，网球拍（TENNIS RACKET）不能填写运动用品（SPORTING GOODS）。发票上如有多种品名，应尽量合并，不一定与发票一样具体（除非信用证有要求）。包装数量及种类要按具体单位填写，在英文表述后注明阿拉伯数字。有包装的不能笼统地写几件；散装的，加注"IN BULK"。对于要求与信用证一致的仅有简单描述的情况须在括号内加注详细的品名描述。电子申请书品名须与证书品名一致。商品名称列完后，应在下一行加结束符。信用证如要求填具合同、信用证号码，可填在结束符下空白处。

第8栏：商品编码。同一份证书包含有几种商品，应将相应的品目全部填写上。此栏不得留空。

第9栏：数量。填写出口货物的数量并与商品的计量单位联用。一般默认为毛重重量，如为净重应注明"NW"。

第10栏：发票号码及日期。应按照出口正式商业发票（议付发票即结汇发票）填写，日期应早于或同于实际出口日期。此栏不得留空。

第11栏：出口方申明。申领员签字，中英文印章，填写申请地点和日期。该栏日期不得早于发票日期。

第12栏：签证机构证明。由签证机构签字、盖章并填写签证地点、日期。签发日期不能早于发票日期和申请日期。

ORIGINAL

1. Exporter (full name and address) BRIGHT SHINE TOY CO., LTD.	Certificate No. 1955566622 **CERTIFICATE OF ORIGIN OF THE PEOPLE'S REPUBLIC OF CHINA**
2. Consignee (full name and address) BURGEON INTERNATIONAL TRADING CO., LTD.	
3. Means of transport and route ON/AFTER DEC. 23, 2013 FROM GUANGZHOU TO NEWYORK BY SEA	5. For certifying authority use only
4. Country/region of destination NEWYORK	

6. Marks and numbers of packages	7. Number and kind of packages; description of goods	8. H.S. Code	9. Quantity	10. Number and date of invoices
G.B. HY05CS007 NEW YORK C/No. 1-345	6911.1010 PLUSH TOY TOTAL: THREE HUNDRED FORTY FIVE CNTS ONLY	GZ6688	345 cartons	TC030707 July 18, 2013

11. Declaration by the exporter	12. Certification
The undersigned hereby declares that the above details and statements are correct; that all the goods were produced in China and that they comply with the Rules of Origin of the People's Republic of China. GUANGZHOU Oct. 25, 2014 张雨 --- Place and date, signature and stamp of authorized signatory	It is hereby certified that the declaration by the exporter is correct. GUANGZHOU Oct. 25, 2014 周亿 --- Place and date, signature and stamp of authorized signature

 Section 3　Inspection Certificate

商品检验（Commodity Inspection）是指商品的卖方、买方或者第三方在一定条件下，借助于某种手段和方法,按照合同、标准或国内外有关法律、法规、惯例,对商品的质量、规格、重量、数量、包装、安全及卫生等方面进行检查,并做出合格与否或通过验收与否的判定或为维护买卖双方合法权益,避免或解决各种风险损失和责任划分的争议,便于商品交接结算而出具各种有关证书的业务活动。

进出口商品检验简称商检,是由国家设置的检验管理机构或由经政府注册批准的第三方民间公证鉴定机构,对进出口商品的品质、数量、重量、包装、安全、卫生、检疫及装运条件等进行的检验、鉴定和管理工作。

中华人民共和国广州进出口商品检疫局
GUANGZHOU IMPORT & EXPORT COMMODITY INSPECTION BUREAU OF THE PEOPLE'S REPUBLIC OF CHINA

地址:广州市珠江新城花城大道 66 号
Address: No. 66 Huacheng Avenue, Zhujiang, Xincheng Guangzhou City

编号:
No.: 058763

电报:
Cable: INSPECT YUE 1122 0033

日期:
Date: Sep. 26, 2014

电话:
Tel: 020-83356071

检 验 证 书
INSPECTION CERTIFICATE

发货人:
Consignor   Bright Shine Toy Co., Ltd.

收货人:
Consignee   Burgeon International Trading Co., Ltd.

品名:
Commodity   Three items of plush toys: BG2046, BG2053, BG2054

标记及号码:
Marks & No.   G.B.-HY05CS007-NEW YORK-C/No. 1-345

报验数量/重量:
Quantity/Weight   BG2046 (1,000); BG2053 (2,500); BG2054(1,800)

Declared _____
_____
_____

检验结果:

Results of Inspection	
GRADE A	
	主任检验员
	Chief Inspector
	Xin Ling 辛绫

华东××贸易有限公司（310991××××）与美国××贸易有限公司签订不同款式 PU 面休闲鞋（属法检商品，法定计量单位：双）出口合同，出具商业发票如下。

HUADONG XXX TRADING LTD.

INVOICE

Messrs: XXX

INV. No.: WVI8180
DATE: 28-April-2014
S/C No.: WVI8180
PAYMENT: T/T

SHIPPED FROM   SHANGHAI, CHINA   TO   NY, USA PER S.S. STAR

GOODS DESCRIPTION				QUANTITY		UNIT PRICE	TTL. AMOUNT
LOT NO.	STYLE	ORDER NO.	SIZE	CTNS	PRS	USD	USD
CASUAL SHOES WITH PU UPPER						TRADE TERMS: FOB SHANGHAI	
WV8021	FT00052	307879-1329	4-12	8	CTNS	96	PRS	USD19.70	USD1,891.2
WV8038	FT00052	307768-1313	4-12	84	CTNS	1,008	PRS	USD19.70	USD19,857.6
WV8020	FT00051	307879-1329	4-12	5	CTNS	60	PRS	USD21.00	USD1,260.0
WV8037	FT00051	307768-1313	4-12	102	CTNS	1,224	PRS	USD21.00	USD25,704.0
TTL				199	CTN	2,388	PRS		USD 48,712.8

```
MARKS & NO.
         ◇ ABC ◇
            NY
         CTN 1-100

REF NO.:
STYLE CODE:
SIZE:
QUANTITY:
CTN NO.:
COUNTRY OF ORIGIN: CHINA

SAY: TOTAL US DOLLARS FORTY EIGHT THOUSAND SEVEN HUNDRED AND TWELVE AND
EIGHT CENTS ONLY
```

请根据商业发票的内容,缮制下列单据。

(1) 出口许可证。

中华人民共和国出口许可证
EXPORT LICENSE OF THE PEOPLE'S REPUBLIC OF CHINA

No.

1. 出口商: Exporter	2. 出口许可证号: Export license No.
3. 发货人: Consignor	4. 出口许可证有效截止日期: Export license expiry date
5. 贸易方式: Terms of trade	6. 进口国/地区: Country/Region of purchase
7. 合同号: Contract No.	8. 付款方式: Payment
9. 报关口岸: Place of clearance	10. 运输方式: Mode of transport
11. 商品名称: Description of goods	商品编码: Code of goods

12. 规格、型号 Specification	13. 单位 Unit	14. 数量 Quantity	15. 单价（　　） Unit price	16. 总值（　　） Amount	17. 总值折美元 Amount in USD
18. 总计 Total					
19. 备注 Supplementary details			20. 发证机关签章 Issuing authority's stamp & signature		
			21. 发证日期 License date		

（2）一般原产地证明书。

ORIGINAL

1. Exporter (full name and address)	Certificate No.
	CERTIFICATE OF ORIGIN **OF** **THE PEOPLE'S REPUBLIC OF CHINA**
2. Consignee (full name and address)	
3. Means of transport and route	5. For certifying authority use only
4. Country/region of destination	

6. Marks and numbers	7. Number and kind of packages; description of goods	8. H.S. Code	9. Quantity	10. Number and date of invoices

11. Declaration by the exporter
    The undersigned hereby declares that the above details and statements are correct; that all the goods were produced in China and that they comply with the Rules of Origin of the People's Republic of China.
 	
-- 	
Place and date, signature and stamp of authorized signatory
	12. Certification
	    It is hereby certified that the declaration by the exporter is correct.
	
	-- 	
	Place and date, signature and stamp of certifying authority

Chapter 12 Financial Documents

Section 1 Commercial Invoice

商业发票（Commercial Invoice）是出口方向进口方开列的发货价目清单，是买卖双方记账的依据，也是进出口报关交税的总说明。商业发票是一笔业务的全面反映，内容包括商品的名称、规格、价格、数量、金额、包装等，同时也是进口商办理进口报关不可缺少的文件。因此，商业发票是全套出口单据的核心，在单据制作过程中，其余单据均需参照商业发票缮制。

（1）卖方栏目要按合同和信用证的规定填写名称和地址的全称。一般来说，名称和地址要分行打印。

（2）买方栏目又称发票的收货人或抬头人。当采用信用证方式付款时，商业发票必须以信用证申请人为抬头，除非信用证另有规定。跟单托收业务下，发票上的收货人应根据合同所列买方或指定名称缮制，并列明详细地址。

（3）发票号码。发票号码由出口商自行编制，一方面便于出口商的查询，同时又代表了全套单据的号码和某批货物，如缮制汇票时的号码就是按发票号码填写，所以在缮制时不能遗漏。

（4）发票日期。即发票的出票日期。信用证方式下，发票日期一般在信用证开证日期之后、装运日期之前，或至少在交单或有效期之前。

（5）信用证号码。按信用证填写。

（6）合同号码。应与信用证上所列的一致，须在发票上列明，若一笔交易有几个合同号码，都应打印在发票上。

（7）起运地。按信用证规定填写，并与提单所列明的一致。

（8）目的地。按信用证填写，同时要注意目的地的规定要明确具体，不能笼统；有重名的目的地后面要加列国别。

（9）运输工具。在得到海运公司或运输代理的配载通知后，按其配载内容列明运输工具和航次。

（10）唛头。凡是信用证上规定唛头的，必须逐字逐行按规定缮制，并与其他单据的唛头相一致。信用证中没有规定唛头的，则按合同条款中指明的唛头或买方已提供的唛头缮制；如果都没有规定，则由卖方自行设计，并注意单单相符。

（11）商品名称及规格。必须与合同和信用证一致。如果是在信用证方式下制单，应特别注意以下几点。

① 发票的品名不能超出信用证的内容。
② 货名不能遗漏和随便减缩。如果来证货物名称写得详细具体，应照抄。
③ 要正确缮制中文和外文品名。
④ 来证品名开错时，如果是实质性问题，应及时修改。如果是次要问题，可采用照抄并括号加注的办法来说明。但严格来说，这也是单证不符，最好还是修改信用证。

⑤ 来证所要求的规格必须在单据上充分体现出来。

（12）数量或重量。既要与实际装运货物相符，又要符合信用证的规定。以件数计算价格的商品，发票要列明件数；以重量计算价格的，必须列明重量。如果货品规格较多，每种商品应写明小计数量，最后表示出总数量。

（13）价格术语要严格按信用证规定填制，有时含佣金，有时不含佣金。

（14）单价和总值是发票的重点，特别要注意发票金额不超过信用证金额，发票的货币要与信用证相一致。

（15）出具人和签章。一般发票必须经出口商正式签字盖章才有效，并注意使用的图章和签字要与其他单据相一致。如果对方国家要求手签时，要注意各国的习惯。

亮光玩具有限公司
BRIGHT SHINE TOY CO., LTD.

商业发票
COMMERCIAL INVOICE

TO: Burgeon International Trading Co., Ltd.
3804 New Sharon Rd, 18/F Commercial Center,
New York 20815, USA
VIA: S.S. "Prince"
FROM:　　Guangzhou

INVOICE NO.: TC030707
DATE:　　July 18, 2014
L/C NO.: AM/VA0513ILC
S/C NO.:　HY05CS007
TO:　　New York

MARKS AND NUMBERS	QUANTITIES AND DESCRIPTIONS OF GOODS		UNIT PRICE (FOB Shanghai)	AMOUNT
BG2046	Dalmatian Dog	1,000	US$20.00	US$20,000
BG2053	Teddy Bear	2,500	US$9.00	US$22,500
BG2054	Teddy Bear in Sweater	1,800	US$15.00	US$27,000

亮光玩具有限公司
BRIGHT SHINE TOY CO., LTD.
NO. 2-8-30 JINHUI BUILDING,
NO. 71 SOUTH ZHONGSHANG ROAD,
TIANHE DISTICT, CHUANGZHOU 510000, P.R. CHINA

Section 2 Draft

汇票是由一人开致另一人的书面的无条件命令，由发出命令的人签名，要求接受命令的人立即，或在固定的时间，或在可以确定的将来时间，把一定金额的货币支付给一个特定的人，或他的指定人，或来人。

汇票的必要项目如下。
（1）写明"汇票"字样。
（2）书面的无条件支付命令。
（3）出票地点和日期。
（4）付款时间。
（5）一定金额的货币。
（6）付款人的名称和地点。
（7）收款人的名称。
（8）出票人的名称和签字。

BILL OF EXCHANGE

凭
Drawn Under CITY BANK, NEW YORK BRANCH   不可撤销信用证
Irrevocable L/C No. AM/VA0513ILC

日期   Payable with interest   20   % 按息付款
Date Oct. 8, 2014
号码   汇票金额
No. HY05cs007   Exchange for US$69,500.00
见票   日后（本汇票之副本未付）
at ************   sight of this FIRST of   Exchange (Second of Exchange Being unpaid)
付交
Pay to the order of BANK OF CHINA, GUANGZHOU BRANCH

金额
The sum of SAY US DOLLARS SIXTY NINE THOUSAND FIVE HUNDRED ONLY

此致
To
  CITIBANK, NEW YORK BRANCH

Section 3 T/T order

电汇汇款（Telegraphic Transfer，T/T）是汇款人委托银行以电报、电传、SWIFT（环球

同业银行金融电讯协会）等方式，指示出口地某一银行作为汇入行，解付一定金额给收款人的汇款方式。

```
FM: BANK OF CHINA, TIANJIN

TO: THE HONG KONG AND SHANGHAI BANKING CORP. H.K.

DD: 1ST MAR., 2014

TEST 12358 OUR REF 208TT0517 NO ANY CHARGES FOR US PAY USD20,000.00.
VALUE 1ST MAR., 2014 TO YOUR HAY BUILDING BR. H.K. FOR ACCOUNT NO.
004-110-106028-001 FAVOUR PRECISION PHOTO EQUIPMENT LTD., HK MESSAGE
CONTRACT NO. P10158 ORDER PHOTOGRAPH CO., TIANJIN COVER DEBIT OUR
HO ACCOUNT.
```

 Section 4　L/C

跟单信用证是开证银行根据进口商的请求，对出口商发出的，授权出口商签发以该行为付款人的汇票，保证交来符合条款规定的汇票和单据必须承兑或付款的保证文件。银行付款是以出口商提交符合信用证规定的单据为条件的，因此又称跟单信用证（Documentary L/C）。

```
TO: BANK OF CYPRUS LTD
LETTERS OF CREDIT DEPARTMENT
NTCOSIA COMMERCIAL OPERATIONS CENTER
INTERNATIONAL DIVISION

TEL: ******
FAX: ******
TELEX: 2451 & 4933 KYPRIA CY
SWIFT: BCYPCY2N

DATE: 23 MARCH 2014

APPLICATION FOR THE ISSUANCE OF A LETTER OF CREDIT

SWIFT MT700 SENT TO:
STANDARD CHARTERD BANK
UNIT 1-8 52/F SHUN NIND SQUARE
```

01 WANG COMMERCIAL CENTRE, SHEN NAN
ROAD EAST, SHENZHEN 518008-CHINA
TEL: 0755-82461688

:27: SEQUENCE OF TOTAL
1/1
:40A: FORM OF DOCUMENTARY CREDIT
IRREVOCABLE
:20OCUMENTARY CREDIT NUMBER
00143-01-0053557
:31C: DATE OF ISSUE
:31DATE AND PLACE OF EXPIRY
050622 IN CHINA 1-0622
:50: APPLICANT
******* NICOSIA
:59: BENEFICIARY
CHAOZHOU HUALI CERAMICS FACTORY
FENGYI INDUSTRIAL DISTRICT, GUXIANG TOWN, CHAOZHOU CITY,
GUANGDONG PROVINCE, CHINA
:32B: CURRENCY CODE, AMOUNT
USD***7841,89
:41D: AVAILABLE WITH ... BY ...
STANDARD CHARTERED BANK
CHINA AND/OR AS BELOW
BY NEGOTIATION
:42CRAFTS AT
SIGHT
:42A: DRAWEE
BCYPCY2NO10
BANK OF CYPRUS LTD.
:43PARTIAL SHIPMENTS
NOT ALLOWED
:44C: LATEST DATE OF SHIPMENT
1-0601
:045A: DESCRIPTION OF GOODS AND/OR SERVICES
SANITARY WARE
FOB SHENZHEN PORT, INCOTERMS 2000
:046A: DOCUMENTS REQUIRED
*FULL SET (AT LEAST THREE) ORIGINAL CLEAN SHIPPED ON BOARD BILLS OF LADING ISSUED TO THE ORDER OF BANK OF CYPRUS PUBLIC COMPANY LTD., CYPRUS, NOTIFY PARTIES APPLICANT AND OURSELVES, SHOWING.

*FREIGHT PAYABLE AT DESTINATION AND BEARING THE NUMBER OF THIS CREDIT.

*PACKING LIST IN 3 COPIES.

*CERTIFICATE ISSUED BY THE SHIPPING COMPANY/CARRIER OR THEIR AGENT STATING THE B/L NO(S) AND THE VESSEL(S) NAME CERTIFYING THAT THE CARRYING VESSEL(S) IS/ARE:

A) HOLDING A VALID SAFETY MANAGEMENT SYSTEM CERTIFICATE AS PER TERMS OF INTERNATIONAL SAFETY MANAGEMENT CODE AND

B) CLASSIFIED AS PER INSTITUTE CLASSIFICATION CLAUSE 01/01/2001 BY AN APPROPRIATE CLASSIFICATION SOCIETY

*COMMERCIAL INVOICE FOR USD11,202,70 IN 4 COPIES DULY SIGNED BY THE BENEFICIARY/IES, STATING THAT THE GOODS SHIPPED:

A) ARE OF CHINESE ORIGIN.

B) ARE IN ACCORDANCE WITH BENEFICIARIES PROFORMA INVOICE NO. HL1-0307 DATED 07/03/2014.

:047A: ADDITIONAL CONDITIONS

*THE NUMBER AND DATE OF THE CREDIT AND THE NAME OF OUR BANK MUST BE QUOTED ON ALL DRAFTS (IF REQUIRED).

*TRANSPORT DOCUMENTS TO BE CLAUSED: VESSEL IS NOT SCHEDULED TO CALL ON ITS CURPENT VOYAGE AT FAMAGUSTA, KYRENTA OR KARAVOSTASSI, CYPRUS.

*INSURANCE WILL BE COVERED BY THE APPLICANTS.

*ALL DOCUMENTS TO BE ISSUED IN ENGLISH LANGUAGE.

*NEGOTIATION/PAYMENT: UNDER RESERVE/GUARANTEE STRICTLY PROHIBITED.

*DISCREPANCY FEES USD80, FOR EACH SET OF DISCREPANT DOCUMENTS PRESENTED UNDER THIS CREDIT, WHETHER ACCEPTED OR NOT, PLUS OUR CHARGES FOR EACH MESSAGE CONCERNING REJECTION AND/OR ACCEPTANCE MUST BE BORNE BY BENEFICIARIES THEMSELVES AND DEDUCTED FROM THE AMOUNT PAYABLE TO THEM.

*IN THE EVENT OF DISCREPANT DOCUMENTS ARE PRESENTED TO US AND REJECTED, WE MAY RELEASE THE DOCUMENTS AND EFFECT SETTLEMENT UPON APPLICANT'S WAIVER OF SUCH DISCREPANCIES, NOTWITHSTANDING ANY COMMUNICATION WITH THE PRESENTER THAT WE ARE HOLDING DOCUMENTS AT ITS DISPOSAL, UNLESS ANY PRIOR INSTRUCTIONS TO THE CONTRARY ARE RECEIVED.

*TRANSPORT DOCUMENTS BEARING A DATE PRIOR TO THE L/C DATE ARE NOT ACCEPTABLE.

*DIFFERENCE OF USD3363.81(T.E.30 PERCENT OF INVOICE VALUE) BETWEEN L/C AMOUNT AND INVOICES AMOUNT REPRESENTS AMOUNT PAID BY APPLICANTS DIRECT TO BENEFICIARIES OUTSIDE THE L/C TERMS WITHOUT ANY RESPONSIBILITY ON OURSELVES AND TO BE SHOWN ON INVOICES AS SUCH.

:71B: CHARGES

BANK CHARGES OUTSIDE CYPRUS INCLUDING THOSE OF THE REIMBURSING BANK ARE FOR BEN. A/C.

:48: PERIOD FOR PRESENTATION

DOCUMENTS MUST BE PRESENTED WITHIN

21 DAYS AFTER B/LADING DATE, BUT

WITHIN THE VALIDITY OF THE CREDIT.

:49: CONFIRMATION INSTRUCTIONS

WITHOUT

:53A: REIMBURSING BANK

BCYPGB2L

BANK OF CYPRUS UK

INTERNATIONAL DEPARTMENT,

87/93 CHASE SIDE, SOUTHGATE N14 5BU

LONDON — UNITED KINGDOM.

:78: INSTRUCTIONS TO THE PAY/ACCEP/NEG BANK

NEGO OF DOCS THRU BANK OF CHINA LIMITED CHINA IS ALLOWED. PLEASE DEDUCT RROM YOUR PAYMENT TO BENEFICIARIES THE AMOUNT OF USD1,500 REPRESENTING RECORDING FEES. NEGOTIATION BANK TO OBTAIN REIMBURSEMENT FROM OUR ACCOUNT WITH REIMBURSING BANK 3 BUSINESS

DAYS FOLLOWING THEIR AUTHENTICATED TELEX/SWIFT ADVICE TO US, STATING A) OUR CREDIT NUMBER, B) AMOUNT CLAIMED, C) VALUE OF DOCUMENTS, D) SHIPMENT/DISPATCH DATE AND E) THAT DOCS ARE IN STRICT COMPLIANCE WITH CREDIT TERMS. ON EXECUTION FORWARD TO US, BANK OF CYPRUS PUBLIC COMAPNY LTD, NICOSIA COMMERCIAL OPER. CENTER INTERN. DIV., 10 KYRIACOS MATSI AV. 1082 AY. OMOLOYITES, NIGOSIA, CYPRUS, ALL DOCS IN ONE LOT BY COURIER SERVICE AT BENEFICIARIES EXPENSE.

:72: SENDER TO RECEIVER INFORMATION

CREDIT IS SUBJECT TO U.C.P. 1993

I.C.C. PUBL. NO. 500. SUBJECT TO URR

ICC 525. COLLECT YOUR CHARGES FROM

BENE. PLEASE ACKN. RECEIPT.

CUMSTOMER'S APPROVAL.

1. 秦皇岛造船厂进口一批油漆，USD2.00/LTR CIF TIANJIN，运费为 USD8 000，保险费率 0.25%，付款方式为"T/T 60 days from B/L Date"，装箱单如下：

PACKING LIST

Seller: KOREA CHEMICAL CO., LTD. 1031-4, SEOCHOODONG, SEO-CHO-KU SEOUL KOREA	Invoice No. and Date: EX80320 MAR. 12, 2014
	Buyer (if other than consignee): AS PER CONSIGNEE
Consignee: TO THE ORDER OF QINHUANGDAO BOATYARD CO., LTD. 154 WUSI ROAD, QINHUANGDAO, CHINA	Other Reference:
	Contract No.: SFEC/KCC803-1
Departure Date: MAR. 16, 2014	
Vessel: ESSEN EXPRESS V.28 ED09 / From: SINGAPORE	
To: TIANJIN, CHINA	

Shipping Marks	No. & Kinds of Packing: Goods Description	Quantity	N/W	G/W	Measurement
	PAINT	LTR 114,056	KG 136,256	KG 161,492	

请根据上述信息，缮制下列单据：

Seller	商业发票 **COMMERCIAL INVOICE**	
Consignee		
	No.	Date
Transport details Departure date Vessel From To	S/C No.	L/C No.
	Terms of Delivery & Payment	

Marks and numbers	Number and kind of packages; description of goods	Quantity	Unit price	Amount

2. 根据所给的英文信息填写汇票。

Suppose that China Machinery Trading Company in Xia'men is exporting to Jone's Corporation in Canada under the L/C issued by Bank of China Toronto Branch with the L/C No. 37659 dated on May 10, 2014. Please fill in the following <u>time</u> draft with the amount of USD8,200.

EXCHANGE for ① _____   China Xia'men at ② _____ sight of this First of Exchange (Second of Exchange being unpaid)
Drawn under Bank of China, Toronto
Irrevocable L/C No. 317659   Dated May 10, 2014 No. 1234
pay to the order of Bank of China the sum of US dollars ③ _____.
To ④ _____

⑤ _____

Chapter 13

Commercial Documents

Section 1 Purchase Order and Sales Confirmation

外贸订单即客户（买方）下的订货单，用以购买商品或服务，由进口商自行缮制，一般以"purchase order"或"sales confirmation"的形式出现，包含的要素如下。
（1）买方（含进口商名称、地址、联系方式等）。
（2）卖方（含出口商名称、地址、联系方式等）。
（3）货物信息（含货物名称、规格、数量、单价、总价等）。
（4）其他条款（如包装条款、运输条款、保险条款、付款条款等）。
（5）注明"purchase order"或"sales confirmation"字样。
如果使用"sales confirmation"，一般一式两份，买卖双方需签字盖章认可。

Samuelsson Company Ltd.
PO BOX 1234, Narre Warren South
Tel: Fax: E-mail:

Purchase Order

Purchase from:	*Deliver to:*		
ABC Pty. Ltd.	Samuelsson Company Ltd.	P.O. #	10111
204 Collins Street,	1234 High Street	Your Ref #	EF1123
Melbourne 3000	London	Our Ref #	
Australia	UK	Credit Terms	30

Attention: Mr. Joe Lynn   Salesperson
                                                       Job Code

We are pleased to confirm our purchase of the following items:

SN	Product ID	Description	QTY UM	Unit price	Amount
1	P1001	Pencils—HB	50 Dozen	$10.00	500.00
2	P1002	Pencils—2B	50 Dozen	$10.00	500.00
3	P1003	Pen—blue	50 Dozen	$12.00	600.00
4	P1004	Pen—yellow	50 Dozen	$12.00	600.00
5	P1005	Pen—pink	50 Dozen	$12.00	600.00
6	P1006	Pen—while	50 Dozen	$12.00	600.00

Comments:	Total before Tax: 3,400.00
	Tax: 400.00
	Total after Tax: 3,800.00

Terms and Conditions: Shipment must be made before May; We reserve the right to reject the goods that are not in good conditions or order as determined by our quality control.

亮光玩具有限公司

BRIGHT SHINE TOY CO., LTD.

NO. 2-8-30 JINHUI BUILDING, NO. 71 SOUTH ZHONGSHANG ROAD, TIANHE DISTICT, CHUANGZHOU 510000, P.R. CHINA

正本

销售确认书

SALES CONFIRMATION

编号
No.: **HY05CS007**

日期
Date: **July 18, 2014**

买方
Buyer: **Burgeon International Trading Co., Ltd.**

地址
Address: **3804 New Sharon Road, 18/F Commercial Center, New York 20815, USA**

电话
Tel: **478309 Burgeon USA**

传真
Fax: **(1)320-816**

兹经买卖双方同意成交下列商品，订立条款如下：
The undersigned Sellers and Buyers have agreed to close the following transaction according to the terms and conditions stipulated below:

货物名称及规格 NAME OF COMMODITY AND SPECIFICATION	数量 QUANTITY	单价 UNIT PRICE	金额 AMOUNT
BG2046 (Dalmation Dog)	1,000	US$20.00	US$20,000
BG2053 (Teddy Bear)	2,500	US$9.00	US$22,500
BG2054 (Teddy Bear in Sweater)	1,800	US$15.00	US$27,000
总值 TOTAL VALUE			US$ 69,500

装运
SHIPMENT: Goods should be shipped not later than October5. Partial shipment and transshipment prohibited.

付款条件
PAYMENT: The Buyer should open through a bank acceptable by the Seller an irrevocable sight letter of credit to reach the seller before July 25, 2014 valid for negotiation in China until the 20th day after date of shipment.

包装
PACKING: Each packed in a plastic bag, 10 of BG2046 in a carton, 20 of BG2053 in a carton, 15 of BG2054 in a carton.

唛头
MARKS & NOS.: G.B.-HY05CS007-NEW YORK-C/No. 1-345.

保险
INSURANCE: 110% of the invoice value against All Risk and WPA.

买方（签章）	卖方（签章）
THE BUYER	THE SELLER
Bill D. H.	Jin Taya
Burgeon International Trading Co., Ltd.	BRIGHT SHINE TOY CO., LTD.

Section 2　Quotation and Price List

报价单是卖方向买方提供的所销售商品或服务的相关信息，由卖方自行缮制，以"Quotation"或"Price List"的形式出现。具体包含的要素如下。

（1）卖方（出口商名称、地址、联系方式等）。
（2）"Quotation"或"Price List"字样。
（3）货物信息（含货物名称、规格、数量、单价等）。
（4）其他信息（如包装条款、运输条款、保险条款、付款条款和报价有效期等）。

ABC Pty. Ltd.
204 Collins Street, Melbourne 3000
Tel:　　　　　Fax:　　　　　E-mail:

Quotation

Dear Sir or Madam,

We are pleased to quote our following items:

SN	Product ID	Description	QTY UM (minimum)	Unit Price
1	P1001	Pencils HB	50 Dozen	$10.00
2	P1002	Pencils 2B	50 Dozen	$10.00
3	P1003	Pen-blue	50 Dozen	$12.00
4	P1004	Pen-yellow	50 Dozen	$12.00
5	P1005	Pen-pink	50 Dozen	$12.00
6	P1006	Pen-while	50 Dozen	$12.00

Remarks:
1. All goods are available from stock.
2. Shipment could be made as instructed.

PRICE LIST

OUR REF: 12N-0002-3B

PACKING: STANDARD EXPORT PACKING   DATE: MARCH 27, 2014
PAYMENT: BY IRREVOCABLE SIGHT L/C IN OUR FAVOR
SHIPMENT: WITHIN 30 DAYS AFTER RECEIPT OF L/C
TERM: FOB SHANGHAI
VALIDITY: 30 DAYS

MODEL NO.	DESCRIPTION	MIN. QTY	FOB SHANGHAI
110S/BP	110 MICRO POCKET CAMERA NEW FOLDING TYPE VIEW FINDER WINDING WHEEL FILM ADVANCE	1,440 PCS	US$2.30/PC
110S/OE	110 MICRO POCKET CAMERA NEW FOLDING TYPE VIEW FINDER WINDING WHEEL FILM ADVANCE	2,000 PCS	US$2.30/PC
110H/OE	110 POCHET MINI CAMERA WITH NEW FOLDING TYPE VIEW FINDER BUILD-IN FLASH SHUTTER: 1/125 SEC. LENS F: 11	1,000 PCS	US$7.50/PC
110H/BP	110 MICRO POCKET MINI CAMERA WITH BUILD-IN FLASH SHUTTER: 1/125 SEC LENS F: 11	1,000 PCS	US$7.65/PC
2000/OE	110 MICRO POCKET MINI CAMERA WITH BUILD-IN FLASH SHUTTER: 1/125 SEC	1,000 PCS	US$6.35/PC
2000T	110 POCKET CAMERA WITH BUILD-IN FLASH SHUTTER:1/125 SEC.	1,000 PCS	US$7.30/PC

F301/OB	FLASHGUN GUIDE NEMBER:16 ASA 100 SYNCHRONIZATION: X	1,000 PCS	US$6.35/PC
EV11/OE	35MM CAMERA WITH BUILD-IN FLASH WITHOUT LOW LIGHT SENSOR SHUTTER SPEED: 1/100 SEC LENS F: 5.6 PLASTIC LENS	500 PCS	US$13.8/PC

NOTE: (1) COLOR AVAILABLE FOR #200 & 2000 T: BLACK, RED, YELLOW, BLUE, SILVER

(2) COLOR AVAILABLE FOR 110H, 110S, EVO, EV11: BLACK, RED, YELLOW, BLVE, PINK

(3) PACKAGE ABBREVIATION
OE: SLEEVE BOX, BP: BLISTER PACK, VP: CLAM SHELL+BLISTER

杭州蓝海实业有限公司与西班牙客户进行贸易，开列以下发票。

ZHEJIANG BLUE SEA IMPORT AND EXPORT CO., LTD.
200 HEDONG ROAD, HANGZHOU, CHINA

COMMERCIAL INVOICE

Invoice No.: 08OIC08002
L/C No.: 9005BTY118934
Date: 9-Jan.-2014

GAYNER, S.A.
C/PALAU DE PLEGAMANS,15
08213-PULINYA
(BARCELONA, SPAIN)

From SHANGHAI, CHINA To BARCELONA, SPAIN

Marks	Quantity and Descriptions	Amount
N/M FOB NINGBO PORT CHINA PACKED IN 10 CASES	GEAR PACK AS PER PROFORMA N/W: 12,628 KGS G/W: 12,828 KGS Measurement: 4.5 CBM	EUR 12,053.60

ZHEJIANG BLUE SEA IMPORT AND EXPORT CO., LTD.

程晓

请根据上述发票内容,缮制下列票据。

(1) 报价单。

Fax to:　　　　　　　　　　　Date:

Our REF: CI-300　　　Your Fax REF. No.: Sw3302

Attn: JENNY LI

Subject:

Many thanks for your inquiry for the subject valve and are glad to quote you our best price and term as below:

QUTATION				
Item	Description	Qty	Unit Price	Total Amount

Packing:

Shipment:

Payment:

Approx. Weight:

Validity:

Very truly yours,

（2）销售确认书。

杭州蓝海实业有限公司
ZHEJIANG BLUE SEA IMPORT AND EXPORT CO., LTD.
200 HEDONG ROAD, HANGZHOU, CHINA

销售确认书
SALES CONFIRMATION

编号 No.

日期 Date

买方
Buyer: _____

地址
Address: _____

电话　　　　　　　　　　　传真
Tel: _____　Fax: _____

兹经买卖双方同意成交下列商品，订立条款如下：
The undersigned Sellers and Buyers have agreed to close the following transaction according to the terms and conditions stipulated below:

货物名称及规格 NAME OF COMMODITY AND SPECIFICATION	数量 QUANTITY	单价 UNIT PRICE	金额 AMOUNT
			总值 TOTAL VALUE

装运
SHIPMENT：

付款条件
PAYMENT：

包装
PACKING：

唛头
MARKS & NOS.：

保险
INSURANCE：

买方（签章）　　　　　　　　　　　　　　　　　　卖方（签章）
THE BUYER　　　　　　　　　　　　　　　　　　　THE SELLER

Chapter 14

Shipping Documents

Section 1 Booking Note

订舱单（Booking Note）的全称为订舱委托书，是承运人或其代理人在接受发货人或货物托运人的订舱时，根据发货人的口头或书面申请货物托运的情况安排货物运输（以集装箱运输为主）而制订的单证。

填写时应注意以下事项。

（1）订舱单是承运货物、安排运输和制作舱单的依据，各项内容必须认真填写。

（2）货物的各项资料，如唛头、件数、货名、重量、尺码等，必须填全。

（3）运费与附加费栏必须认真填写金额，如有协议或合约，则加填协议或合约号，切勿空白。

（4）运费预付、到付栏不填的，一律按预付处理；运输条款不填的，一律视作 CY-CY 条款；是否中转及中转港口栏必须填写清楚。

（5）因订舱单填写错误或资料不全引起的货物不能及时出运、运错目的地、舱单制作错误、不能提货等而产生的一切责任、风险、纠纷、费用等概由托运人承担。

大连市骏诚物流有限公司出口货物订舱单

To	From
Shipper: JUN CHENG LOGISTICS CO., LTD.	Booking No.:
Consignee: JI XIANG APPLE CO., LTD.	TEL: 0755-26891871 Tony Lin E-MAIL: real@jcsz.net FAX: 0411-83831963
Notify Party: HAO YUN LAI FRUIT CO., LTD.	FREIGHT & CHARGES: RMB5,000 合约/编号: L12345
Pre-carriage by	PREPAID	COLLECT
Place of Receipt: NO. 6, UL. DRUZHBY, MOSCOW, RUSSIA	OF	
Ocean Vessel: MOL GARLAND	ORC	
Voy. No.: 0308A	文件费	
Port of Loading: DALIAN, CHINA	其他	

Port of discharge BANGKOK	Place of delivery NO. 6 TROK RONG MAI BANGKOK		Final Destination for the Merchant's Reference: BANGKOK	
Marks & Nos: 0599UI Container/Seal No.: COC31A08	No. of container's package: 5	Description of Goods: LS1006 40 mm apple	Gross W: 7630	Measurement: 33.2
箱型/箱量：40 MM		运输条款：		
货类：	蔬果类			
提柜时间：2014-4-25		拖车公司：JUN CHENG LOGISTICS CO., LTD.		
是否中转：是		中转港口：BUSAN		
装货地点：DALIAN, CHINA		装货时间与联系人：4月3日装货，王景卫		
☆ 注 意 事 项 ☆	1. 订舱单是承运货物、安排运输和制作舱单的依据，各项内容必须认真填写。 2. 货物的各项资料，如唛头、件数、货名、重量、尺码等，必须填全。 3. 运费与附加费栏必须认真填写金额，如有协议或合约，则加填协议或合约号，切勿空白。 4. 运费预付、到付栏不填的，一律按预付处理；运输条款不填的，一律视作CY-CY条款；是否中转及中转港口栏必须填写清楚。 5. 危险品货物，除填本单危险品一栏内容外，出运时还须提供产品说明书，包装容器使用性能鉴定书。 6. 因订舱单填写错误或资料不全引起的货物不能及时出运、运错目的地、舱单制作错误、不能提货等而产生的一切责任、风险、纠纷、费用等概由托运人承担。		托运人签章： 日期：	

Section 2　Shipping Advice

　　如成交条件为FOB、FCA、CFR、CPT等，出口商还需要向进口国保险公司发出装船通知，以便其为进口商办理货物保险手续。出口装船通知应按合同或信用证规定的时间发出，该通知的副本常作为向银行交单议付的单据之一。在进口方派船接货的交易条件下，进口商为了使船、货衔接得当，也会向出口方发出有关通知。装船通知以英文制作，无统一格式，内容一定要符合信用证的规定，一般只提供一份。装船通知的内容主要包括所发运货物的合同号或信用证号、品名、数量、金额、运输工具名称、开航日期、启运地和目的地、提运单号码、运输标志等，并且与其他相关单据保持一致。如信用证提出具体项目要求，应严格按规定出单。此外,装船通知中还可能出现包装说明、船舶预离港时间(ETD)、船舶预抵港时间(ETA)、预计开始装船时间(ETC)等。

装运通知(Shipping Advice)是由出口商(受益人)发给进口商(申请人)的;"shipping instructions"的意思是"装运须知",一般是进口商发给出口商的;"shipping note/bill"指装货通知单或船货清单;"shipping order"简称 S/O,含义是装货单、关单或下货纸(是海关放行和命令船方将单据上载明的货物装船的文件)。

Sample 1

Invoice No.	TC030707		
L/C No.	AM/VAO1513ITC	B/L No.	cos9815222
SHIPPING ADVICE			
To	Order		
Marks	亮光玩具有限公司		
Commodity	3 items of plush toy		
Packing conditions	Each packed in a plastic bag, 20 of BG2053 in a carton, 15 of BG2054 in a carton, 10 of BG2046 in a carton		
Quantity	345 cartons		
Gross weight	13.26 M/T		
Net weight	11.8 M/T		
Total value	USD69,500		
Please be informed that these goods have been shipped From Guangzhou to New York by sea Shipment date October 5, 2014			
Ocean vessel	Star	Voy. No.	0011w
We herewith certify this message to be true and correct.			
Special conditions in shipping advice			
Place: Guangzhou		Date: 2014-10-1	
Company name: China Ocean Shipping Co. Guangzhou Branch			
Address:		Signature:	

Sample 2

SHIPPING ADVICE

Messrs:

Re: Invoice No. <u>TC030707</u>   L/C No. <u>AM/VAO1513ITC</u>

We hereby inform you that the goods under the above mentioned credit have been shipped. The details of the shipment are as follows:

Commodity: 3 items of plush toy
Quantity: 345 cartons
Amount: USD69,500
Bill of Lading No.: cos9815222
Ocean Vessel: Star S.S. 0011w
Port of Loading: Guangzhou
Port of Destination: New York
Date of Shipment: 2014-10-5

We hereby certify that the above content is true and correct.

Company name: BRIGHT SHINE TOY CO., LTD.

Address: No. 2-8-30 Jinhui Building, No. 71 South Zhongshan Rd, Tianhe District, Guangzhou 510000, China

Signature:

Jin Taya

 Section 3　Packing List

　　装箱单是发票的补充单据，它列明信用证（或合同）中买卖双方约定的有关包装事宜的细节，便于国外买方在货物到达目的港时供海关检查和核对货物，通常可以将其有关内容加列在商业发票上，但是在信用证有明确要求时，就必须严格按信用证约定制作。因缮制的出口公司不同，装箱单的内容也大不相同，但主要包括：包装单名称、编号、日期、唛头、货名、规格、包装单位、件数、每件的货量、毛净重、包装材料、包装方式、包装规格及签章等。

　　缮制装箱单时的注意事项如下。

　　（1）装箱单名称（Packing List）。应按照信用证规定使用，通常用"Packing List"、"Packing

Specification"、"Detailed Packing List"。如果来证要求用中性包装单（Neutral Packing List），则包装单名称用"Packing List"，但包装单内不写卖方名称，且不能签章。

（2）编号（No.）。应与发票号码一致。

（3）合同号或销售确认书号（Contract No./ Sales Confirmation No.）。要注明此批货的合同号或者销售合同书号。

（4）唛头（Shipping Mark）。应与发票一致，有时注实际唛头，有时也可以只注"as per invoice No. XXX"。

（5）箱号（Case No.），又称包装件号码。在单位包装货量或品种不固定的情况下，需注明每个包装件内的包装情况，因此包装件应编号。例如：Carton No. 1-5，Carton No. 6-10。

有的来证要求此处注明"CASENO.1—UP"，UP是指总箱数。

（6）货号（Name of Commodity）。按照发票制作，与发票内容一致。

（7）货物描述（Description；Specification）。要求与发票一致。货名如有总称，应先注总称，然后逐项列明详细货名。

（8）数量（Quantity）。应注明此箱内每件货物的包装件数，例如"bag 10"、"drum 20"、"bale 50"。

（9）出票人签章（Signature）。应与发票相同。

Issuer BRIGHT SHINE TOY CO., LTD. No. 2-8-30 Jinhui Building No. 71 South Zhongshan Rd, Tianhe District, Guangzhou 510000, China		PACKING LIST	
To Burgeon International Trading Co., Ltd. 18/F Commercial Center, 3804 New Sharon Rd, New York 20815, USA		Invoice No. TC030707	Date July 18, 2014
Marks and numbers G.B. HY05CS007 NEW YORK C/No.1-345	Number and kind of packages; Each packed in a plastic bag 10 of BG2046 in a carton 15 of BG2054 in a carton 20 of BG2053 in a carton	Description of goods 3 items of plush toy	
Signature			

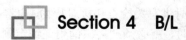

Section 4　B/L

提单是承运人和托运人之间处理运输中双方权利和义务的依据。虽然一般它不是由双方共同签字的一项契约，但构成契约的主要项目如船名、开航日期、航线、靠港及其他有关货运项目等是众所周知的；有运价和运输条件的，承运人也是事先规定的。因此，在托运人或其代理人向承运人订舱的时候就被认为契约即告成立，所以虽然条款内容是由承运人单方拟订，托运人也应当认为双方已认可，即成为运输契约，习惯上成了日后处理运输中各种问题的依据。

提单的缮制方法如下。

（1）提单编号（B/L No）。一般列在提单右上角，以便于工作联系和查核。发货人向收货人发送装船通知（Shipment Advice）时，也要列明船名和提单编号。

（2）托运人（Shipper）。此栏填写托运人的名称、地址，必要时也可填写代码。托运人一般为信用证中的受益人（出口商）。

（3）收货人（Consignee）。此栏填写收货人的名称、地址，必要时可填写电话、传真或代码。如要求记名提单，此栏可填上具体的收货人的名称；如属指示提单，则填"To order"或"To order of ×××"。

（4）通知方（Notify party）。这是船公司在货物到达目的港时发送到货通知的收件人，有时即为进口商。在信用证项下的提单，如信用证上对提单通知方有具体规定，则必须严格按照信用证要求填写。如果是记名提单或收货人指示提单，且收货人又有详细地址的，则此栏可以不写。如果是空白指示提单或托运人指示提单，则此栏必须填写通知方的名称与详细地址，否则船方就无法与收货人联系，收货人也不能及时报关提货。通知方一般为预定的收货人或收货人的代理人。

（5）船名（Name of Vessel）。此栏填写装运货物的船名及航次。若是已装船提单，必须填写船名；若是待运提单，待货物实际装船完毕后记载船名。

（6）接货地（Place of Receipt）。此栏在多式联运方式下填写，表明承运人接收到货物的地点，其运输条款可以是：门—门、门—场、门—站。

（7）装货港（Port of Loading）。此栏应填写实际装船港口的具体名称。

（8）卸货港（Port of Discharge）。此栏应填写实际卸下货物的港口的具体名称。如属转船，第一程提单上的卸货港填转船港，收货人填二程船公司；第二程提单上的装货港填上述的转船港，卸货港填最后的目的港。如由第一程船公司签发联运提单（Through B/L），则卸货港即可填写最后目的港，并在提单上列明第一和第二船名。如经某港转运，要显示"via ××"字样。填写此栏要注意同名港口的问题，如属选择港提单，要在此栏中注明。

（9）交货地（Place of Delivery）。此栏在多式联运方式下填写，表明承运人交付货物的地点，其运输条款可以是：门—门、场—门、站—门。

（10）货名（Description of Goods）。在信用证项下，货名必须与信用证上规定的货名一致。

（11）件数和包装种类（Number and kind of Package）。此栏按箱子的实际包装情况填写。在集装箱整箱货运输下，此栏通常填写集装箱的数量、型号（如：1×20 FT DC）；如果是在拼箱货运输下，此栏应填写货物件数（如：10 Cases Machinery）。

（12）唛头（Shipping Marks）。信用证上有规定的，必须按规定填写；否则可按发票上的唛头填写。

（13）毛重、尺码（Gross Weight，Measurement）。信用证上有规定的，必须按规定填写；否则一般以公斤为单位列出货物的毛重、以立方米列出货物的体积。

（14）运费与费用（Freight and Charges）。一般为预付（Freight Prepaid）或到付（Freight Collect）。如为CIF或CFR出口，一般均填上"运费预付"字样，千万不可漏填，否则收货人会因为运费未清问题而晚提货或提不到货。如系FOB出口，则运费可制作"运费到付"字样，除非收货人委托发货人垫付运费。

（15）提单的签发地点、日期和份数（Place and Date of Issue, Number of Original B(s)/L）。提单签发的地点原则上是装货地点，一般是在装货港或货物集中地签发。提单的签发日期应该是提单上所列货物实际装船完毕的日期，也应该与收货单上大副所签发的日期是一致的。如果是在跟单信用证项下结汇，提单上所签发的日期必须与信用证或合同上所要求的最后装船期一致或先于装船期。如果卖方估计货物无法在信用证规定的期限内装船，应尽早通知买方，要求修改信用证，而不应该利用"倒签提单"、"预借提单"等欺诈行为取得货款。提单份数一般按信用证要求出具，如"Full Set of"，一般理解为正本提单一式三份，每份都有同等效力，收货人凭其中一份提取货物后，其他各份自动失效。副本提单的份数可视托运人的需要而定。

（16）承运人或船长，或由其授权的人签字或盖章。

Shipper BRIGHT SHINE TOY CO., LTD.		B/L NO. cos 9815222	
Consignee CHINA OCEAN SHIPPING (GROUP) CO.		中国远洋运输（集团）总公司 **CHINA OCEAN SHIPPING (GROUP) CORP.** **Combined Transport BILL OF LADING**	
Notify Party BRIGHT-SHINE TOY CO., LTD.				
Pre-carriage by	Place of Receipt Guangzhou China		
Ocean Vessel Voy. No. Star 0011w	Port of Loading Guangzhou China		
Port of Discharge New York USA.	Place of Delivery New York USA.	Final Destination of the Goods New York USA.	
Marks & Nos. Container/Seal No.	No. of Containers or P'kgs	Kind of Packages; Description of Goods	Gross Weight	Measurement
G.B. HY05CS007 NEW YORK C/No. 1-345	345 CARTONS IN CT8684 CT8685 CT8686 CT3231	3 items of plush toy	13.26 ton	830 M^3
Total Number of Containers or Packages (In Words)				
Freight & Charges Freight prepaid US$14,851.2	Revenue Tons	Rate	Per	Prepaid All prepaid at Guangzhou	Collect
Exchange Rate	Prepaid at Guangzhou	Payable at	Place and Date of Issue Guangzhou, 2014-9-24	
	Total Prepaid	No. of Original B(S)/L THREE	Signed for the Carrier	
LADEN ON BOARD THE VESSEL DATE_____				

Section 5　Cargo Receipt

　　承运货物收据是指承运人出具给托运人的收据，也是承托双方的运输合同。收据背面印有"承运简章"，表明它适用于铁路、轮船、公路、航空等单种和多种联合运输。我国内地通过铁路运往港澳地区的出口货物，不论是以港澳为目的地还是为中转站的，发货人都委托中国外贸运输公司或其在各地的分公司承运货物。装车后，由上述部门签发"承运货物收据"，发货人据此连同其他相关单据结汇，而收货人凭以提货。承运货物收据一般出具一份正本，主要内容有：编号、托运人、收货人、被通知人、车号、运单号、装车日期、起运地、目的地、货物名称、件数、毛重、标记、运费支付声明、签发日期、承运人印章等。如果信用证要求出具正本两份，应照办。承运货物收据的签发日一定要与运单上的发车日一致，且一定要在实际发运以后或同日签发。

China National Foreign Trade Transportation Corporation Nanjing Branch

CARGO RECEIPT
承运货物收据

货运编号 No. 13475

第一联　（凭提货物）
发票号　No. 2433
合约号　No. 13542

委托人 Shipper
BRIGHT SHINE TOY CO., LTD.

收货人 Consignee
BRIGHT-SHINE TOY CO., LTD.

通知 Notify
BRIGHT SHINE TOY CO., LTD.

From **Nanjing**　Via　　To **HK**

发货日期：June 13, 2014
装运日期：June 13, 2014

车号：332

标记	件数	货物名称	附记
G.B. HY05CS007 HK C/No. 1-345	345 CARTONS	plush toy	

运费缴付地点
Freight Payable
全程运费在南京付讫

请向下列地点接洽提货
香港中国旅行社有限公司
CHINA TRAVEL SERVICE (HK) LTD.

FREIGHT PREPAID AT NANJING ROAD. CENTRAL. HONGKONG 押汇银行签收 Bank's Endorsement	CHINA TRAVEL BUILDING 77 QUEEN'S 收货人签收 Consignee's Signature
	中国对外贸易运输总公司南京分公司

杭州蓝海实业有限公司与西班牙客户进行贸易，签订 CIF 合同 HT078，将货物交由中国远洋运输（集团）总公司 [CHINA OCEAN SHIPPING (GROUP) CO.] 运输，L/C 指定的付款行为 Citibank，BARCELONA Branch，开列以下发票。

ZHEJIANG BLUE SEA IMPORT AND EXPORT CO., LTD.
ADD: 200 HEDONG ROAD, HANGZHOU, CHINA

COMMERCIAL INVOICE

Invoice No.: 08OIC08002
L/C No.: 9005BTY118934
Date: 9-Jan.-2014

GAYNER, S.A.
C/PALAU DE PLEGAMANS, 15
08213-PULINYA
(BARCELONA, SPAIN)

From SHANGHAI, CHINA To BARCELONA, SPAIN

Marks	Quantity and Descriptions	Amount
N/M FOB NINGBO PORT CHINA PACKED IN 10 CASES	GEAR PACK AS PER PROFORMA N/W: 12,628 KGS G/W: 12,828 KGS Measurement: 4.5 CBM	EUR12,053.60
	ZHEJIANG BLUE SEA IMPORT AND EXPORT CO., LTD. 程晓	

请根据上述发票内容，缮制下列票据。

（1）装箱单。

Issuer	
	PACKING LIST
To	
	Invoice No. / Date
Marks and numbers	Number and kind of packages / Description of goods

（2）提单。

Shipper	
	B/L NO.
Consignee	
	中国远洋运输（集团）总公司 **CHINA OCEAN SHIPPING (GROUP) CORP.**
Notify Party	
Pre-carriage by / Place of Receipt	**Combined Transport BILL OF LADING**
Ocean Vessel Voy. No. / Port of Loading	

Port of Discharge	Place of Delivery	Final Destination of the Goods (not the ship) see article 7 par (2)		
Marks & Nos. Container/Seal No.	No. of Containers or P'kgs	Kind of Packages; Description of Goods	Gross Weight	Measurement
Total Number of Containers or Packages (In Words)				
Freight & Charges	Revenue Tons	Rate	Per	Prepaid	Collect
Exchange Rate	Prepaid at	Payable at	Place and Date of Issue		
	Total Prepaid	No. of Original B(S)/L	Signed for the Carrier		
LADEN ON BOARD THE VESSEL DATE_____					

Chapter 15

Insurance Documents

在国际货物买卖业务中，海上保险是一个不可缺少的条件和环节。其中，业务量最大、涉及面最广的海上保险是海洋运输货物保险。进行货物投保时需要填写保单申请书，申请书的填写和保险单缮制的内容有重复，主要内容如下。

（1）正本保险单的份数。全套保险单包括三份正本和二份副本。在正本保险单上写有"The First Original"、"The Second Original"和"The Third Original"。

（2）发票号码。填写"As per invoice"或实际的发票号码。

（3）保单号次。填写由保险公司编制的保单号码

（4）被保险人。通常为出口商。如果信用证规定被保险人为凭指示抬头，填写"To order"。

（5）标记。填写唛头或"As per invoice No. XXXX"，如无唛头，填写"N/M"。

（6）数量。填写最大包装的总件数。

（7）被保险货物项目。填写商品名称，如果所有的单据要求指明信用证号码，应在此栏中标明。

（8）保险金额。可小写，一般按发票金额的110%投保。

（9）总保险金额。用大写的英文填写，用 only 结尾。

（10）保费/费率。通常不注明具体数字而分别印就"As arranged"（按协商）。有时"保费"栏可按信用证要求填写"Paid"、"Prepaid"。

（11）装载运输工具。填写"As per B/L"。海运方式下填写船名，最好再加航次，例如"FENG NING" V.9103；如整个运输由两次完成时，应分别填写一程船名及二程船名，中间用"/"隔开。此处可参考提单内容填制。例如，提单中一程船名为"Mayflower"，二程船名为"Dongfeng"，则填写"Mayflower/Dongfeng"。

（12）开航日期。填写"As per B/L"。如果需要转船，填写"Via XXX"。也可根据提单签发日具体填写。按照跟单信用证 600 号出版物规定，也允许填写提单签发前 5 天之内任何一天的日期。也可暂时不填，待签发提单后再填。

（13）承保险别。至少填写一种基本险，如有附加险，也应填明。投保的险别除注明险别名称外，还应注明险别适用的文本和日期。

（14）勘查理赔代理人。由保险公司选定，代理人的地址应详细填写。发生损失时，收货人通知其代理人进行勘查和赔款事宜。

（15）赔款偿付地点。根据合同或信用证填写，应标明偿付货币名称，如"At London in USD"。信用证要求，如发生货损，赔款付给×××公司（Loss if any, pay to … Co.），则在保险单"赔款偿付地点"栏后加注"Pay to … Co."。

（16）日期和地点。保险单签发的日期应早于提单日期。签发地点一般在受益人所在地。

Sample 1 Application Form for Marine Cargo Insurance

PICC 中国人民保险公司广州分公司
The People's Insurance Company of China, Guangzhou Branch

货物运输保险投保单
APPLICATION FORM FOR CARGO TRANSPORTAION INSURANCE

被保险人 INSURED: <u>BRIGHT SHINE TOY CO., LTD.</u>
发票号 (INVOICE NO.): TC030707
合同号 (CONTRACT NO.): HY05CS007
信用证号 (L/C NO.): AM/VAO1537ILC
发票金额 (INVOICE AMOUNT): <u>US$69,500</u>   投保加成（PLUS）: <u>110</u> %

兹有下列货物向 <u>as arranged</u> 投保。(INSURANCE IS REQUIRED ON THE FOLLOWING COMMODITIES.)

标记 MARKS & NOS.	数量及包装 QUANTITY	保险货物项目 DESCRIPTION OF GOODS	保险金额 AMOUNT INSURED
G.B. HY05CS007 NEW YORK C/No. 1-345	345 cartons	3 items of plush toy	US DOLLARS 75,450

启运日期：   装载运输工具：
DATE OF COMMENCEMENT <u>October 5, 2014</u>   PER CONVEYANCE <u>Star 0011w</u>
自   经   至
FROM <u>Guangzhou</u>   VIA_____   TO <u>New York, America</u>
提单号：   赔款偿付地点：
B/L NO. <u>COS9815222</u>   CLAIM PAYABLE AT <u>New York, America</u>
投保险别：(PLEASE INDICATE THE CONDITIONS AND/OR SPECIAL COVERAGES:)
<u>Covering Institute Cargo Clauses (A) and WPA clause of Institute Cargo Clauses</u>
请如实告知下列情况：（如"是"在［　］中打"√","不是"打"×"。）
IF ANY, PLEASE MARK "√" OR "×".

1. 货物种类：	袋装 [√]		散装 [ ]	冷藏 [ ]		液体 [ ]		活动物 [ ]		
	GOODS:	BAG/JUMBO	BULK	REEFER		LIQUID		LIVE ANIMAL		
	机器/汽车 [ ]			危险品等级 [ ]						
	MACHINE/AUTO			DANGEROUS CLASS						
2. 集装箱种类：	普通 [√]		开顶 [ ]	框架 [ ]		平板 [ ]		冷藏 [ ]		
	CONTAINER:	ORDINARY	OPEN	FRAME		FLAT		REFRIFERATOR		
3. 转运工具：	海轮 [√]		飞机 [ ]	驳船 [ ]		火车 [ ]		汽车 [ ]		
	BY TRANSIT:	SHIP	PLANE	BARGE		TRAIN		TRUCK		
4. 船舶资料：			船籍 [China]		船龄 [6]					
	PARTICYULAR OF SHIP:		REGISTRY		AGE					

备注：被保险人确认本保险合同条款和内容已经完全了解。
THE ASSURED CONFIRMS HEREWITH THE TERMS AND CONDITIONS OF THIS INSURANCE CONTRACT FULLY UNDERSTOOD.

投保人（签名盖章）
APPLICANT'S SIGNATURE

BRIGHT SHINE TOY CO., LTD.

Jin Taya

电话（TEL）：020-77658866
投保日期（DATE）：September 26, 2014
地址（ADD）：No. 2-8-30 Jinhui Building No. 71 South Zhongshan Rd, Tianhe District, PRC

Sample 2 Cargo Transportation Insurance Policy

中国人民财产保险股份有限公司货物运输保险单
PICC PROPERTY AND CASUALTY COMPANY LIMITED CARGO TRANSPORTATION INSURANCE POLICY

总公司设于北京　　　　一九四九创立
Head Office: Beijing　　　Established in 1949

印刷号（Printed Number）　　　　保险单号（Policy No.）PICCGI 054321
合同号（Contract NO.）HY05CSO07
发票号（Invoice NO.）TC030707
信用证号（L/C NO.）AM/VAO1537ILC
被保险人（Insured）BRIGHT SHINE TOY CO., LTD.

中国人民财产保险股份有限公司（以下简称本公司）根据被保险人的要求，以被保险人向本公司缴付约定的保险费为对价，按照本保险单列明条款承保下述货物运输保险，特订立本保险单。

THIS POLICE OF INSURANCE WITNESSES THAT PICC PROPERTY AND CASUALTY COMPANY LIMITED (HEREINAFTER CALLED "THE COMPANY") AT THE REQUEST OF THE INSURED AND IN CONSIDERATION OF THE AGREED PREMIUM PAID TO THE COMPANY BY THE INSURED, UNDERTAKES TO INSURE THE UNDERMENTIONED GOODS IN TRANSPORTATION SUBJECT TO THE CONDITION OF THIS POLICY AS PER THE CLAUSES PRINTED BELOW.

标 记 MARKS & NOS.	包装及数量 QUANTITY	保险货物项目 GOODS	保险金额 AMOUNT INSURED
G.B. HY05CSO07 NEW YORK C/NO. 1-345	345 Cartons	3 items of plush toy	US DOLLARS 75,450

总保险金额：
Total Amount Insured: Say US DOLLARS Seventy-five thousand four hundred and fifty Only

保费（Premium）： AS ARRANGED

启运日期（Date of Commencement）： AS OER B/L

装载运输工具（Per Conveyance）： S.S. STAR 0011W

自　　　　　　　　　　经　　　　　　　　　到
From　　Guangzhou　　　Via　　　　　　　　To New York, America

承保险别（Conditions）: Covering Institute Cargo Clause (A) and WPA Cargo Clause

所保货物，如发生保险单项下可能引起索赔的损失，应立即通知本公司或下述代理人查勘。如有索赔，应向本公司提交正本保险单（本保险单共有___3___份正本）及有关文件，如一份正本已用于索赔，其余正本自动失效。

IN THE EVENT OF LOSS OR DAMAGE WHICH MAY RESULT IN A CLAIM UNDER THIS POLICY, IMMEDIATE NOTICE MUST BE GIVEN TO THE COMPANY'S AGENT AS MENTIONED. CLAIMS, IF ANY, ONE OF THE ORIGINAL POLICY WHICH HAS BEEN ISSUED IN _____3_____ ORIGINAL(S) TOGETHER WITH THE RELEVENT DOCUMENTS ALL BE SURRENDERED TO THE COMPANY. IF ONE OF THE ORIGINAL POLICY HAS BEEN ACCOMPLISHED, THE OTHERS TO BE VOID.

保险人：中国人民保险公司广州市分公司
Underwriter: PICC, Guangzhou Branch

电话（TEL）：		
传真（FAX）：		
地址（ADD）：		
赔款偿付地点：		
Claim Payable at ___New York in US Dollars___	授权人签字： ___李明明___	
签单日期（Issuing Date）___September 26, 2014___	Authorized Signature _____	
核保人：	制单人：	经办人：

请根据下列资料制作保险单。

L/C NO. AND DATE: 2AG8-325001 DATED MAY 10, 2014
INVOICE NO. AND DATE: 004858 DATED JUNE 25, 2014
BENEFICIARY: ZHEJIANG SUNFLOWER FOREING TRADE CORP.
APPLICANT: TRADEPORT AB. INDUSTRIESTRASSE 65, BETZDORT, GERMANY
EVIDENCING SHIPMENT OF: WORK CLOTHES AS PER CONTRACT NO. HX091112, 1,500 SETS AT EUR20 PER SET, CIF HAMBURG
SHIPMENT: FROM SHANGHAI, CHINA TO HAMBURG, GERMANY
NOT LATER THAN JULY 12, 2014 BY SEA
DOCUMENTS REQUIRED:
+ INSURACE POLICY OR CERTIFICATE IN DUPLICATE ENDORSED IN BLAND FOR 110PCT OR INVOICE VALUE COVERING MARINE INSTITUTE CARGO CLAUSES ALL RISKS AND WAR RISKS AS PER OCEAN MARINE CARGO CLAUSES 1/1/81 OF THE PICC. INSURANCE CLAIMS TO BE PAYABLE IN GERMANY IN THE CURRENCY OF THE DRAFTS.
+ A CERTIFICATE OF ORIGING ISSUED BY AN AUTHORITY IN CHINA

中国人民保险公司上海分公司

海洋货物运输保险单

发票号次	保单号次
Invoice No. 07SHGD3029	NP47/12

中国人民保险公司（以下简称本公司）根据（以下简称被保险人）的要求，由被保险人向本公司缴付约定的保险费，按照本保险单承保险别和背面所载条款与下列特殊条款承

保下述货物运输保险，特立本保险单。

This Policy of Insurance witnesses that People's Insurance Company of China (hereinafter called "the Company") at the request of _____ (hereinafter called "the Insured") and in consideration of the agreed premium being paid to the Company by the Insured, undertakes to insure the under-mentioned goods in transportation subject to the condition of this Policy as per the Clause printed overleaf and other special clauses attached hereon.

标记 Marks and Nos.	包装及数量 Quantity	保险货物项目 Description of Goods	保险金额 Amount Insured
N/M	1500 SETS	_____	_____

总保险金额：
Total amount insured: _____

保费　　　　　　　　　费率　　　　　　　　　装载工具运输
Premium　as arranged　Rate　as arranged　Per Conveyance　S.S. EVERBRIGHT 0056W

开航日期　　　　　　　　自　　　　　　　　　　至
Sailing on　July 10, 2014　from _____　　　to _____

承保险别
Conditions: _____

所保货物，如遇出险，本公司凭第一正本保险单及其有关证件给付赔偿款。所保如发生本保险单项下负责赔偿的损失或事故，应立即通知本公司代理人勘察。

Claims, if any, are payable on surrender of the first original of the Policy together with other relevant documents. In the event of accident whereby loss or damage may result in a claim under this Policy, immediate notice applying for survey must be given to the Company's Agent.

Claims payable at _____
Date _____

中国人民保险公司上海分公司

Part 4

Simulation Training in Business Correspondence

Chapter 16

Simulation Training in Business Correspondence (1)

1. Background Information

Ms. Joanne Zhang, sales manager of Poseidon Trading Co., Ltd., sourced the following information.

Company Name: Roslyns Emporium

About Us: We are selling gifts in the UK, but want to buy Ladies Fashion, Jewelry, Handbags, Gifts, Greeting Cards, etc. from other countries.

Contact Person: Ms. Roslyn Calder, Overseas Department Manager

Telephone: 44-01651-851260

Address: 3 Pringle Avenue, Tarves, Aberdeenshire, ab417nz, United Kingdom

Website: http://www.RoslynsEmporium.co.uk

The following are details of Joanne Zhang's company.

Company Name: Poseidon Trading Co., Ltd.

Main Markets: South America, Asia and USA currently

Product: 100% Handmade EMB Camisole, 100% Handmade Beads EMB Slim Bag, 100% Handmade Beads EMB Handbag, 100% Handmade Beads EMB Top

Contact Person: Ms. Joanne Zhang, Sales Manager

Telephone: 86-755-88261899

Fax: 86-755-88261880

Address: 4/F, Bonham Centre, 79-85 Bonham Strand East, Sheung Wan, Hong Kong

Website: public.fotki.com/Handbag/

2. Training Procedures
Step One

Joanne logins on the website of this company and finds it is reliable, so she writes a letter of inquiry to Roslyn.

To: "Ms. Roslyn Calder" <RoslynCalder@RoslynsEmporium.com>
From: "Ms. Joanne Zhang" <PoseidonTrading@hotmail.com>
Date: January 10, 2014
Subject: Establishing Business Relationship

Step Two

Roslyn Calder replies immediately after receiving the letter.

To: "Ms. Joanne Zhang" <PoseidonTrading@hotmail.com>
From: "Ms. Roslyn Calder" <RoslynCalder@RoslynsEmporium.com>
Date: January 11, 2014
Subject: Establishing Business Relationship

Dear Joanne,

Thank you for your letter of January 10. We are glad to enter into business relations with you.

As you know, we have been specializing in gifts in the UK for years, and are interested in Ladies Fashion, Jewelry, Handbags, Gifts, Greeting Cards, etc. from other countries.

We are currently interested in your 100% Handmade Beads EMB Slim Bag and 100% Handmade Beads EMB Handbag. Pricelist and your illustrated catalogue will be greatly appreciated.

We are looking forward to your early reply.

Sincerely yours,

Roslyn Calder
Overseas Department Manager

Step Three

Upon getting the reply from Roslyn, Joanne sends an e-mail back immediately.

To: " Ms. Roslyn Calder "< RoslynCalder@RoslynsEmporium.com>
From: "Ms. Joanne Zhang"< PoseidonTrading@hotmail.com >
Date: January 11, 2014
Subject: Pricelist and Catalogues

Step Four

Roslyn thinks the prices are a little higher than expected, so she replies, asking for 10% less than the original ones and FOB price rather than CIF price. She says the prices for beads EMB bags are dropping in international market. She hopes to get delivery within one month after order confirmed.

To: "Ms. Joanne Zhang"< Poseidon Trading@hotmail.com >
From: " Ms. Roslyn Calder "< RoslynCalder@RoslynsEmporium.com>
Date: January 12, 2014
Subject: Price Term

Dear Joanne,

Thanks for the offer attached in your last e-mail. We appreciate the good quality of your goods, but unfortunately, we are not in a position to accept the offer on your terms. Your price appears to be on rather high side. Actually we can obtain the products with similar quality through another channel at a much lower price than you quoted us.

As you know, the market for Beads EMB Bags is declining.

May we suggest that you make some allowance, say 10% on your quoted price, which would help to push the sales of your goods in our markets. If you can do so, we will possibly make regular orders from you. We hope you will take advantage of this chance so that both of us will benefit from the expanding market.

We will appreciate it very much if you will consider our counter offer favorably and fax us your acceptance as soon as possible.

We can only do business on FOB basis, and would like you to convert your CIF prices into FOB prices. In addition, we hope to get delivery within one month after order confirmed.

Sincerely yours,

Roslyn

Step Five

Joanne sends an e-mail back immediately.

To: "Ms. Roslyn Calder"< RoslynCalder@RoslynsEmporium.com>
From: "Ms. Joanne Zhang"< Poseidon Trading@hotmail.com >
Date: January 13, 2014
Subject: Price Term

Step Six

Roslyn accepts Joanne's offer and places an order: 100% Handmade Beads EMB Slim Bag: Item No. SB356: 200 bags, SB357: 100 bags, SB358: 150 bags; 100% Handmade Beads EMB Handbag: Item No. HB202: 150 bags, HB203: 200 bags, HB204: 200 bags, HB205: 250 bags. She also refers to shipment and terms of payment — by 30-day L/C instead of sight L/C.

To: "Ms. Joanne Zhang"< Poseidon Trading@hotmail.com >
From: "Ms. Roslyn Calder"< RoslynCalder@RoslynsEmporium.com>
Date: January 14, 2014
Subject: Our Order No. JB369 for Handmade Beads EMB Bags

Dear Joanne,

Thank you for your quotation of January 13. We are glad to place an order with you for the captioned goods on the terms and conditions as below:

Article: 100% handmade beads EMB slim bag and handbag

Item No.	Quantity (bag)	Unit Price (in USD)
SB356	150	8.5
SB357	100	10
SB358	120	11
HB202	130	12
HB203	100	13
HB204	150	15
HB205	100	16

Payment: payable by irrevocable confirmed sight L/C on FOB Hong Kong
Shipment: not later than February 29
Packing: each in an air bubble plastic bag, 10 in a box and 50 boxes in a carton

Since this is the first order, we will pay special attention to the quality.

Looking forward to receiving our order early.

Sincerely yours,

Roslyn

Step Seven

Joanne acknowledges acceptance of the order and promises to fulfill the order as required. She reminds Roslyn to open the L/C timely.

To: "Ms. Roslyn Calder"< RoslynCalder@RoslynsEmporium.com>
From: "Ms. Joanne Zhang"< Poseidon Trading@hotmail.com >
Date: January 16, 2014
Subject: Your Order No. JB369

Step Eight

Roslyn opens the L/C and sends details to Joanne

To: "Ms. Joanne Zhang"< Poseidon Trading@hotmail.com >
From: "Ms. Roslyn Calder"< RoslynCalder@RoslynsEmporium.com>
Date: January 19, 2014
Subject: Opening L/C

Dear Joanne,

We are pleased to inform you that we have opened L/C No. 116369 for USD10,350 under our order No. JB369 on CIF basis on January 18 through "Bank of China, London Branch" to your bank.

Please check and confirm us by cable.

Sincerely yours,

Roslyn

Step Nine

Joanne opens the e-mail, but she finds some discrepancies in the L/C: the total amount is wrong: not USD10,350, but USD10,305, price terms not CIF, but FOB. Joanne sends Roslyn an e-mail immediately, requiring her to amend the L/C soon.

To: "Ms. Roslyn Calder"< RoslynCalder@RoslynsEmporium.com>
From: "Ms. Joanne Zhang"< Poseidon Trading@hotmail.com >
Date: January 20, 2014
Subject: L/C Amendment

Step Ten

Roslyn makes amendment of the L/C, feeling very sorry for her carelessness.

To: "Ms. Joanne Zhang"< Poseidon Trading@hotmail.com >
From: "Ms. Roslyn Calder"< RoslynCalder@RoslynsEmporium.com>
Date: January 21, 2014
Subject: L/C Amendment

Dear Joanne,

We are so sorry to learn from your last letter that there are some discrepancies in the L/C No. 116369.

We have made the relevant amendments as required and to save time, we have cabled the amended L/C to you. Please check and confirm by fax.

Thank you for your consideration and we apologize for the inconvenience and trouble caused.

Sincerely yours,

Roslyn

Step Eleven

Joanne receives the correctly amended L/C, and ships the goods. Then she dispatches shipping documents immediately and asks for payment.

To: "Ms. Roslyn Calder"< RoslynCalder@RoslynsEmporium.com>
From: "Ms. Joanne Zhang"< Poseidon Trading@hotmail.com>
Date: February 2, 2014
Subject: Asking for Payment

Step Twelve

Roslyn received the goods, but found a mistake of the number ordered for: Article No. SB356 is 100, not 150 and Article No. SB357is 150 not 100.

To: "Ms. Joanne Zhang"< Poseidon Trading@hotmail.com>
From: "Ms. Roslyn Calder"< RoslynCalder@RoslynsEmporium.com>
Date: March 16, 2014
Subject: Wrong Delivery of Order No. JB369

Dear Joanne,

We are pleased to inform you that the handmade EMB bags under our order No. JB369 have arrived. However, on unpacking the boxes, we found serious mistakes in the number of Article No. SB356 and Article No. SB357. For your detailed information, we attach a copy of our order and one of the packing list.

Please confirm the problem and solve it soon, instructing us how we should deal with the surplus in our hands currently.

Sincerely yours,

Roslyn

Step Thirteen

Receiving Roslyn's e-mail, Joanne replies immediately, explaining the reason for the mistake: a newly-employed college employee caused the error when the order was outbound. Joanne also provides ways to solve the problem.

To: "Ms. Roslyn Calder"< RoslynCalder@RoslynsEmporium.com >
From: "Ms. Joanne Zhang"< Poseidon Trading@hotmail.com >
Date: March 19, 2014
Subject: Complaint Settlement

Step Fourteen

Receiving Joanne's e-mail, Roslyn replies to accept the additional 50 bags of Article No. SB356 for 10% discount but cancel the 50 bags of Article No. SB357.

To: "Ms. Joanne Zhang"< Poseidon Trading@hotmail.com >
From: "Ms. Roslyn Calder"< RoslynCalder@RoslynsEmporium.com>
Date: March 21, 2014
Subject: Settlement of Order No. JB369

Dear Joanne,

Thanks for your last e-mail. After careful consideration, we have made a decision to accept the additional 50 bags of Article No. SB356 for 10% discount. However, for the sake of your convenience, we have to cancel the 50 bags of Article No. SB357.

If this trial order proves successful, we will place substantial orders with you.

Sincerely yours,

Roslyn

Step Fifteen

Joanne replies, expressing her appreciation for Roslyn's help to solve the problem and hoping for more business in the future.

To: "Ms. Roslyn Calder"< RoslynCalder@RoslynsEmporium.com>
From: "Ms. Joanne Zhang"< Poseidon Trading@hotmail.com >
Date: March 23, 2014
Subject: Thanks for Your Consideration

Chapter 17

Simulation Training in Business Correspondence (2)

1. Background Information

Abbott Shan from Sales Department of Good Fortune Trade Company, at 165 Zhongshan Road, Yuexiu District, Guangzhou, China, puts an advertisement on alibaba.com, introducing his company as follows:

Company Name: Good Fortune Trade Company

About Us: Our company is one of the greatest import and export companies in China . We mainly export electronic and electrical appliances, light industrial products and chemicals. Our imported goods include information technology products, luxurious automobiles and cosmetic products.

Contact Person: Abbott Shan, Sales Department

Telephone: 86-020-3895689   **Fax:** 86-020-3895688

Address: 165 Zhongshan Road, Yuexiu District, Guangzhou, China,
Zip Code 510600

Website: http://www.gftc.com

By chance, Abbott Shan read about Hunter & Co., Ltd. as below:

Company Name: Hunter & Co., Ltd., a 15-year's experience importer

Product: Electronic products

Contact Person: Lucas Stephan (Mr.), Overseas Department Manager

Telephone: 0064-4-3895678

Fax: 0064-4-3895679

Address: 320 Royal Parades, Wellington, 6011, New Zealand

Then, Abbott Shan writes a letter of inquiry to Hunter & Co., Ltd. Thus, in order to succeed in trading with each other, Abbott Shan and Lucas Stephan exchange correspondence.

2. Training Procedures

Step One

Abbott Shan writes a letter of inquiry to Hunter & Co., Ltd.

Good Fortune Trade Company
165 Zhongshan Road, Yuexiu District, Guangzhou, China, Zip Code 510600
Telephone: 86-020-3895689   Fax: 86-020-3895688

March 20, 2014

Hunter & Co., Ltd.
320 Royal Parade,
Wellington, New Zealand

Dear Sirs,

From the Chamber of Commerce of Beijing, we have learned your firm. We take the pleasure of addressing this letter in the hope of establishing direct business relations with you.

Our company is one of the greatest import and export companies in China and has wide experience in all the lines we handle. We mainly export electronic and electrical appliances, light industrial products and chemicals.

Our imported goods include information technology products, luxurious automobiles and cosmetic products.

We are looking forward to a productive trade between us.

Yours faithfully,

Abbott Shan
Sales Department

Step Two

Upon receiving the letter, Lucas Stephan writes a letter in reply, expressing his willingness to enter into business relationship, making a brief self-introduction, asking for some information and material. Now, please write a letter for Hunter & Co., Ltd.

Hunter & Co., Ltd.
320 Royal Parade, Wellington, 6011, New Zealand
Telephone: 0064-4-3895678   Fax: 0064-4-3895679

March 21, 2014

Good Fortune Trade Company
165 Zhongshan Road,
Yuexiu District, Guangzhou, China

Step Three

Now, Abbott Shan writes a letter in reply.

Good Fortune Trade Company
165 Zhongshan Road, Yuexiu District, Guangzhou, China, Zip Code 510600
Telephone: 86-020-3895689   Fax: 86-020-3895688

March 22, 2014

Hunter & Co., Ltd.
320 Royal Parade,
Wellington, New Zealand

Dear Lucas,

Thank you for your letter of March 21 of your willingness to trade with us.

Please read the attached files for specific information required in your last letter. Also attached you will find our latest catalogue and pricelist.

We usually accept irrevocable sight L/C.

We hope to receive your reply soon.

Best regards.

Abbott Shan

Step Four

Lucas Stephan writes a letter, showing interest in Electronic Products Catalogue, Model No. 0369, 0370 and Item No. 0381, 0382, and 0383. Lucas asks Abbott to make him an offer. Now, please write a letter for Lucas.

Hunter & Co., Ltd.
320 Royal Parade, Wellington, 6011, New Zealand
Telephone: 0064-4-3895678   Fax: 0064-4-3895679

March 24, 2014

Good Fortune Trade Company
165 Zhongshan Road,
Yuexiu District, Guangzhou, China

Step Five

Now, Abbott Shan makes an offer.

Good Fortune Trade Company
165 Zhongshan Road, Yuexiu District, Guangzhou, China, Zip Code 510600
Telephone: 86-020-3895689   Fax: 86-020-3895688

March 24, 2014

Hunter & Co., Ltd.
320 Royal Parade,
Wellington, New Zealand

Dear Lucas,

Thank you for your letter of this morning of your interest in our Electronic Products.

We are in a position to supply electronic products in various models and functions. We take pleasure in making you an offer as follows:

Price: Model No. 0369, USD12/set; 0370, USD12.8/set
    Item No. 0381, USD10/piece; 0382, USD10/piece and 0383, USD10.5/piece
    FOB Guangzhou
Payment: by irrevocable confirmed sight L/C
Discount: 3% for total amount of USD5,000, another 0.5% for every USD1,000 more, with 10% as the highest, no discount for total amount less than USD5,000
Shipment: within one month after order confirmed
Validity: one week from the date quoted

We hope the above terms and conditions are acceptable to you and may become the basis of our future business.

Looking forward to receiving your order early.

Sincerely yours,

Abbott

Step Six

After receiving the offer, Lucas replies immediately, placing an order.

Hunter & Co., Ltd.
320 Royal Parade, Wellington, 6011, New Zealand
Telephone: 0064-4-3895678   Fax: 0064-4-3895679

March 26, 2014

Good Fortune Trade Company
165 Zhongshan Road,
Yuexiu District, Guangzhou, China

Step Seven

Abbott confirms receipt of the order and writes a letter to Lucas.

Good Fortune Trade Company

165 Zhongshan Road, Yuexiu District, Guangzhou, China, Zip Code 510600

Telephone: 86-020-3895689   Fax: 86-020-3895688

March 27, 2014

Hunter & Co., Ltd.
320 Royal Parade,
Wellington, New Zealand

Dear Lucas,

Re: Your order No. EP5398

We are pleased to receive your order. It is almost ready for shipment. Please arrange the payment and open the relevant L/C timely so as to avoid any delay in shipment.

Thanks.

Sincerely yours

Abbott

Step Eight

Lucas opens the L/C as required and gives Abbott a notification.

Hunter & Co., Ltd.
320 Royal Parade, Wellington, 6011, New Zealand
Telephone: 0064-4-3895678   Fax: 0064-4-3895679

March 31, 2014

Good Fortune Trade Company
165 Zhongshan Road,
Yuexiu District, Guangzhou, China

Step Nine

Having learned the information from Abbott that the L/C has reached Bank of China, Guangzhou Branch, Lucas writes a letter to Abbott, giving him details concerning shipping vessel.

Hunter & Co., Ltd.
320 Royal Parade, Wellington, 6011, New Zealand
Telephone: 0064-4-3895678   Fax: 0064-4-3895679

April 3, 2014

Good Fortune Trade Company
165 Zhongshan Road,
Yuexiu District, Guangzhou, China

Dear Abbott,

We are glad to learn that the L/C has reached you. Please be noted that we have authorized AIRNET INTERNATIONAL LOGISTICS CO., LTD. for the transportation of the order. Details are as follows:

OCEAN VESSEL VOY. NO. : Princess, OSC 3289
PORT OF LOADING: Guangzhou
LAYTIME: Weather Working Days of 24 Hours, from April 10 to 15
ETD: April 16

Please check and make necessary arrangement for shipment ASAP.

Sincerely,

Lucas

Step Ten

As soon as the order is delivered, Abbott writes a letter to Lucas, informing him of the detailed shipment information, dispatching transportation documents.

Good Fortune Trade Company
165 Zhongshan Road, Yuexiu District, Guangzhou, China, Zip Code 510600
Telephone: 86-020-3895689   Fax: 86-020-3895688

April 14, 2014

Hunter & Co., Ltd.
320 Royal Parade,
Wellington, New Zealand

Dear Lucas,

We are glad to inform you that your Order No. EP5398 has been shipped on board S.S. Princess as required, which is scheduled to sail for Guangzhou on April 16.

The relevant shipping documents are enclosed herewith. Please check.

As agreed, we will draw upon you a sight draft. Please honor it.

We look forward to your further orders.

Yours sincerely,

Abbott

Step Eleven

A month later, Lucas takes delivery of the goods and writes to Abbott, expecting to have further deals.

Hunter & Co., Ltd.
320 Royal Parade, Wellington, 6011, New Zealand
Telephone: 0064-4-3895678   Fax: 0064-4-3895679

May 20, 2014

Good Fortune Trade Company
165 Zhongshan Road,
Yuexiu District, Guangzhou, China

Chapter 18

Simulation Training in Business Correspondence (3)

1. Background Information

Alisa, sales manager of Nanjing Textile Import & Export Co., Ltd., releases profile information of her company online as follows, in the hope of establishing business relationship with overseas buyers.

Company Name: Nanjing Textile Import & Export Co., Ltd.
Address: 77, North Yunnan Road, Nanjing China, Nanjing, Jiangsu, China
Telephone: 025-83305588   Fax: 025-83300-518
E-mail: nantex@nantex.com.cn
Website: http://www.nantex.com.cn
Brief Introduction: Nanjing Textiles I/E Co., Ltd, established in 1978, and now we are a leading company specializing in textiles and garments manufacturing and exporting. Our products range from textiles, garments and toys. And our department, Garment Dept. 2, has more than 20 years' experience in cooperation with European, USA, Canadian and Australian clients. We are in a position to accept orders against customers' samples, specifying designs and packing requirements. We are also prepared to accept orders with customers own trademarks and brand names. And our strong items are jackets, skiwear, activewear, pants, jeans, children wear, and ect. (mainly woven). If you have buying office in China, Could you inform us their contact information? We can bring samples there. If you have any problem, please feel free to contact us.

Nicola Alu, General Manager of NENON INTERNATIONAL GARMENTS & TEXTILES, makes an advertisement as follows on alibaba.com, hoping to purchase textile products.

Company Name: NENON INTERNATIONAL GARMENTS & TEXTILES
About Us: We are the importer of all kinds of garments/textiles, such as t-shirts, polo shirts, jeans wears, all kinds of ladies wears, all kinds of children's wears, bed sheets etc. So we are looking for strong standard manufacturers and exporters of the above mentioned products to have a long trust mutual business transaction.
Product/Service in Demand: T-shirts, shirts & blouses, Polo Shirts
Country/Region: American Samoa
Contact Person: Mr. Nicola Alu, General Manager
E-mail: nigt@nigt.com.cn
Telephone: 684-228-9226604

Fax: 684-228-2218125

Address: 32 Rue Chemin De Fer, Lome, American Samoa, 41922

Alisa, sales manager of Nanjing Textile Import & Export Co., Ltd. reads Mr. Nicola Alu's advertisement and writes an inquiry letter and e-mails it to Mr. Nicola Alu. Mr. Nicola Alu is glad to receive Alisa's e-mail.

Now, writes to one of your classmates, who is supposed to be Mr. Nicola Alu. And you are required to write to each other, simulating every procedure of a transaction, including inquiry, offer, counter-offer, ordering, confirming the order, payment issues, packing requirement/proposal, shipment, insurance and complaint or claim.

2. Training Procedures

Step One Inquiry

Alisa writes an inquiry letter and e-mails it to Mr. Nicola Alu, making a brief self-introduction of her company, in the hope of establishing business relationship with this overseas buyer.

To:
From:
Date:
Subject:

Step Two Reply to the Inquiry

Nicola Alu receives the e-mail from Alisa and replies to express his willingness to establish business relations, showing interest in textiles and garments, inviting an offer and asking for the latest pricelists and catalogues.

To:
From:
Date:
Subject:

Step Three   An Offer

Upon getting the reply from Nicola Alu, Alisa sends an e-mail back immediately, making an offer to Mr. Nicola Alu, giving payment requirement — confirmed, irrevocable letter of credit, proving the information and material needed.

To:
From:
Date:
Subject:

Step Four Counter-offer

Upon receipt of the offer from Alisa, Nicola Alu makes a counter-offer, considering the price on the high side, asking for a 15% discount for a total purchase of USD10,000, confirming a 60-day confirmed, irrevocable letter of credit for terms of payment.

To:
From:
Date:
Subject:

Step Five A Firm Offer

Following Alu's counter-offer, Alisa makes a firm offer subject to reply within one week — **Price:** as shown in the pricelist, for a 15% discount; **Total amount:** at least USD10,000; **Payment:** confirmed, irrevocable letter of credit payable by draft at sight to be opened 30 days before the time of shipment; **Shipment:** within 30 days after receipt of the relevant L/C.

To:
From:
Date:
Subject:

Step Six   Order

Nicola Alu accepts the firm offer and places an order: Oder No. 289.

QNTY	Item No.	Description	Unit Price
500	CW121	Cotton	USD6 FOB Nanjing
500	CW122	Cotton	USD8 FOB Nanjing
1,000	PS108	Silk	USD25 FOB Nanjing
1,000	PS109	Cotton	USD20 FOB Nanjing
1,000	JW209	Cotton	USD15 FOB Nanjing
1,000	TS202	Cotton	USD15 FOB Nanjing
1,000	TS203	Silk	USD20 FOB Nanjing

All the other terms should be applicable as agreed.

To:
From:
Date:
Subject:

Step Seven Order Acknowledgment

Alisa loses no time to acknowledge the order with expression of thanks, assuring Alu of prompt and careful execution of order, expressing her desire for future orders, restating the key contents of the order, the shipping instructions, the terms of payment and attaching catalogues of other products likely to be of interest and a Sales Confirmation in duplicate for counter-signature.

To:
From:
Date:
Subject:

Step Eight Urging the Establishment of L/C

Two weeks after acknowledging the order, Alisa still has not received any information about the opening of the L/C from Nicola Alu, she writes an e-mail to urge the establishment of the L/C.

To:
From:
Date:
Subject:

Step Nine Informing the Establishment of L/C

Nicola Alu replies Alisa, explaining the reasons for delaying opening of the L/C, informing her of the details of the relevant L/C, such as L/C No., the amount, the opening date, opening bank, advising bank, and etc.

To:
From:
Date:
Subject:

Step Ten L/C Amendment & Extension

Alisa receives the L/C, finding some discrepancies concerning terms of payment and total amount in figure. So, she writes Nicola Alu a letter immediately, requiring the L/C to be amended by cable accordingly soon, and the shipment date and L/C expiry date to be extended.

To:
From:
Date:
Subject:

Step Eleven Giving Shipping Instructions and Packing Requirements

After receiving Alisa's confirmation of the L/C amendment, Nicola Alu writes Alisa an e-mail, giving shipping instructions, shipping mark and packing requirements: each in an inner box and 10 boxes in an export carton, lined with waterproof plastic sheet.

To:
From:
Date:
Subject:

Step Twelve Giving Shipping Advice and Dispatching Shipping Documents

Alisa, having gotten Alu's shipping instructions and packing requirements, makes arrangement of the shipping of the order immediately. Then she gives Alu shipping advice: ETD and ETA, name of the vessel, packing Nos. shipping mark and etc, asking Alu to cover the order for insurance. She also dispatches the shipping documents, asking for acceptance of the 30-day draft.

To:
From:
Date:
Subject:

Step Thirteen   Sending Information about Insurance Coverage

Nicola Alu receives the details about shipment from Alisa and arranges insurance immediately. Then he replies, informing Alisa of the insurance coverage of the order.

To:
From:
Date:
Subject:

Step Fourteen Complaint

Nicola Alu takes delivery of the goods. But on unpacking, he finds some errors: for item No. TS203, the 1,000 articles are cotton not silk. He writes an e-mail to Alisa, requiring her to reship the goods needed soon, also asking the way to deal with the wrongly-delivered t-shirts.

To:
From:
Date:
Subject:

Step Fifteen Reply to the Complaint

Alisa replies to make an apology and proposes ways to solve the problems, ensuring him to avoid such mistakes, promising to offer special allowance.

To:
From:
Date:
Subject:

Step Sixteen Acceptance of the Complaint Settlement

Nicola Alu receives Alisa's reply and accepts her way to solve the problem on the condition that a 5% percent discount should be offered.

To:
From:
Date:
Subject:

Step Seventeen   Settlement of the Complaint

Alisa replies to accept Alu's requirement, providing more information about the latest products, hoping for more business between each other, ensuring Alu to fulfill the future order accurately.

To:
From:
Date:
Subject:

参 考 文 献

[1] DWYER J. The business communication handbook. 4th ed. New Jersey: Prentice Hall, 2003.
[2] PERELMAN L, PARADIS J, BARRETT E. The mayfield handbook of technical and Scientific Writing. Mountain View, CA: Mayfield Publishing Company, 1998.
[3] STIRK N. 商务英语写作王. 西安：陕西师范大学出版社，2010.
[4] 曹菱. 商务英语信函. 北京：外语教学与研究出版社，2000.
[5] 陈良璇. 商务英语函件与单证. 郑州：河南人民出版社，2004.
[6] 陈庆勋，耿纪永，程浩东. 英语应用文写作大全. 北京：社会科学文献出版社，2003.
[7] 程同春. 新编国际商务英语函电. 南京：东南大学出版社，2001.
[8] 冯祥春，刘卓林. 外贸英语函电句型 150 例. 南京：南京大学出版社，1994.
[9] 胡亦武. 实用商务英语写作. 广州：华南理工大学出版社，2003.
[10] 黄玛莉. 现代商务英文写作. 北京：世界图书出版社，2004.
[11] 戚云方. 新编外经贸英语函电与谈判. 杭州：浙江大学出版社，2005.
[12] 王兴孙. 新编进出口英语函电. 上海：上海交通大学出版社，2001.
[13] 诸葛霖. 外贸业务英文函电. 北京：对外经济贸易大学出版社，2003.
[14] http://bbs.cnool.net/cthread-2551990.html.
[15] http://www.ezysoft-dev.com/blog/purchase-order.
[16] www.picc.com.cn.
[17] http://www.lupinworks.com/roche/pages/memos.php.
[18] http://www.omafra.gov.on.ca/english/rural/facts/05-037.htm.
[19] http://www.ehow.com/info_7758187_definition-business-reports.html#ixzz30Kp3QVBG.
[20] http://baike.baidu.com/view/302972.htm?fr=aladdin.
[21] http://www.hz.ziq.gov.cn/bsdt/View.aspx?id=4614.
[22] http://zhidao.baidu.com/link?url=l6nEIyqWycnuvIBbby93pMfQsxmoTZdTUiYqtbvY2Hw4m.
[23] http://baike.baidu.com/view/101711.htm?fr=aladdin.
[24] http://baike.baidu.com/view/472563.htm?fr=aladdin.
[25] http://baike.baidu.com/link.
[26] http://baike.baidu.com/view/160979.htm?fr=aladdin.
[27] http://baike.baidu.com/view/66743.htm?fr=aladdin.
[28] http://wiki.mbalib.com/wiki/Cargo_Receipt.
[29] http://www.lawtime.cn/info/hetong/hetongzhishi/baoxian/2010120684412.html.